Professional Education at Historically Black Colleges and Universities

This book focuses on the significant role that professional education programs play at Historically Black Colleges and Universities (HBCUs) and these programs' impact on society. Chapter authors discuss the contexts and experiences of students who have attended these programs, including their relationships with faculty, research opportunities, professional growth, personal enrichment, and institutional support. Taking into account social supports, identity development, and doctoral student socialization patterns, this book sheds light on what development and status of such professional education programs mean for future research and practice, while emphasizing issues of race, oppression, and marginalization.

Tiffany Fountaine Boykin is Assistant Director of Student Services at Anne Arundel Community College.

Adriel A. Hilton is Director of the Myrtle Beach Metropolitan Campus at Webster University.

Robert T. Palmer is Interim Chair and Associate Professor in the Department of Educational Leadership and Policy Studies at Howard University.

Routledge Research in Higher Education

For a full list of titles in this series, please visit www.routledge.com

Transnational Education Crossing 'Asia' and 'the West'
Adjusted desire, transformative mediocrity, neo-colonial disguise
Phan Le-Ha

Experiencing Master's Supervision
Perspectives of international students and their supervisors
Nigel Harwood and Bojana Petrić

The Design of the University
German, American, and "World Class"
Heinz-Dieter Meyer

The Politics of Widening Participation and University Access for Young People
Making educational futures
Valerie Harwood, Anna Hickey-Moody, Samantha McMahon and Sarah O'Shea

Narrative, Identity, and Academic Community in Higher Education
Edited by Brian Attebery, John Gribas, Mark K. McBeth, Paul Sivitz, Kandi Turley-Ames

Learning Community Experience in Higher Education
High-Impact Practice for Student Retention
Susan Mary Paige, Amitra Wall, Joe Marren, Amy Rockwell, and Brian Dubenion

Academics Engaging with Student Writing
Working at the Higher Education Textface
Jackie Tuck

Professional Education at Historically Black Colleges and Universities
Past Trends and Outcomes
Edited by Tiffany Fountaine Boykin, Adriel A. Hilton, and Robert T. Palmer

Professional Education at Historically Black Colleges and Universities
Past Trends and Outcomes

Edited by Tiffany Fountaine Boykin, Adriel A. Hilton, and Robert T. Palmer

LONDON AND NEW YORK

First published 2018 by Routledge

2 Park Square, Milton Park, Abingdon, Oxfordshire OX14 4RN

52 Vanderbilt Avenue, New York, NY 10017

Routledge is an imprint of the Taylor & Francis Group, an informa business

First issued in paperback 2019

Copyright © 2018 Taylor & Francis

The right of Tiffany Fountaine Boykin, Adriel A. Hilton, and Robert T. Palmer to be identified as editors of this work has been asserted by them in accordance with sections 77 and 78 of the Copyright, Designs and Patents Act 1988.

All rights reserved. No part of this book may be reprinted or reproduced or utilised in any form or by any electronic, mechanical, or other means, now known or hereafter invented, including photocopying and recording, or in any information storage or retrieval system, without permission in writing from the publishers.

Notice:
Product or corporate names may be trademarks or registered trademarks, and are used only for identification and explanation without intent to infringe.

British Library Cataloguing-in-Publication Data
A catalogue record for this book is available from the British Library

Library of Congress Cataloging-in-Publication Data
A catalog record for this book has been requested

ISBN: 978-1-138-22951-8 (hbk)
ISBN: 978-0-367-88484-0 (pbk)

Typeset in Sabon
by Apex CoVantage, LLC

Contents

About the Editors	vii
About the Contributors	ix
Acknowledgments	xix

1 Introduction—Professional Education at Historically Black Colleges and Universities: Trends, Experiences, and Outcomes   1
TIFFANY FOUNTAINE BOYKIN, ADRIEL A. HILTON, AND ROBERT T. PALMER

2 Historically Black Colleges' and Universities' Role in Preparing Professional Students for the Global Workforce   13
LARRY J. WALKER AND RAMON B. GOINGS

3 Securing the Future: Creating "Social Engineers" for Societal Change at Historically Black College and University Law Schools   29
STEVE D. MOBLEY, JR., SUNNI L. SOLOMON II, AND A.C. JOHNSON

4 Factors for Effective Recruitment, Development, Mentorship, and Retention of Education Doctoral Students   47
CHERON H. DAVIS

5 Historically Black Medical Schools: Addressing the Minority Health Professional Pipeline and the Public Mission of Care for Vulnerable Populations   57
NYCAL ANTHONY-TOWNSEND, BETTINA M. BEECH, AND KEITH C. NORRIS

6 Staying in Focus: Research Self-Efficacy and Mentoring Among HBCU Professional Doctorates   75
NADIELKA BISHOP, COMFORT OKPALA, AND C. DEAN CAMPBELL

7 Social Work Education and Cultural Competence: The Role
  of Historically Black Colleges and Universities   91
  JENNIFER M. JOHNSON AND ZULEKA HENDERSON

8 Mentoring Experiences of Graduate Students in HBCU
  Professional Programs   103
  SEAN ROBINSON AND CHARMAINE TROY

9 Beyond Respectable: Why Earn an Advanced Degree
  from an Historically Black College and University   123
  RIKESHA L. FRY BROWN, ALONZO M. FLOWERS III, ADRIEL A.
  HILTON, AND MICHELLE DEJOHNETTE

10 In Excess of Legitimate Need: Title III and the Development
   of Graduate and Online Degree Programs at Morgan
   State University   141
   MAURICE C. TAYLOR

11 Emerging Themes, Questions, and Implications
   for Professional Education at Historically Black
   Colleges and Universities   155
   ADRIEL A. HILTON, TIFFANY FOUNTAINE BOYKIN,
   AND ROBERT T. PALMER

   Index   165

About the Editors

Tiffany Fountaine Boykin is assistant dean of Student Services at Anne Arundel Community College in Arnold, Maryland. Dr. Boykin engages in strategic planning and promotes creative ideas that enable student support services programs and the College to be more innovative, productive, and efficient. She also interprets, articulates, and monitors institutional compliance with appropriate laws, regulations, and policies. Dr. Boykin's research examines Black graduate student experiences, the role of Historically Black Colleges and Universities, and legal aspects of higher education. A noted author and presenter, Dr. Boykin has numerous publications and proceedings to her credit. She's also been recognized by the American Education Research Association for her efforts in producing scholarship which advances multicultural and multiethnic education, and for her continued commitment to underserved communities.

Dr. Boykin was recently named as Director of Legal Counsel for the Center for African American Research and Policy. She also serves as an editorial reviewer for the *Journal of College Student Retention* and the *Journal of Negro Education*. Dr. Boykin earned a BA in Communication from the University of Maryland, College Park, an MS in Communications Management from Towson University, a PhD in Higher Education from Morgan State University, and a JD from the University of Baltimore School of Law. Dr. Boykin is licensed to practice in Maryland state courts.

Adriel A. Hilton is director of the Webster University Myrtle Beach Metropolitan Extended Campus. As the chief administrative officer, he is charged with implementing programs and policies to achieve Webster University's overall goals and objectives at the extended campus. Dr. Hilton's most recent positions include chief of staff and executive assistant to the president at Grambling State University and assistant professor and director of the Higher Education Student Affairs program at Western Carolina University.

Dr. Hilton was the inaugural assistant vice president for inclusion initiatives at Grand Valley State University. He honed his expertise in higher education administration and teaching at Upper Iowa University (UIU) as executive assistant to the president and assistant secretary to the board of trustees. He was the school's first chief diversity officer and an adjunct faculty member at both UIU and the University of Northern Iowa. Dr. Hilton holds a bachelor's degree in business administration (finance) from Morehouse College, Atlanta, GA; a master's of applied social science degree (public administration emphasis) from Florida A&M University, Tallahassee, FL; and a PhD in higher education (administration) from Morgan State University, Baltimore, MD. His award-winning dissertation and research was titled, *The Perceptions of Administrators Concerning the One Florida Initiative.*

Robert T. Palmer is interim chair and associate professor of Educational Leadership and Policy Studies at Howard University. His research examines issues of access, equity, retention, persistence, and the college experience of racial and ethnic minorities, particularly Black men as well as other student groups at Historically Black Colleges and Universities (HBCUs). Since earning his PhD in 2007, Dr. Palmer has authored/co-authored well over 100 academic publications. Dr. Palmer's work has been published in leading journals in higher education, such as *The Journal of College Student Development, Teachers College Record, Journal of Diversity in Higher Education, Journal of Negro Education, College Student Affairs Journal, Journal of College Student Retention, The Negro Educational Review,* and *Journal of Black Studies,* among others. In 2009, the American College Personnel Association's (ACPA) Standing Committee for Men recognized his excellent research on Black men with its Outstanding Research Award. Dr. Palmer was named an ACPA Emerging Scholar in 2012 and an ACPA Senior scholar in 2017. Furthermore, in 2012, he was awarded the Association for the Study of Higher Education (ASHE)-Mildred García Junior Exemplary Scholarship Award. In 2015, Diverse Issues in Higher Education recognized Dr. Palmer as an Emerging Scholar. Later that year, he also received the SUNY Chancellor's award for Excellence in Scholarship and Creative Activities. This prestigious award is normally given to a full professor. Dr. Palmer earned his PhD in Higher Education Administration from Morgan State University in 2007, MS in Counseling with an emphasis on Higher Education at West Chester University of Pennsylvania in 2003, and a BS in History at Shippensburg University of Pennsylvania in 2001.

About the Contributors

Nycal Anthony-Townsend has nearly 30 years of professional experience in education and human services management for government and non-profit agencies. As President of AQE Solutions, a management consulting firm, she determines the company's strategic vision and implements business development priorities. Mrs. Anthony-Townsend is currently a doctoral student of the University of Maryland Eastern Shore (UMES). At UMES, she majors in Educational Leadership. She has a proven history of commitment to reducing educational inequities and health disparities among underserved communities. Mrs. Anthony-Townsend has secured grant funding totaling more than $100 million for community service, education, and health programs nationally. For over a decade, she served as a Board of Director member for National Black College Hall of Fame Foundation, Creed Arts Academy Charter School, and Mentoring Matters. Mrs. Anthony-Townsend is the Board Vice President for the Boys and Girls Club of Greater Washington, Prince George's County Region. Prior to founding AQE Solutions, Mrs. Anthony-Townsend served as a senior administrator for universities and non-profit organizations. She studied Biology at Simmons College and earned a Master's of Human Services from Lincoln University and completed an Education Policy Fellowship from Institute of Educational Leadership.

Bettina M. Beech is professor and founding dean of the John D. Bower School of Population Health, and Executive Director of the Myrlie Evers-Williams Institute for the Elimination of Health Disparities at the University of Mississippi Medical Center. She has an interdisciplinary background integrating public health, sociology, and population health science to address disparities in "diabesity" among pediatric populations. Dr. Beech holds a BA and MPH from Temple University, and a Dr.P.H. in Community Health Science from University of Texas Health Science Center, School of Public Health. She completed a postdoctoral fellowship in behavioral science at the M.D. Anderson Cancer Center and was 2011–2012 Fellow in the Hedwig van Amerigen Executive Leadership in Academic Medicine (ELAM) Program for Women (Drexel University) and a 2016–2017 American Council on Education (ACE) Fellow.

Dr. Beech has been principal investigator for multiple studies funded by National Institutes of Health, including an R25 funded by the National Heart, Lung, and Blood Institute (NHLBI) to provide a research training and mentoring program for early career faculty who are either employed at, or graduates of, HBCUs. She is a standing member of the Community Level Health Promotion (CLHP) study section and has chaired several ad hoc study sections for NIH and CDC. She has reviewed for over 30 peer-reviewed journals, and is a member of several editorial boards, including *Ethnicity and Disease, American Journal of Health Promotion, Journal of Childhood Obesity, Journal of Population Health Management* and serves as Editor-in-Chief for the *Journal of Family and Community Health*.

Nadielka Bishop works to develop and direct academic support initiatives in higher education. Her primary work has included writing centers and discipline-specific instruction. She currently directs academic training and supplemental instruction for an urban initiative community scholarship program at Belmont University in Nashville, Tennessee.

Dr. Bishop's conference presentations include the subjects of peer-to-peer tutoring in university writing centers, peer mentoring among HBCU doctoral women, research training of HBCU doctoral students, and graduate enrollment management as a community of practice.

Rikesha L. Fry Brown is the co-founder and clinician of the Kindred Family Wellness Group, a counseling, consulting, and coaching practice in the Atlanta area. In addition, Dr. Fry Brown is an adjunct professor in the psychology departments of Clark Atlanta University and Spelman College. Dr. Fry Brown graduated cum laude from Hampton University, where she earned a Bachelor of Arts degree in psychology with an emphasis in education. She earned a Master of Counselor Education degree with concentrations in both school guidance and mental health counseling from Florida Agricultural and Mechanical University. Dr. Fry Brown earned a PhD in Counseling Psychology from Howard University. Dr. Fry Brown's primary research focuses on the psychological and social implications of mediated images for African American women.

C. Dean Campbell has served as Assistant Dean for Academic Services in The Graduate School at North Carolina A&T State University (NCAT) since 2012. Dr. Campbell participates in leadership and management of the unit with a focus on developing strategic direction and managing the implementation of admission and enrollment activities to meet strategic services provided to students throughout their matriculation. Dr. Campbell is a member of the graduate faculty and teaches as an adjunct instructor in the NCAT School of Education's Adult Education Master's degree program.

Prior to coming to NCAT, Dr. Campbell worked for over a decade in a variety of professional administrator roles in graduate education, including Morgan State University's School of Graduate Studies and the University of Southern California's Graduate School and Enrollment Services Division. A published scholar, his research interests include organizational effectiveness in higher education, workplace learning, administrator professional development, and qualitative methods in the study of adult and higher education administration. He earned his Bachelor's degree in Political Science from Yale University, Master's degree in Higher Education Administration and Student Development from Boston College, and Doctorate in Educational Leadership-Higher Education Administration from the University of Southern California.

Cheron H. Davis is an assistant professor of reading education at Florida A&M University. Most recently, Dr. Davis was appointed as the director of student teaching and is charged with coordinating field placements and internships between the University and local school systems. Having earned her doctorate degree in reading education from Auburn University, Dr. Davis has worked in higher education for nearly 10 years. She is a former elementary teacher who thrives on creating meaningful, sustainable partnerships with K-12 staff, faculty, and administrators with whom she works. Her research interests include multicultural literature, culturally conscious pedagogy, and early literacy intervention. When she is not working with preservice teachers in elementary schools, Dr. Davis enjoys reading, attending sporting events, and spending time with her family.

Michelle DeJohnette is currently a PhD student in the Joint Doctoral Program in Education with San Diego State University (SDSU) and Claremont Graduate University (CGU), where she has been selected as a Chancellor Doctoral Incentive Program (CDIP) Scholar. Her research interests include Critical Race Theory, African American children in early childhood, culturally relevant pedagogy, and social justice issues. The primary focus of her research is eliminating the gap between the academic achievement of African American children and their highest potential. Additionally, Michelle's theory is that addressing this gap should begin in early childhood, before children begin Kindergarten. Recent research has been focused on fostering African American Science Technology Engineering and Mathematics (STEM) identity in early childhood. She has earned a Bachelor's degree in Child and Family Development, with Distinction in the major, from San Diego State University (SDSU), and a Master's degree in Human Development, with a specialization in Early Childhood Education, at Pacific Oaks College and Children's School in Pasadena, CA. During the time Michelle has been pursuing her education, she has also devoted her time to children and families by owning and operating a family child care home for the past 19 years and is a sitting board member of the San Diego Association for the Education of Young Children.

Alonzo M. Flowers III is an assistant professor in the School of Education at Drexel University. Dr. Flowers specializes in educational issues including academic identity development of men of color (MoC) in STEM education. He also focuses on issues including diversity, teaching and learning, and college student development in higher education. Specifically, Dr. Flowers' research focuses on the academic experiences of academically gifted African American male students in the STEM disciplines.

Dr. Flowers currently serves as Senior Research Fellow with The Massachusetts Institute for College and Career Readiness (MICCR) at Boston University. To date, he has completed 50 peer-reviewed national conference presentations, including several presentations at the Association for the Study of Higher Education (ASHE) and American Educational Research Association (AERA). Dr. Flowers is also a member of the *Journal of Race and Policy* editorial board. Additionally, he is a reviewer for several educational journals, including the *Journal of African American Males in Education* (JAAME). Dr. Flowers' research continues to impact the needs of underrepresented students in education: he has authored or co-authored several book chapters and articles that focus on students of color and their academic experiences. Dr. Flowers has recently co-authored the book, *The African American Student's Guide to STEM Careers*, which focuses on practical educational tools for African American students to navigate the STEM pipeline.

Ramon B. Goings is an assistant professor of educational leadership at Loyola University Maryland. His research interests are centered on exploring the academic and social experiences of gifted/high-achieving Black males PK-PhD, nontraditional student success, diversifying the teacher and school leader workforce, and investigating the contributions of Historically Black Colleges and Universities. Dr. Goings is the co-editor of *Graduate Education at Historically Black Colleges and University: A Student Perspective* (2016, Routledge Press) and the upcoming book *How Obama Changed the Political Landscape* (Prager). Along with his scholarship, Dr. Goings serves as the Editor-In-Chief of the *Journal of African American Males in Education*. Dr. Goings was named a 2017 Emerging Scholar by *Diverse: Issues in Higher Education* and received the 2016 College Board Professional Fellowship.

Prior to working in higher education, Dr. Goings was a music education and special education teacher in several urban school districts, including Baltimore City Public Schools, and was a foster care and youth probation counselor/advocate in New Haven, Connecticut. In 2013 he served as a fellow with the White House Initiative on Educational Excellence for African Americans. He earned his Doctor of Education degree

About the Contributors xiii

in urban educational leadership from Morgan State University, Master of Science in human services from Post University, and Bachelor of Arts in music education from Lynchburg College.

Zuleka Henderson is an assistant professor of social work at Bowie State University. Her research and writing have focused on addressing research and statistics anxiety among social work students at HBCUs and examining the implications of historical trauma theory for the development of culturally relevant research pedagogy. Dr. Henderson is also a licensed social worker with clinical and research experience focusing on trauma, mental health service use, and intergenerational healing among Black adolescents and families. She is a graduate of the Howard University School of Social Work PhD program.

A.C. Johnson is a doctoral student of higher education administration in the Department of Educational Leadership, Policy, and Technology Studies at the University of Alabama. She currently serves as an editorial assistant for the *International Journal for Researcher Development* and is also a graduate research assistant in the College of Education at the University of Alabama. Her research interests include Historically Black Colleges and Universities, Black women in higher education, first generation students, developmental education and bridge programs, and P-20 educational access for underrepresented students. Before entering the field of higher education, she taught English composition, speech, American literature, and academic success skills courses at several diverse post-secondary contexts. During that time, she also served on many committees at these institutions that focused on English proficiency and student retention. A. C. earned her BS in Psychology and her MA in English from Jacksonville State University, and although she has resided in many areas across the country, Birmingham, AL is where she calls home.

Jennifer M. Johnson Jennifer M. Johnson is an Assistant Professor in the Department of Policy, Organizational and Leadership Studies at Temple University. Her scholarly agenda is to promote the college access and persistence of traditionally underrepresented populations (e.g., first generation college students, lower-income individuals, and racial/ethnic minorities) through the qualitative examination of the experiences and outcomes of students across institutional contexts in higher education. Her work has highlighted the experiences of Black women at selective colleges and universities, Black and Latina/o graduate students pursuing STEM degrees, and alumni of Historically Black Colleges and Universities.

Steve D. Mobley, Jr. is assistant professor of higher education in the Department of Educational Leadership, Policy, and Technology Studies at the University of Alabama. His scholarship focuses on the contemporary placement of Historically Black Colleges and Universities (HBCUs). Particularly, Dr. Mobley's research underscores and highlights the understudied facets of HBCU communities, including issues surrounding race, social class, and student sexuality. Dr. Mobley also has extensive experience in the field of higher education. Most recently, he served as Associate Director of the undergraduate program at Georgetown University's McDonough School of Business. Prior to arriving at Georgetown, he held appointments in academic affairs at the University of Maryland and taught courses in The College of Education, Undergraduate Studies, and the Academic Achievement Programs (A TRiO Initiative). A proud native of Washington, DC, prior to his time in the academy, he served his home community as a college counselor and spearheaded numerous higher education initiatives in conjunction with several non-profits geared toward increasing college access for DC students. He earned his BA in Communication and Culture from Howard University. Upon graduating from Howard, he completed his Master's in Higher Education Management from the University of Pennsylvania, and most recently he earned his PhD in Higher Education from the University of Maryland.

Keith Norris is an internationally recognized clinician scientist and health policy leader who has been instrumental in shaping national health policy and clinical practice guidelines for chronic kidney disease (CKD). He did his undergraduate work at Cornell University followed by medical school at Howard University. He is board certified in internal medicine and nephrology, and is an American Society of Hypertension, Specialist in Clinical Hypertension. In 2014 he received his doctorate in religious, spiritual, and metaphysical philosophy. After serving as Executive VP for Research and Health Affairs for six years and Interim President at Charles Drew University (CDU) for two years, he returned to UCLA as a Professor of Medicine and Co-Director of the Clinical and Translational Science Institute Community Engagement Research Program.

Dr. Norris was the founding Principal Investigator for the first national translational research network dedicated to reducing health disparities, the National Institutes of Health (NIH)-Research Centers in Minority Institutions Translational Research Network. Presently, he co-directs an NIH grant to provide research training and mentoring for early career faculty who are either employed at, or graduates of, HBCUs. Finally, he directs the NIH Diversity Program Consortium Coordination and Evaluation Center at UCLA, the centerpiece of a new $230 million NIH initiative to enhance diversity in the biomedical workforce.

Dr. Norris has co-authored over 300 articles in peer-reviewed journals and 30 book chapters. He currently serves as the Editor-in-Chief of the international journal *Ethnicity and Disease*, and as an associate editor for the *Journal of the American Society of Nephrology*.

Comfort Okpala is a professor and Chair in the Department of Leadership Studies, School of Education at North Carolina A&T State University. Her teaching interest includes qualitative research, quantitative research, higher education finance, leadership theory, and community college leadership. Dr. Okpala is a noteworthy researcher who has been cited over 380 times by international and national researchers. Her research agenda is grounded in leadership training and development, social justice, resource equity, and African American education and social issues.

Sean Robinson is an associate professor of higher education and student affairs at Morgan State University, in Baltimore, MD. He has over 25 years' experience on university campuses in both academic affairs and student affairs. Dr. Robinson's teaching interests include: higher education administration, student affairs administration, organizational development and change management, leadership development, and qualitative research methodology. His two primary research areas include an exploration of the lived experiences of LGBTQ faculty and administrators within colleges and universities, and understanding the socialization and mentoring experiences of minority graduate students, particularly those attending HBCUs.

Sunni L. Solomon II is a fourth-year doctoral student pursuing his PhD in higher education administration as part of the Department of Advanced Studies in Leadership and Policy at Morgan State University in Baltimore, MD. His research interests include the written and unwritten dynamics of faculty diversity at White institutions, the impacts of elitism on African American community cohesion, and the role of tradition in sustaining viable Historically Black Colleges and Universities.

In addition to his academic pursuits, Mr. Solomon also serves in a full-time professional capacity as the Special Program Administrator for the Vice President for Student Affairs at the University of Baltimore. He is the architect and current director of University of Baltimore's Brotherhood, Mentorship, Achievement, Leadership, and Enterprise (BMALE) Academy, which focuses on closing the achievement and opportunity gaps for undergraduate men of color by providing mentoring, professional development, academic enrichment services, and social/cultural programming opportunities to students beginning in the first year of enrollment. Prior to his current role, Mr. Solomon served as the Director for Fraternity and Sorority Life at Union College in Schenectady, NY. He earned his BS in Business Administration with a marketing concentration from Cheyney University of Pennsylvania, and also possesses a Master's degree in College Student Affairs from Eastern Illinois University.

Maurice C. Taylor is Vice President for Academic Outreach and Engagement at Morgan State University and the former Dean of Morgan's

School of Graduate Studies. As Vice President, Morgan Online is one of several departments for which he has supervisory responsibility. He has served as Morgan liaison to the Maryland Higher Education Commission (MHEC) and was a member of a number of MHEC task forces, including: the 2009 and 2013 Maryland State Plan for Post-Secondary Education Subcommittees on Diversity, Northeast Maryland Higher Education Task Force Facilities Working Group, Segmental Task Force on Program Approval Process, and the Historically Black Institutions Task Force on Best Practices for Improving Retention and Graduation Rates. He also served as a member of a MHEC's subcommittee charged with the final review of the 2005 Partnership Agreement between Maryland and the United States Department of Education Office of Civil Rights.

Presently, Dr. Taylor is a member of: the State of Maryland's African American Museum Corporation Board of Directors, the Board of Trustees, Mercy High School, the Walters Art Museum Engagement Committee, Maryland-District of Columbia Campus Compact Senior Advisory Group for Engagement (SAGE), and Visit Baltimore Multicultural Advisory Committee (MAC). He also chairs the Prince George's County Financial Advisory Committee responsible for oversight of the county's $50 million Economic Development Incentive Fund. Dr. Taylor earned a Bachelor's of Arts degree from Juniata College and the Master of Arts and Doctor of Philosophy degrees in Sociology from Bowling Green State University. He earned the Juris Doctorate from Duke University's School of Law and practiced labor law in the firm of Gordon, Feinblatt, Rothman, & Hoffberger.

Charmaine E. Troy is a doctoral candidate in higher education administration at Morgan State University. She is an academic advisor and instructor for the first-year seminar course at Georgia Gwinnett College. Her research focus areas are student success, persistence, student development, and the college experience of minorities, particularly first-year, first generation Black females at Historically Black Colleges and Universities (HBCUs) and minority serving institutions (MSIs). She is co-editor of the book *Graduate Education at Historically Black Colleges and Universities (HBCUs): A Student Perspective*. Charmaine earned her Master of Public Administration from North Carolina Central University and BA in Journalism and Mass Communication from the University of North Carolina at Chapel Hill.

Larry J. Walker is a researcher and HBCU advocate. Previously, Dr. Walker was selected as a Congressional Fellow with the Congressional Black Caucus Foundation. After completing his fellowship, Dr. Walker served as the Legislative Director for Congressman Major R. Owens. During his tenure on Capitol Hill, Dr. Walker worked on amendments to the Higher Education Act and fought for additional funding for HBCUs. Dr. Walker has authored/co-authored articles and book chapters on HBCUs. He is the coeditor of *Graduate Education at Historically Black Colleges and Universities: A Student Perspective*. In addition, he moderated a discussion on HBCUs sponsored by the Congressional Black Caucus titled, *A Legacy of Excellence: Examining the Unique Role HBCUs will Play in the 21st Century Economy*. Dr. Walker completed his doctorate at Morgan State University.

Acknowledgments

I would first like to thank Adriel A. Hilton and Robert T. Palmer for continuing to serve as great colleagues, friends, coaches, and collaborative partners. I would also like to extend a sincere thank you to each of the contributors for working tirelessly to meet numerous deadlines and for helping bring this volume to fruition.

This book is dedicated to my husband Aram C. Boykin, Sr. Thank you for being my inspiration when my vision wavered, for being my rock when I was unsteady, and for pushing me when I've wanted to stand still. We did it!

Tiffany Fountaine Boykin

This book is dedicated to those who are closest to me: my parents, Alphonso and Sarah Hilton, Jr.; my sister, Shay Blanding; and my beautiful niece, Sarah Nicole Penn. Had it not been for your support, sacrifice, guidance, and unwavering love, I would not have been able to accomplish this goal.

In addition, I would like to thank Tiffany F. Boykin and Robert T. Palmer for their leadership and support while working on this project. Also, I would like to thank the contributors for working diligently to meet the many deadlines for this project.

Adriel A. Hilton

I would like to thank Tiffany F. Boykin for her leadership on this project and Adriel A. Hilton for thinking of the need for this project.

Robert T. Palmer

1 Introduction—Professional Education at Historically Black Colleges and Universities
Trends, Experiences, and Outcomes

Tiffany Fountaine Boykin, Adriel A. Hilton, and Robert T. Palmer

Introduction

Over the last two decades, scholars have learned a considerable amount about the enrollment, completion, and experiences of Black students who attend Historically Black Colleges and Universities (HBCUs). In general, HBCUs have been credited with cultivating supportive and engaging environments where Black students have a strengthened self-esteem and stronger sense of racial pride.[1] Further, the literature is clear that Black students who attend HBCUs perform better academically, build more meaningful relationships with faculty and staff, are more engaged in the campus environment, and have a better sense of belonging and connection than Black students who attend predominantly White institutions [PWIs].[2] Simply put, HBCUs have been cited as being able to provide Black students, at both undergraduate and graduate levels, with an exceptional educational experience, often unachievable at PWIs.[3]

However, much of the aforementioned research has concentrated on HBCU student experiences at the undergraduate level, often examining the comparative experiences and outcomes of Black undergraduate students attending HBCUs to those attending PWIs.[4] That is not to say the literature is absent of research that has considered racial and ethnic minority student populations exclusive to the doctoral level. Recent studies have explored the experiences and lives of persons of color in STEM doctoral programs,[5] the advancement of the pipeline or school choice-related matters,[6] and the cultural experiences of Black and Latino students.[7] But, despite the important contributions of these studies, research about the experiences of graduate students at HBCUs is generally limited. In fact, many scholars in the higher education community may have erroneously assumed that the research on undergraduate students at HBCUs defined the experiences of graduate students at HBCUs. Such an assumption cannot be further from the truth. For example, in his theory of student departure, Tinto[8] discussed the importance of undergraduate students becoming academically and socially integrated into the university to facilitate retention and persistence. Because graduate students may have different needs, obligations, experiences, and expectations than undergraduate students,[9] certain aspects of his theory may be less applicable to graduate students,[10] specifically at HBCUs.

Though national data on doctoral degree attainment are generally available, extant research has often failed to examine key dimensions of doctoral students' experiences regarding their development and progress in academic programs.[11] In addition, when examining the literature as a whole, relatively few studies have concentrated on specific factors influencing the experiences and outcomes for Black doctoral students, despite continuing evidence of growth in Black doctoral program enrollment and attainment.[12] Notwithstanding, there is a recent growing body of literature examining experiences and factors that impact the success of Black doctoral students.[13] But, much of the research that actually has examined Black doctoral students has not necessarily investigated the implications of an HBCU setting.[14] And, while the aforementioned scholarship does indeed provide considerations for understanding doctoral education from multiple lenses, it falls short of a comprehensive view on doctoral education exclusive to the professions—or doctoral programs focused on preparing graduates for specific careers in areas such as medicine, law, and social work—at HBCUs. This research is important, particularly since earning an advanced degree, particularly in a professional area of study, has significant implications on our [US] competitiveness in the global economy. In fact, scholars have argued that a graduate degree will become the new bachelor's degree, serving as the minimal education credential that high-skills employers require.[15]

The foci of research on graduate study for students of color have been relatively narrow. Thus, substantial gaps in the knowledge base exist. Given that HBCUs, in particular, play a significant role in the number of Blacks who earn doctorates, additional study is warranted.[16] Even when examining Black doctoral education in an HBCU setting, researchers have often concentrated on traditional liberal arts or STEM programs of study, and less on professional programs such as medicine, law, or dentistry.[17] These gaps in the literature fail to expand the knowledge base of Black student trends, outcomes, and experiences at HBCUs that could prove critical to matriculation and completion of professional advanced degrees for these students. In addition, the literature offers minimal understanding for current and prospective Black students to deal with the personal and professional challenges of doctoral study, as well as limited strategies and best practices for faculty and administrators to best support these students. Thus, this monograph serves several critical purposes. First, it provides a critical review of the historical nature of professional programs at HBCUs and the programs' impact on a global society. Second, research study findings, personal narratives, and theoretical analyses are offered to provide further context about the experiences of Black doctoral students in specific disciplines, outcomes for enrollment and degree attainment, relationships with faculty and advisors, research opportunities, and the role of faculty and socialization processes in promoting positive Black doctoral student development and professional growth. Finally, the monograph addresses the future of professional education at HBCUs and what fundamental aspects are needed to ensure their survival, competitiveness, and growth.

Having established the relevancy and necessity of this monograph, the subsequent sections of this introductory chapter will better contextualize the need for this volume by providing a brief history on HBCUs in America, a review of the extant literature on Black graduate education, inclusive of the role of HBCUs and their professional programs of study, and the organization of the monograph's content.

Brief History of HBCUs in America

Historically Black Colleges and Universities (HBCUs) are federally designated as educational institutions, founded prior to 1964, that provide access to education for Black students.[18] Three HBCUs—two in Pennsylvania (Cheyney University and Lincoln University), and one in Ohio (Wilberforce University)—were among the first HBCUs established before the Civil War.[19] The *Morrill Act* of 1890, which required states to establish separate land grant colleges for Blacks if they were precluded from attending existing land grant schools, played a vital role in the proliferation of HBCUs. Specifically, this legislation resulted in the establishment and financing of 17 public HBCUs.[20] Today, there are 105 HBCUs represented in six distinct Carnegie Classifications that include Research Universities (10%), Master's Universities (23%), Baccalaureate Universities (48%), Medical Schools (2%), Seminaries (4%), and Associates Institutions (13%).[21]

While most HBCUs primarily serve undergraduate students, the majority of HBCUs (60%) offer graduate or professional degrees.[22] America's HBCUs, in their history, have traditionally been the institutions with the largest impact on the production of minorities with graduate and professional degrees. This was largely because in the early years, African Americans and other minorities were not welcomed to apply at most PWIs, whether graduate or professional.[23] Graduate and professional schools emerged during the 1940s because of several court cases brought by African Americans who had been denied entry into graduate school at all-White public universities in their states.[24] As a result of the lawsuits, legislators in these states opted to open publicly supported graduate and professional schools at HBCUs rather than integrate the all-White schools.[25] This led to the birth of a number of professional and graduate schools at HBCUs.

Examining Black Graduate Education

In general, recent trends have shown indicators for continual and impressive progress for the future of Blacks in graduate programs, especially at the doctoral level.[26] In fact, there has been a 70% increase in the number of doctorates awarded to Blacks over the past 20 years.[27] The literature has offered a variety of factors that may have contributed to this increase, including strengthening the pipeline of aspiring Black doctorates, particularly in STEM, at the undergraduate level;[28] employing a Black feminist approach to doctoral advising;[29] and providing comprehensive support for doctoral students who are at the intersection of identities, especially gay men.[30] In addition, research has confirmed that institutional characteristics such as type, racial and ethnic composition, selectivity, and geographic location also matter in terms of producing successful minority doctoral students.[31] In fact, it has been suggested that earlier aspects of a doctoral student's educational pipeline, specifically attending an HBCU, also play a significant role in preparing Black students for doctoral success.[32]

While HBCUs represent just 3% of US higher education institutions, and despite relatively smaller endowments and lower institutional resources, HBCUs have been a critical force in the production of Black advanced degree recipients. For example, the National Center for Education Statistics [NCES] reported that HBCUs produced 6,900 master's recipients (5,034 for Blacks), accounting for roughly 10% of master's degrees awarded to Black students that year.[33] HBCUs have also been a principal producer of Black doctorates; between 1992–1993 and 1997–1998, HBCUs increased their number of doctoral graduates by 15.2%.[34] By 2012–13, the percentage of Black doctoral degree recipients who received their degrees from HBCUs was approximately 12%.[35]

Between 2005 and 2009, Howard University, Morgan State University, Jackson State University, and Clark Atlanta University—all HBCUs—placed first, fourth, sixth, and eighth, respectively, among top ten universities awarding doctorate degrees to Blacks.[36] These statistics are remarkable given that, at times, doctoral degree production among Blacks at these aforementioned HBCUs has exceeded doctoral degree production among Blacks at institutions that have enjoyed much longer histories of graduate education and have considerably better publicly funded research profiles, including such notables as Harvard University, Temple University, Georgia State University, and Columbia University.[37]

In addition, HBCUs are a powerhouse in Black professional doctorate production. In fact, more than 80% of all Black Americans who received degrees in medicine and dentistry were trained at the two traditionally Black institutions of medicine and dentistry—Howard University and Meharry Medical College.[38] And, when examining data for professional doctorates in general (i.e., medicine, law, veterinary medicine, etc.), HBCUs remain leaders; in 2016, Howard University, Florida Agricultural and Mechanical University, Meharry Medical College, Texas Southern University, Southern University Law Center, and North Carolina Central University ranked first, second, third, fifth, seventh, and eighth, respectively.[39]

Organization of this Monograph

This introductory chapter notes the critical purposes of this monograph, contextualizes the need for this volume by providing a brief history on HBCUs in America, including the establishment and proliferation of professional education programs, and reviews the extant literature on Black graduate education, inclusive of the role of HBCUs and their professional programs of study. In Chapter Two, "Historically Black Colleges' and Universities' Role in Preparing Professional Students for the Global Workforce," Larry Walker and Ramon Goings affirm the enduring relevancy of HBCUs through an exploration of HBCU exosystems and how they contribute to positive outcomes for Black graduate students after they enter the workforce. This chapter concludes with recommendations for administrators, faculty, and staff.

Chapter Three, "Securing the Future: Creating 'Social Engineers' for societal Change at Historically Black College and University Law Schools," authored by Steve D. Mobley, Jr., Sunni L. Solomon II, and A. C. Johnson, discusses the impact of HBCU law schools. The authors argue that though small in number, HBCU law schools occupy the role of training social engineers in the nuances of legal practice. Specifically, the authors critically note that HBCU law schools do not just produce lawyers. Instead, they generate leaders who are primed and ready to advance the cause of civil rights with the same passion and commitment of previous generations of graduates, faculty, and administrators. This chapter concludes with thought provoking implications for practice.

In Chapter Four, "Factors for Effective Recruitment, Mentorship, Development, and Retention of Education Doctoral Students," Cheron Davis examines teacher education programs at HBCUs. Today's 21st century K-12 school classrooms are microcosmic representations of the increasingly diverse population that characterizes much of the United States. The post-racial narrative suggests that we, as teacher educators, are training teachers to create learning environments that enable student members to engage in dialogue reflective of the unique sociocultural experiences that they bring to the setting. Research and anecdotes from the field suggest that the reality is far different. Davis proposes a reconceptualization of the current model of recruitment, mentorship, development, and retention of HBCU education doctoral candidates who will eventually become teacher educators and educational leaders, as well as policymakers.

In Chapter Five, "Historically Black Medical Schools: Addressing the Minority Health Professional Pipeline and the Public Mission of Care for Vulnerable Populations," Nycal Anthony-Townsend, Bettina M. Beech, and Keith C. Norris discuss the historical nature of health professional education at HBCUs and the impact of these programs on society. Their chapter concludes with recommendations regarding how HBCUs can best design the future of education programs to optimize the preparation and contribution of future Black doctoral health professionals.

Nadielka Bishop, Comfort Okpala, and C. Dean Campbell highlight the importance of research training and research mentoring in doctoral programs at Historically Black Colleges and Universities in Chapter Six, "Staying in Focus: Research, Self-Efficacy, and Mentoring among HBCU Professional Doctorates." Considering that Historically Black Colleges and Universities are the highest producers of Black doctoral degree recipients, it is valuable to evaluate the research training that occurs between major professors/advisors and PhD candidates. The themes in this chapter implore concepts of research self-efficacy, the purpose and responsibilities of HBCUs, mentoring relationships, and research training environment theory. By highlighting the relationship as well as the method utilized to increase research self-efficacy through proper research training, the authors argue that HBCUs can find additional methods designed to increase diverse researchers as well as researchers with diverse cultural perspectives.

Chapter Seven, entitled "Social Work Education and Cultural Competence: The Role of Historically Black Colleges and Universities," focuses on social work programs at HBCUs. Authors Jennifer Johnson and Zuleka Henderson focus on the history of social work education at HBCUs, their focus on culturally relevant pedagogy, and the ways their core missions are reflected in the mission/vision of PhD programs at HBCUs. Their chapter concludes with recommendation on what PWIs can learn from this approach in the ways they design/structure social work education programs (MSW/PhD) to meet the demands of the profession and the needs of individuals and communities from diverse backgrounds.

In Chapter Eight, "Mentoring Experiences of Graduate Students in Professional Programs," Sean Robinson and Charmaine Troy draw on a series of phenomenological interviews with minority students attending professional degree programs at HBCUs to highlight the essential support structures that might aid in their retention and persistence, organizational fit, and career decisions, as well as point out HBCUs' opportunities for better expenditure of individual and institutional resources.

In Chapter Nine, Rikesha L. Fry Brown, Alonzo M. Flowers III, Adriel A. Hilton, and Michelle DeJohnette utilized ethnographic narrative case studies to extract themes from ten individuals about their experiences pursuing graduate and professional education at HBCUs. Findings indicated that students attend HBCUs for a variety of reasons, including location, cost, and convenience. However, beyond these common rationales for college choice, respondents also indicated that they attended HBCUs as a result of their historical contribution to African American communities as well as the supportive environment fostered within these institutions. Finally, findings also indicated that, while students often select HBCUs for graduate and professional school, because they are HBCUs, they are aware of challenges associated with those decisions.

Introduction   7

In Chapter Eleven, "In Excess of Legitimate Need: Title III and the Development of Online and Degree Programs at Morgan State University," Maurice C. Taylor discusses creative alternatives for advancing professional doctorate programs at a public HBCU, in the absence of state funding and support. Maryland's failure to provide funding and to support program development for Morgan State University and the state's other three Historically Black Colleges and Universities (HBCUs) comparable to that of the state's traditionally White universities is grounded in the enduring history of de jure and de facto segregation throughout Maryland. The racial animus was particularly acute in Baltimore, where both Morgan and Coppin State Universities are located. The Corporation for Enterprise Development notes that policymakers at all levels have influenced current economic and racial disparities in Baltimore. The focus of this chapter is how, in the absence of state support, Morgan was able to utilize the Department of Education's Title III Program to develop its graduate, particularly its doctoral, and its online degree programs.

In the final chapter, "Emerging Themes, Questions, and Implications for Professional Education at Historically Black Colleges and Universities," Adriel A. Hilton, Tiffany Fountaine Boykin, and Robert T. Palmer note the importance of policymakers' use of research to ensure that HBCUs are funded adequately. In addition, this chapter highlights how HBCUs continue to play a vital role in advancing the Black intelligentsia. Finally, this chapter concludes by noting that HBCUs are not only essential to Black professional degree attainment, but also to the nation's preservation and continuation of its global leadership role.

Conclusion

Although HBCUs have made considerable strides in the production of Black doctorates over the last 30 years, progress has not kept pace with national and global needs. Blacks' total share of doctorate recipients increased from 3.8% in 1977 to only 4.8% in 2000. And, as of 2010, Blacks' share increased to just 7.4%, considerably lagging behind that of White students. In fact, in 2010, Blacks earned 10,417, or 7.4%, of all doctorates conferred; Whites earned 104,426, or 74.3%.[40] Student outcomes at HBCUs have a national impact on the number of Blacks who are primed to enter into and advance within the workforce and contribute to the American economy, and ultimately America's ability to compete globally.[41] Thus, the HBCU remains a vital necessity for increasing Blacks' share of earned advanced degrees, and careful examination of the factors that serve to support or restrain the capacity of HBCUs to develop professional education programs is warranted.

This monograph does not attempt to uncover or identify a disparity between doctoral student achievements at HBCUs versus predominantly White, and other, institutions; nor is it designed to compare the experiences of doctoral students at one HBCU over another. Independent of comparisons, the influences that promote (or challenge) success among HBCU Black doctoral students in professional graduate programs are independently important, and thus warrant continued examination and visibility in the larger higher education conversation. This monograph does serve as a champion of advocacy for the continued necessity and relevance of the HBCU. The HBCU has and continues to serve as a bold catalyst in the production of Black advanced professional degree holders, thus adding to the success of higher education, the economy, and to the civic and social order of future generations in America.

Notes

1. Hall and Closson 2005; Hirt et al. 2006; Palmer and Gasman 2008
2. Jackson 2001; Palmer and Gasman 2008; Terenzini et al. 1997
3. Allen 1992; Fountaine 2012
4. Cooper and Dougherty 2015; Fries-Britt and Turner 2002; Pascarella and Terenzini 2005; Weddle-West, Hagan, and Norwood 2013
5. Upton and Tanenbaum 2014
6. Joseph and Feldman 2009
7. Gildersleeve, Croom, and Vasquez 2011
8. Tinto 1993
9. Bean and Metzner 1985; Ogren 2003
10. Lovitts 2001
11. Nettles and Millett 2006
12. Survey of Earned Doctorates 2014
13. Gildersleeve, Croom, and Vasquez 2011; Felder and Barker 2013; Felder, Stevenson, and Gasman 2014; Okahana et al. 2016
14. Ellis 2000; Palmer, Hilton, and Fountaine 2012; Nerad and Miller 1996; Nettles and Millett 2006; Turner and Thompson 1993
15. Wendler et al. 2010
16. Palmer, Hilton, and Fountaine 2012
17. Fountaine 2012; Palmer, Hilton, and Fountaine 2012
18. Gasman, Baez Turner 2008
19. Albritton 2012
20. Allen and Jewell 2002; Provasnik Shafer, and Snyder 2004
21. Lee, Jr. and Keys 2013
22. Lee, Jr. and Keys 2013
23. Swygert 2004
24. Gannon 1996
25. *Sweatt v. Painter* 1950; *Hawkins v. Board of Control* 1950
26. Golde and Walker 2006; National Opinion Research Center 2007; Roach 1997; Survey of Earned Doctorates 2014; Thompson 1999
27. Survey of Earned Doctorates 2014
28. Maton and Hrabrowski 2004
29. Jones, Wilder, and Lampkin 2013
30. Means et al. 2016
31. Lundy-Wagner Vultaggio, and Gasman 2013
32. Lundy-Wagner, Vultaggio, and Gasman 2013
33. National Center for Education Statistics 2005
34. St. John 2001

35 National Center for Education Statistics 2015
36 Taylor 2012
37 Taylor 2012
38 US Department of Education, Office of Civil Rights 1991
39 *Top 100 Degree Producers 2016*: Graduate and Professional
40 National Center for Education Statistics 2012
41 Lee, Jr. and Keys 2013

Bibliography

Albritton, Travis. "Educating our own: The historical legacy of HBCUs and their relevance for educating a new generation of leaders." *Urban Review*, 44 no. 2 (2012): 311–331.

Allen, Walter R. "The color of success: African American college student out-comes at predominantly White and historically black public colleges and universities." *Harvard Educational Review*, 62 no. 1 (1992): 26–44.

Allen, Walter R., and Joseph O. Jewell. "A backward glance forward: Past, present, and future perspectives on historically black colleges and universities." *Review of Higher Education*, 25 no. 3 (2002): 241–261.

Bean, John P., and Barbara Metzner. "A conceptual model of nontraditional undergraduate student attrition." *Review of Educational Research*, 55 (1985): 485–540.

Cooper, Joseph N., and Shaun Dougherty. "Does race still matter? A post bowl championship series (BCS) Era examination of student athletes' experiences at a division I Historically Black College/University (HBCU) and Predominantly White Institution (PWI)." *Journal of Issues in Intercollegiate Athletics*, 8 (2015): 74–10.

Ellis, Evelynn M. *Race, gender, and the graduate student experience: Recent research*, 2000. Retrieved February 10, 2007, from www.diversityweb.org/Digest/F00/ graduate.html

Felder, Pamela P., and Marco Barker. "Extending Bell's concept of interest convergence: A framework for understanding the African American doctoral student experience." *International Journal of Doctoral Studies*, 8 (2013): 1–20.

Felder, Pamela P., Howard Stevenson, and Marybeth Gasman. "Understanding race in doctoral student socialization." *International Journal of Doctoral Studies*, 9 (2014): 21–42. Retrieved from http://ijds.org/Volume9/IJDSv9p021-042Felder0323.pdf

Fountaine, Tiffany Patrice. "The impact of faculty–Student interaction on black doctoral students attending historically black institutions." *The Journal of Negro Education*, 81 no. 2 (2012): 136–147.

Fries-Britt, Sharon, and Bridget Turner. "Uneven stories: Successful black collegians at a black and a white campus." *The Review of Higher Education*, 25 no. 3 (2002): 315–330.

Gannon, Michael. *The new history of Florida*. Gainesville, FL: University of Florida Press, 1996.

Gasman, Marybeth, Benjamin Baez, Caroline Sotello, and Viernes Turner. *Understanding minority-serving institutions*. Albany, NY: State University of New York Press, 2008.

Gildersleeve, Ryan E., Natasha N. Croom, and Phillip L. Vasquez. "Am I going crazy?! A critical race analysis of doctoral education." *Equity & Excellence in Education*, 44 no. 1 (2011): 93–114.

Golde, Chris, and George Walker. Envisioning the future of doctoral education: Preparing stewards of the discipline. San Francisco: Jossey-Bass, 2006.

Hall, Brenda, and Rosemary Closson. "When the majority is the minority: White graduate students' social adjustment at a historically black university." *Journal of College Student Development*, 46 no. 1 (2005): 28–42.

Hawkins v. Board of Control 1950.

Hirt, Joan B., Terrell L. Strayhorn, Catherine Amelink, and Belinda Bennett. "The nature of student affairs work at historically black colleges and universities." *Journal of College and Student Development*, 47 no. 6 (2006): 661–676.

Jackson, Jerlando F. L. Retention of African American administrators at pre- dominantly White institutions: Using professional growth factors to inform the discussion. Paper presented at the Annual Meeting of the Association for the Study of Higher Education, Richmond, VA. (ERIC Document Reproduction Service No. ED 457 818), 2001.

Jones, Tamara B., JeffriAnne Wilder, and La'Tara Osborne-Lampkin. "The race against time: Preparing black students for the changing landscape of higher education." *The Journal of Negro Education*, 82 no. 3 (2013): 326–338.

Joseph, Mark, and Jessica Feldman. "Creating and sustaining successful mixed-income communities: Conceptualizing the role of schools." *Education and Urban Society*, 41 no. 6 (2009): 623–652.

Lee Jr., John Michael, and Samaad Wes Keys. Repositioning HBCUs for the future: Access, success, research & innovation. APLU Office of Access and Success Discussion Paper, 1, 2013.

Lovitts, Barbara E. "Being a good course-taker is not enough: A theoretical perspective on the transition to independent research." *Studies in Higher Education*, 30 no. 2 (2005): 137–154.

Lovitts, Barbara E. Leaving the ivory tower: The causes and consequences of departure from doctoral study. New York: Rowman and Littlefield Publishers, Inc., 2001.

Lundy-Wagner, Valerie, Julie Vultaggio, and Marybeth Gasman. "Preparing underrepresented students of color for doctoral success: The role of undergraduate institutions." *International Journal of Doctoral Studies*, 8 (2103): 151–172. Retrieved from http://ijds.org/Volume8/IJDSv8p151-172Lundy-Wagner0381.pdf

Maton, Kenneth I., and Freeman Hrabrowski III. "Increasing the number of African American PhDs in the sciences and engineering: A strengths-based approach." *American Psychologist*, 59 no. 6 (2004): 547–556.

Means, Darris R., Cameron C. Beatty, Reginald A. Blockett, Michael Bumbrey, Robert Canida II, and Tony Cawthorn. "Resilient scholars: Reflections from black gay men on the doctoral journey." *Journal of Student Affairs, Research and Practice*, 54 no. 1 (2016): 109–120. Retrieved from http://dx.doi:org/10.1080/19496591.2016.1219265

National Center for Education Statistics. Selected statistics on degree-granting historically black colleges and universities, y control and level of institution: Selected years, 1990 through 2013, 2015. Retrieved from http://nces.ed.gov/programs/digest/d14/tables/dt14_313.30.asp?current=yes

National Center for Education Statistics. The condition of education 2012. Washington, DC: US Department of Education, 2012. Retrieved from https://nces.ed.gov/fastfacts/display.asp?id=72

National Center for Education Statistics. Doctor's degrees conferred by degree-granting institutions, by sex, racial/ethnic group, and major field of study: 2003–04, 2005. Retrieved from http://nces.ed.gov/programs/digest/d05/tables/xls/tabn268.xls

National Opinion Research Center. (2007). Survey of earned doctorates: Summary re- port 2006. Washington, DC: National Academy Press. Retrieved from www.norc.org/NR/rdonlyres/C22A3F40-0BA2-4993-A6D3-5E65939EEDC3/0/06SRFinalVersion.pdf

Nerad, Maresi, and Debra S. Miller. "Increasing student retention in graduate and professional programs." *New Directions in Institutional Research*, 92 (1996): 61–76.

Nettles, Michael T., and Catherine M. Millet. *Three magic words: Getting to Ph.D.* Baltimore, MD: The Johns Hopkins University Press, 2006.

Ogren, Christine A. "Rethinking the 'nontraditional' student from a historical perspective: State normal schools in the late nineteenth and early twentieth centuries." *The Journal of Higher Education*, 74 no. 6 (2003): 640–664.

Okahana, Hironao, Jeff Allum, Pamela P. Felder, and Renata Tull. Implications for practice and research from Doctoral Initiative on Minority Attrition and Completion (CGS Data Sources PLUS #16–01). Washington, DC: Council of Graduate Schools, 2016.

Palmer, Robert T., Adriel A. Hilton, and Tiffany P. Fountaine (Eds.). *Black graduate education at historically black colleges and universities: Trends, experiences, and outcomes*. New York/London: Information Age Press, 2012.

Palmer, Robert, and Marybeth Gasman. "'It takes a village to raise a child': The role of social capital in promoting academic success for African American men at a black college." *Journal of College Student Development*, 49 no. 1 (2008): 52–70.

Pascarella, Ernest T., and Patrick T. Terenzini. *How college affects students: A third decade of research*. San Francisco: Jossey-Bass, 2005.

Provasnik, Stephen, Linda L. Shafer, and Thomas D. Snyder. *Historically universities, 1976 to 2001 (NCES 2004–062)*. Washington, DC: National Center for Education Statistics, 2004. Retrieved from http://purl.LPS54090

Roach, Ronald. "Clouded optimism." *Black Issues in Higher Education*, 14 no. 11 (1997): 16–19.

St. John, Eric. "More doctorates in the house—More African American students are receiving doctorates." *Black Issues in Higher Education*. Retrieved July 6, 2001, from http://findarticles.com/p/articles/mi_m0DXK/is_10_17/ai_63817017

Survey of Earned Doctorates. *Doctorate recipients from US Universities: 2014*. National Center for Science and Engineering Statistics Directorate for Social, Behavioral and Economic, Arlington, VA. Retrieved from http://www.nsf.gov/statistics/2016/nsf16300/.

Sweatt v. Painter, 1950.

Swygert, H. Patrick. "The accomplishments and challenges of historically Black colleges and universities." 2nd Annual African American Leadership Summit: Washington, DC, 2004.

Taylor, Maurice C. "On a wing and a prayer: The future of graduate education at HBCUs." In Palmer, Robert T., Adriel A. Hilton, and Tiffany P. Fountaine, *Black graduate education at historically black colleges and universities* (pp. 223–252). New York: Information Age Press, 2012.

Terenzini, Patrick T., Patricia. M. Yaeger, Lousie Bohr, Ernest T. Pascarella., and Nora Amaury. *African American college students' experiences in HBCUs and PWIs and learning outcomes*. University Park, PA: National Center on Postsecondary Teaching, Learning, and Assessment,1997.

Thompson, Gail L. "What the numbers really mean: African American under- representation at the doctoral level." *Journal of College Student Retention*, 1 no. 1 (1999): 23–40.

Tinto, Vince. *Leaving college: Rethinking the causes and cures of student attrition* (2nd ed.). Chicago, IL: University of Chicago Press, 1993.

"Top 100 Degree Producers 2016: Graduate and Professional." *Diverse*. Retrieved from http://diverseeducation.com/top100/GraduateDegreeProducers2016.php

Turner, Caroline, Sotello Viernes, and Judith Rann Thompson. "Socializing women doctoral students: Minority and majority experiences." *Review of Higher Education*, 16 no. 3 (1993): 355–370.

Upton, Rachel and Courtney Tanenbaum. The role of historically black colleges and universities as pathway providers: Institutional pathways to the STEM PhD among black students. American Institutes for Research, 2014. Retrieved from www.air.org/sites/default/files/downloads/report/Role%20of%20HBCUs%20in%20STEM%20PhDs%20for%20Black%20Students.pdf

US Department of Education, Office of Civil Rights. *Historically black colleges and universities and higher education desegregation*, 1991. Retrieved from www2.ed.gov/about/offices/list/ocr/docs/hq9511.html

Weddle-West, Karen, Hayden Joseph Waldon, and Kristie M. Norwood. "Impact of college environments on the spiritual development of African American students." *Journal of College Student Development*, 45 no. 3 (2013): 299–314.

Wendler, Cathy, Brent Bridgeman, Fred Cline, Catherine Millett, JoAnn Rock, Nathan Bell, and Patricia McAllister. The path forward: The future of graduate education in the United States: Report from the commission on the future of graduate education in the United States. Princeton, NJ: Educational Testing Service, 2010.

2 Historically Black Colleges' and Universities' Role in Preparing Professional Students for the Global Workforce

Larry J. Walker and Ramon B. Goings

Introduction

Since their inception in the 1800s, Historically Black Colleges and Universities (HBCUs) have played a critical role in increasing the number of Black students enrolled in graduate programs.[1] Despite inadequate state and federal funding, HBCUs provide nurturing environments, committed faculty, and rigorous courses that prepare students to compete in the global workforce.[2] HBCUs are integral to minority and underserved communities because they produce skilled practitioners with similar lived experiences. This is increasingly important because of shifting demographics. For instance, according to the US Census Bureau, the United States will become a majority-minority nation by 2044.[3] Thus, recognizing the connection between HBCUs, workforce diversity, and 21st century skills is more important than ever.

Producing Black lawyers, doctors, dentists, and pharmacists affects treatment rates, access to legal advice, and the overall health of individuals in Black and underserved communities. According to one study on minority physicians and diversifying the workforce, "nonwhite physicians provide a disproportionate share of care to underserved populations. Hence, increasing racial and ethnic diversity of the physician workforce may be key to meeting national goals to eliminate health disparities."[4] Producing more Black graduate students, particularly in health sciences, would have long-term implications for vulnerable populations. HBCUs are the key to closing health disparities in urban and rural communities. In addition, recruiting and training students is vital considering the aging United States population. Moreover, because of globalization, there will be an increasing need for professionals, with specialized skills, who can cross borders and solve complex issues.[5]

Historically Black Colleges and Universities are uniquely suited to help Black students succeed in today's society. Unfortunately, the increasing racialized rhetoric has created a hostile environment at some predominantly White institutions (PWIs).[6] Fortunately, HBCUs offer Black students a respite from hostile academic and social environments, which can increase student anxiety levels. By contrast, students enrolled in graduate programs at PWIs have to navigate microaggressions and macroaggressions that could increase attrition rates.[7] According to Osanloo, Boske, and Newcomb, "macroaggressions occur at a structural level encompassing actions that are meant to exclude, either by action or omission,"[8] while "microaggressions are exemplified by dismissive and often innocuous comments, behaviors or beliefs that minimize, exclude, or render insignificant."[9] The experiences of STEM students can be particularly difficult because of the dearth of Black peers, professors, and mentors at some PWIs.[10] A study examining how STEM undergraduate research experiences influence choices to attend graduate school found that students of color have to navigate "multiple identities"[11] while balancing relationships with mentors.

The findings are important because Black students encounter negative experiences throughout the baccalaureate to post-baccalaureate pipeline that shape their identity and self-confidence.[12] For Black women, and other women of color, their racial and gendered experiences are complicated by relationships with peers or faculty members that cannot see beyond stereotypes and misconceptions. Gibbs and Griffin's study on Biomedical PhD graduates found that women, specifically women of color, encountered an array of racist behavior, and "women of color more often described race as having a direct impact on the quality of their training experiences."[13] While it is important to note that racism and sexism exist at post-secondary institutions throughout the nation, HBCUs have been increasingly successful at producing Black female graduates.[14] For this reason, contextualizing the experiences of Black graduate students regardless of their gender, sexual orientation, gender expression, and identity at HBCUs is important.

For this chapter, the authors utilized Urie Bronfenbrenner's Bioecological Systems Theory as a lens to examine the relationship between Black graduate student experiences on HBCU campuses and workforce readiness skills.[15] This will include delineating how the microsystem and exosystem impact student outcomes. For the purposes of this chapter, the microsystem includes faculty and peer relationships, while the exosystem includes university missions and support systems. Examining each system is critical to understanding HBCUs' success enrolling and graduating students from under-resourced communities. Furthermore, the chapter includes an examination of the Black professional's role in an increasingly borderless world.

Literature Review

In totality, HBCUs offer Black graduate students collegial environments that are culturally centered and committed to preparing alumni to compete with students from ethnically, racially, and linguistically diverse backgrounds.[16] While some HBCUs' financial and structural challenges are considerable, the institutions have built a foundation that prepares students in health and social sciences, among other disciplines, to succeed despite the odds.[17]

Throughout their history, HBCUs have inculcated values and traditions that served students well after graduation.[18] The transfer of ideas and beliefs is what makes HBCUs unique and contributes to student success.[19] For example, a study from Gallup concluded that in comparison to Black alumni from PWIs, HBCU alumni believed they are better prepared to succeed after graduation.[20] The findings can be attributed to an environment that shields Black students from explicit and implicit bias while centering instruction within cultural norms. This sense of familial protectionism is an essential element, which allows Black graduate students to excel at HBCUs. For this chapter, familial protectionism describes a community-centered approach in which HBCUs focus on the individual (emotional wellbeing, spirituality, religiosity, meditation, and physical health) and external factors (racism, classism, and cultural identity) while utilizing African American principles related to family.[21]

Centering instruction on Black students is important because of the challenges they encounter, including racial discrimination.[22] The National Academies Press defines racial discrimination as "differential treatment on the basis of race that disadvantages a racial group."[23] HBCUs play an important role in preparing students to counter systemic barriers. For decades HBCU professional schools have developed a cadre of Black change agents committed to fighting for social justice.[24] For instance, Howard University trained Thurgood Marshall, the nation's first African American Supreme Court Justice, who left an indelible impact on the legal system. Prior to his confirmation to the court, he successfully litigated *Brown v. Board of Education*; post-*Brown*, Marshall stood steadfast against racial animus as a member of the court.

Marshall is one example among many students that successfully navigated the workforce after completing a degree at an HBCU. Students learn valuable skills throughout their tenure, including the importance of community, political skills, and skills for shaping social change.[25] Today they continue their role in preparing students in critical areas, including medicine, dentistry, and law. HBCUs produce 70% of Black physicians and dentists and 35% of the nation's lawyers.[26] Additionally, from 2000 to 2008, the number of pharmacy degrees awarded by HBCUs to Black students rose to 38%.[27]

These aforementioned statistics highlight the role HBCUs play in preparing professionals in key disciplines. In spite of HBCUs' success, the US continues to struggle to prepare Black students for careers in health sciences and STEM disciplines.[28] The failure to recruit, train, and support more students in critical fields, including engineering, may be rooted in systemic failures that create barriers for talented Black students.[29] Consequently, more must be done to identify frameworks and strategies that dramatically increase the number of Black and other minority students in important areas.

Although HBCUs have a successful record of preparing professional students for the global workforce, students encounter some of the same stressors as their counterparts at PWIs. Laurence and Williams' study of 143 students at the Howard University School of Dentistry found that 16.7% were coping with depressive symptomatology.[30] The findings mirror other studies examining the relationship between environmental stressors and academic performance for students at HBCUs.[31] It's important to recognize that while HBCUs do shield students from some societal pressures, they have to overcome mental health challenges related to community, familial, or race based traumas.[32]

While HBCUs provide nurturing environments that sustain students throughout economic and personal struggles, they face challenges that could upend their history of enrolling and graduating students from minority and underserved communities. For example, financial hardships related to historical inequities, mismanagement, and limited fundraising are problematic for institutions with a proud history but small endowments.[33] Some HBCUs are seeking to reverse enrollment declines in an increasingly hostile political environment.[34] More importantly, several HBCUs face leadership changes that reflect disagreements between university leaders, board members, and alumni.[35] Ensuring HBCUs continue to thrive will be predicated on institutional changes, including recruiting Latino students and other subgroups from low- and moderate-income backgrounds.[36]

Overall, HBCUs present opportunities for graduate students with limited financial means to receive a quality education in a supportive environment. However, they cannot allow a singular focus on the past to blind them to the obstacles students have to overcome prior to and after they matriculate.[37] Building sustainable models that focus on student engagement, resource allocation, cultivating new donors, and attrition rates are the key to their success.[38] HBCUs have to be prepared to compete with post-secondary institutions with a reputation for supporting various subgroups. Increasingly, some PWIs are creating institutes or programs targeting marginalized populations. Schools that fail to keep pace risk alienating students and hindering recruitment and retention efforts.

The Importance of Safe Spaces for Black LGBTQ Students Post-Baccalaureate

Over the last few years, several scholars have written treatises discussing the important role safe spaces play at post-secondary institutions. Primarily, these discussions revolve around the experiences of ethnic, racial, religious, and LGBTQ students at PWIs.[39] While it is accurate to suggest that subgroups are forced to navigate challenging spaces on PWI campuses, HBCUs have to take steps to ensure every student on campus feels safe and welcomed. Recently there has been a stronger focus on micro-communities, specifically LGBTQ students on HBCU campuses.[40] Gasman and Harper found LGBTQ students encounter barriers at HBCUs because of their socially conservative histories.[41] The findings suggest that there should be a stronger emphasis on the experiences of LGBTQ students at HBCUs.

Currently, there is scant research that focuses on LGBTQ graduate students at HBCUs. In an increasingly diverse society, there should be a stronger focus on LGBTQ student engagement, allocating resources for programs, and providing mentors with similar experiences. This can be accomplished by school leaders that coordinate with faculty and staff to collect data and identify exemplar programs at other post-secondary institutions. Moreover, some HBCUs may have to consider altering their mission statements or student handbook to ensure they reflect 21st century realities.

HBCUs that choose to amend policies and increase programmatic opportunities for LGBTQ students could recruit talented graduate students seeking inclusive environments. Considering the drop in enrollment at some HBCUs, developing tools via social media and other outlets represent unique openings to broaden appeals to targeted groups. In order to compete for highly qualified students, some HBCUs, similar to Bowie State in Maryland, have to create safe spaces for LGBTQ students.[42]

Far too often, when researchers discuss student diversity, they assume that the Black community is monolithic. Rarely are issues that intersect, including race, sexual orientation, gender expression, and identity examined, particularly on HBCU campuses.[43] To ensure their survival, some HBCUs will have to consider a paradigm shift. This should include actively recruiting LGBTQ students to broaden the applicant pool and diversify the student body. In addition, HBCUs have to be prepared to hire administrators, faculty, and staff to support LGBTQ student needs. This should also include funding for LGBTQ centers that create safe spaces and fund key programs.

Recognizing and actively seeking out LGBTQ graduate students will have several benefits, including: 1) preparing students to work with diverse populations; 2) strengthening linkages between cisgender and LGBTQ students; 3) creating welcoming environments that reflect 21st century work spaces; and 4) creating a diverse alumni base. Moreover, creating an LGBTQ friendly campus will improve the university's standing among the higher education community and employers. HBCUs with antiquated models will struggle to prepare students for an increasingly diverse workforce and could encounter decreasing enrollment. Thus, it is incumbent on school leaders to develop progressive policies and programs which are consistent with Fortune 500 companies. Choosing to ignore the needs of growing communities could hamper HBCUs' efforts to broaden their appeal and prepare students to compete in the global economy.

University Microsystem: Faculty and Peer Relationships

Students that matriculate at HBCUs excel because they are beneficiaries of institutions with a community-centered focus. The relationships between university leaders, faculty, and students are the glue that keeps students from leaving school because of financial, family, or personal obstacles.[44] In addition, HBCUs provide opportunities for students from low socioeconomic backgrounds to graduate and build wealth. According to a study on HBCU graduates, "HBCUs are also essentially responsible for the creation of the Black middle class, as a disproportionately high percentage of Black political leaders, lawyers, doctors, and PhDs were educated at HBCUs."[45] The relationship between Black wealth, HBCUs, and professional schools cannot be ignored. Without HBCUs, the percentage of Black students enrolled in graduate schools would drop dramatically.[46]

For this reason, investigating how and why strong linkages exist between members of the university family is critical. Students at HBCUs benefit from strong student-to-faculty and peer-to-peer relationships that bind the academic community.[47] Hard to reach subgroups, including Black males, succeed because faculty members take time during and after class to mentor scholars. Palmer and Maramba's study on Black males at an HBCU found, "embedded in the relationship that faculty have with students is demonstrating concern not only for students' academic success, but also for their experiences and success outside of the classroom. He emphasized that displaying a caring mentality is more important than implementing a variety of programmatic initiatives to promote student success."[48] The description mirrors empirical research, which highlights the substantive relationships between students and faculty at HBCUs.[49] Faculty don't simply work with students within the confines of the classroom but take time after class, including weekends, to support their efforts.

Faculty members at HBCUs act as surrogate parents, confidantes, and academic advisors,[50] playing a critical role in the lives of graduate students. It is important for aspiring physicians, dentists, and pharmacists to have access to individuals from similar ethnic and racial backgrounds. Specifically, faculty and students can discuss how to navigate homogenous workspaces where they may encounter stereotypes and misconceptions. After graduation, relationships between faculty and former students continue to foster conversations on professional development and future goals as well as aspirations. Support during and after graduate school is important, particularly for Black students that depend on faculty members to help chart their career path.

Without positive feedback and support from faculty members, HBCUs could struggle to retain Black graduate students. For instance, Fountaine's study on Black doctoral students and faculty relationships determined that engagement was linked to student persistence.[51] The findings are noteworthy because there is limited research on the experiences of graduate students at HBCUs. Primarily, the research focuses on undergraduate experiences without considering how HBCUs foster collegial environments for Black students post-baccalaureate.

Similar to faculty-to-student relationships, peer-to-peer relationships play an equally significant role for students at HBCUs. In school settings, students encourage each other to set high expectations and meet academic benchmarks. A participant from Palmer and Gasman's study on social capital and African American students at an HBCU noted, "most of my friends . . . they have goals, they're ambitious, they have drive, passion. I try to keep people like that close to me and I think that's how that's changing me, because I kind of emulated them in a way; it kind of made me become more focused."[52] The participant's response highlights how student relationships are motivating factors and contribute to academic and social success. These peer relationships help undergraduate and graduate students overcome school related challenges that impact attrition rates.

For graduate students, university cohorts can alleviate stressors associated with meeting academic benchmarks.[53] Collectively students complete classroom assignments, prepare for exams, and navigate relationships with faculty. In addition, student cohorts provide opportunities for students to develop interpersonal skills, learn to work in small groups, and collaborate on research opportunities. Partnering on research projects may be particularly important for graduate students that attend HBCUs because of limited departmental and university funding. Overall, HBCUs offer Black graduate students competitive and nurturing settings that encourage students to work together before and after graduation.

University Ecosystem: Mission and Support Systems

Black students that enroll and graduate from professional programs make up a small percentage of the overall numbers. This is particularly true for Black physicians. Today, practicing Black physicians represent only 5% of the profession, while Blacks make up 13% of the US population.[54] The reasons why a small percentage of Black students apply and are currently enrolled in medical school is complex. Recently, researchers have tried to discern why there is a drop in Black males applying to medical school.[55] The trend is troubling and influenced by institutional and structural barriers that negate progress in other areas.[56]

Without medical schools, including Howard, Morehouse, Meharry, and Charles Drew, the number of Black male and female students would dramatically shrink. HBCUs continue to have a prominent role in preparing students for careers in the health sciences. Unfortunately, Black students are less likely to be admitted to medical schools in comparison to their White counterparts. A study conducted by Castillo-Page concluded that African Americans had the lowest acceptance rates for medical school in comparison to other groups.[57]

Acknowledging that African American students struggle to be admitted to medical school is important. Despite the troubling figure, HBCUs are graduating Black students. A study that disaggregated medical school acceptance rates determined that if you remove HBCUs from the data, there would be a dramatic drop in Black medical students.[58] The finding supports evidence that HBCUs admit students that may need additional academic support but are prepared to compete after they graduate.

HBCUs admit students from low- to moderate-income backgrounds because it is consistent with their missions. Gasman and McMickens examined the mission statements of HBCUs and categorized based on the following: liberal arts, professional/practical, or schools that encompass both.[59] A few schools from the list have professional schools, including Texas Southern University, University of the District of Columbia, and Florida A&M University. Based on an analysis, HBCUs' mission statements focused on two core ideas, including a commitment to morals and ethics and dedication to community service.

The areas of emphasis are why HBCUs succeed in producing Black physicians while other post-secondary institutions fail to admit and retain students. Students receive considerable support from individuals from similar backgrounds that care about their long-term growth. Morally, HBCUs feel compelled to give students first or second chances when society turns its back. Very few post-secondary institutions are committed to giving Black students with low MCAT scores an opportunity to develop their skills. This is particularly true because professional schools place a strong emphasis on standardized test scores. However, they don't measure student resiliency or work ethic. HBCUs recognize they play a critical role in enrolling and educating students from diverse backgrounds. Without their commitment, the nation could struggle to train a new cadre of physicians, dentists, pharmacists, and scientists. HBCUs represent an important link between 21st century skills and global competiveness. More than ever the nation needs their expertise providing nurturing environments for Black students.

The Black Professional, HBCUs, and the Global Workforce

The Presidential election between Donald Trump and Hillary Clinton highlighted national fears regarding globalization. Some pundits have reshaped the narrative and suggested that populist views relating to economic anxieties among the White working class contributed to the election result.[60] Issues relating to racism, xenophobia, and sexism are rarely discussed. However, they also fail to understand that economic concerns among some Whites are rooted in a fear of change. Specifically, the belief that trade (NAFTA and TIPP), immigration (ethnocentrism), and borderless countries (European Union) have limited opportunities for working and middle class Whites. Most of these individuals do not have the skills to compete with ethnic and racial groups with skills in high need areas.

Fears regarding globalization, including automation and national and international competition, are driving the narrative.[61] Recent and future HBCU graduates have to be prepared to circumvent workspaces with individuals that may not understand or feel comfortable with a person of color. This could include workplace hostilities, including harassment, demotions, or receiving a separation of service notice.

Fortunately, HBCUs instill a sense of self-confidence and wellbeing that can help alumni avoid or challenge uncomfortable workforce occurrences. Despite the challenges, employers are seeking qualified individuals from diverse backgrounds with important skills. Growth from economies in Africa and Asia may force hospitals, research institutes, post-secondary institutions, and think tanks to hire individuals with culturally rich backgrounds. Change occurs rapidly in today's society. For this reason, HBCUs have to prepare students to be flexible and prepared to seek opportunities outside the United States.

Recommendations and Implications

Advocates for HBCUs have to continue to demonstrate how these institutions contribute to the higher education landscape. From a student services perspective, faculty and staff, including career center staff and advisors, have to help counter deficit narratives that HBCUs are not as "competitive" as PWIs. Moreover, HBCUs have to be prepared to challenge misnomers that HBCUs are institutions that only serve Black students, offer limited opportunities for research, and have poorly trained faculty members. This monograph is a first step in reshaping the narrative regarding professional programs at HBCUs.

From a scholarly perspective, more research is needed that explores the contributions of graduate education programs at HBCUs. Given that a majority of the research has focused on the student experience, it will be critical to arm HBCU advocates with research that delineates the student experience at HBCUs across multiple identities (e.g., race, gender, class). In addition to exploring student experiences, researchers should focus on institutional and programmatic efforts at HBCUs. For instance, what policies, programs, and practices do graduate schools at HBCUs offer that foster student engagement and a sense of community on campus? In addition, how do HBCUs build partnerships with community organizations so their graduate students have the opportunity to apply their coursework in a real-world context while simultaneously contributing to their community?

Lastly, from a policy perspective, it is critical that pro-HBCU policymakers and stakeholders use research on HBCUs to ensure they are adequately funded. For example, policymakers at the state level need to work with higher education commissioners and chancellors to prevent duplicate programs at PWIs. A recent example in the state of Maryland highlights the long-term impact duplicate programs can have on HBCUs. The Coalition for Equity and Excellence in Maryland Higher Education, which represented three HBCUs in Maryland, sued the Maryland Higher Education Commission. Historically the institutions were underfunded in comparison to state PWIs, and the Commission allowed them to duplicate programs offered at HBCUs.[62] As a result, the programs hampered efforts by HBCUs to recruit students. If policymakers in Maryland and other states are concerned with

HBCUs' viability, then there must be stronger efforts to equalize funding and prevent harmful policies and programs.

Considering the recent election results and the increased hostility toward students of color at PWIs, HBCUs are in a unique position to educate prospective professional students who are looking for welcoming school environments. As our nation becomes more racially and ethnically diverse, it is critical that healthcare, finance, and law professionals, among others, reflect the shifting demographics. It is our hope that HBCUs continue to play a vital role shaping the future of professional programs. Without HBCUs, the nation will struggle to recruit, train, and graduate students with untapped potential.

Notes

1. Palmer, Hilton, and Fountaine 2012; Palmer et al. 2016
2. Palmer, Davis, and Gasman 2011
3. Colby and Ortman 2014
4. Marrast et al. 2014, p. 289
5. Okoro and Washington 2012
6. Cabrera 2014; Harper 2012
7. Henfield, Hongryun, and Washington 2013
8. Osanloo, Boske, and Newcomb 2016, p. 6
9. Osanloo, Boske, and Newcomb 2016, p. 3
10. Joseph 2012
11. Eagan et al. 2013, p. 690
12. Boykin 2016
13. Gibbs and Griffin 2013, p. 717
14. Owens, Bloom, and Cavil 2012
15. Bronfenbrenner 1979
16. Palmer and Maramba 2013
17. Wilcox et al. 2014
18. Gasman, Lundy-Wagner, and Bowman III 2010
19. Goings 2015(b)
20. Seymour and Ray 2014
21. Russell-Brown 2005
22. Boysen 2012
23. National Academies Press 2004, p. 55
24. Gasman and Williams 2012
25. Sydnor, Smith-Hawkins, and Edwards 2010.
26. Avery 2009
27. Noonan, Lindong, and Jaitley 2013.
28. McGee, Jr., Saran, and Krulwich 2012
29. Ford 2010; Harper 2010
30. Laurence, Williams, and Eiland 2009
31. Walker 2015
32. Walker (under review)
33. Boland and Gasman 2014; Coupet and Barnum 2010; Johnson 2013
34. Palmer, Davis, and Thompson 2010; Richards, David, and Awokoya 2012
35. Nicholas 2004; Commodore et al. 2016
36. Garcia-McMillian 2014; Palmer et al. 2015
37. Peters et al. 2013

38 Gasman and Bowman III 2011; Gasman and Bowman III 2013; Strayhorn and DeVita 2010
39 Greyerbiehl and Mitchell 2014
40 Patton 2011
41 Harper and Gasman 2008
42 Mobley and Johnson 2015
43 Patton and Simmons 2008
44 Mawhinney 2011
45 Strayhorn et al. 2013
46 Lee 2012
47 Bonner II 2014
48 Palmer and Maramba 2012, p. 105
49 Flowers et al. 2015
50 Bryant-Shanklin and Brumage 2011
51 Fountaine 2012
52 Palmer and Gasman 2008, p. 60
53 Ross et al. 2011
54 Tweedy 2015
55 Goings 2015(a)
56 Butler, Longaker, and Britt 2010
57 Castillo-Page 2012
58 Isaac et al. 2014
59 Gasman and McMickens 2010
60 Johnston 2016
61 Thompson 2015
62 Palmer, Davis, and Gasman 2011

Bibliography

Avery, Sheldon. "Taking the pulse of historically black colleges." *Academic Questions*, 22 no. 3 (2009): 327–339.

Boland, William, and Marybeth Gasman. "America's public HBCUs: A four state comparison of institutional capacity and state funding priorities." 2014.

Bonner II, Fred A. The critical need for faculty mentoring. In Bonner Fred, Aretha Tuitt Marbley, Frank Robinson, Rosa Petra Banda, and Robin Hughes, *Black Faculty in the Academy: Narratives for Negotiating Identity and Achieving Career Success*, (pp. 123–135). New York: Routledge, 2014.

Boykin, T. F. Journey to the PhD: A personal narrative of doctoral studies at an HBCU." In Palmer, Robert T., Larry Walker, Ramone Goings, Charmaine E. Troy, Chaz T. Gipson, and Dr. Felecia Commodore, *Graduate education at historically Black colleges and universities (HBCUs): A student perspective* (pp. 25–38). New York: Taylor & Francis, 2016.

Boysen, Guy A. "Teacher and student perceptions of microaggressions in college classrooms." *College Teaching*, 60 no. 3 (2012): 122–129.

Bronfenbrenner, Urie. "Ecology of human development: Experiments by nature and design." 1979.

Bryant-Shanklin, Mona, & Brumage, Norma W. "Collaborative responsive education mentoring: Mentoring for professional development." *Higher Education. Florida Journal of Educational Administration & Policy*, 5 no. 1 (2011): 42–53.

Butler, Paris D, Michael T. Longaker, and L.D. Britt. Addressing the paucity of underrepresented minorities in academic surgery: Can the "Rooney Rule" be applied to academic surgery? *The American Journal of Surgery,* 2010 no. 199. DOI: 10.1016/j.amjsurg.2009.05.021Cabrera, Nolan León. "Exposing whiteness in higher education: White male college students minimizing racism, claiming victimization, and recreating White supremacy." *Race Ethnicity and Education,* 17 no. 1 (2014): 30–55.

Castillo-Page, Laura. *Diversity in medical education: Facts and figures,* Association of American Medical Colleges, Washington, DC, 2012.

Colby, Sandra L., and Jennifer M. Ortman. *Projections of the size and composition of the U.S. Population: 2014 to 2060.* Washington, DC: Current Population Reports, P25–1143, U.S. Census Bureau, 2014.

Commodore, Felicia, Sydney Freeman, Gasman, Marybeth, & Carter, Courtney M. (2016). "How It's Done": The Role of Mentoring and Advice in Preparing the Next Generation of Historically Black College and University Presidents. Education Sciences, 6 no. 19 (2016): 1–14.

Coupet, Jason, and Darold Barnum. "HBCU efficiency and endowments: An exploratory analysis." *International Journal of Educational Advancement,* 10 no. 3 (2010): 186–197.

Eagan Jr, M. Kevin, Sylvia Hurtado, Mitchell J. Chang, Gina A. Garcia, Felicia A. Herrera, and Juan C. Garibay. "Making a difference in science education: the impact of undergraduate research programs." *American Educational Research Journal,* 50 no. 4 (2013): 683–713.

Flowers, Alonzo, Jameel Scott, Jamie Riley, and Robert T. Palmer. "Beyond the call of duty: An analysis of the effects of othermothering at historically black colleges and universities (HBCUs)." *Journal of African American Males in Education (JAAME),* 6 no. 1 (2015), 59–73.

Ford, Donna. Reversing underachievement among gifted Black students. Waco, TX: Prufrock Press, 2010.

Fountaine, Tiffany Patrice. "The impact of faculty–student interaction on black doctoral students attending historically black institutions." *The Journal of Negro Education,* 81 no. 2 (2012): 136–147.

Garcia-McMillian, Darilis. Latino student perceptions of college experiences at Historically Black Colleges and Universities. Hampton University, 2014.

Gasman, Marybeth, and Nelson Bowman III. A guide to fundraising at Historically Black Colleges and Universities: An all campus approach. Routledge, 2011.

Gasman, Marybeth, and Nelson Bowman III. Engaging diverse college alumni: The essential guide to fundraising. Routledge, 2013.

Gasman, Marybeth, and Tryan L. McMickens. "Liberal or professional education? The missions of public black colleges and universities and their impact on the future of African Americans." *Souls,* 12, no. 3 (2010): 286–305.

Gasman, Marybeth, Valerie Lundy-Wagner, Tafaya Ransom, and Nelson Bowman III. "Special issue: Unearthing promise and potential-our nation's historically black colleges and universities." *ASHE Higher Education Report,* 35 no. 5 (2010): 1–134.

Gasman, Marybeth, and M. S. Williams. "A short history of graduate and professional programs at historically black colleges and universities" In Palmer, Robert T., Adriel A. Hilton, and Tiffany P. Fountaine, *Black graduate education at Historically Black Colleges and Universities: Trends, experiences, and outcomes,* (pp. 9–24). New York: IAP, 2012.

Gibbs, Kenneth D., and Kimberly A. Griffin. "What do I want to be with my PhD? The roles of personal values and structural dynamics in shaping the career interests of recent biomedical science PhD graduates." CBE-Life Sciences Education, 12 no. 4 (2013): 711–723.

Goings, Ramon B. "Increasing the representation of African American medical doctors: A call to action." *The Edvocate* (2015). Retrieved from http://www.theedvocate.org/increasing-the-representation-of-african-american-male-medical-doctors-a-call-to-action/

Goings, Ramon B. "High-achieving African American males at one historically black university: A phenomenological study." PhD diss., Morgan State University, 2015.

Greyerbiehl, Lindsay, and Donald Mitchell Jr. "An intersectional social capital analysis of the influence of historically black sororities on African American women's college experiences at a predominantly White institution." *Journal of Diversity in Higher Education*, 7 no. 4 (2014): 282.

Harper, Shaun R., and Marybeth Gasman. "Consequences of conservatism: Black male undergraduates and the politics of historically black colleges and universities." *The Journal of Negro Education*, 77 no. 4 (2008): 336–351.

Harper, Shaun R. "Race without racism: How higher education researchers minimize racist institutional norms." *The Review of Higher Education*, 36 no. 1 (2012): 9–29.

Harper, Shaun R. "An anti-deficit achievement framework for research on students of color in STEM." *New Directions for Institutional Research*, 2010 no. 148 (2010): 63–74.

Henfield, Malik S., Hongryun Woo, and Ahmad Washington. "A phenomenological investigation of African American counselor education students' challenging experiences." *Counselor Education and Supervision*, 52 no. 2 (2013): 122–136.

Isaac, John, Kendrick Davis, Ruthita Fike, Paul Isaac, Asia Archer, Clement Aroh, and Adaku Ume. "An idea whose time has come: The need for increased diversity in medical practice and education." *Western Journal of Black Studies*, 38 no. 1 (2014): 35.

Johnson, Melvin Norman. "Financial and related issues among historically black colleges and universities." *Journal of Intercollegiate Sport*, 6 no. 1 (2013): 65–75.

Johnston, David. "Why voters elected President Donald Trump and why they'll regret it." *The Daily Beast*, November 9, 2016.

Joseph, Joretta. "From one culture to another: Years one and two of graduate school for African American women in the STEM fields." *International Journal of Doctoral Studies*, 7 (2012): 125–142.

Laurence, Brian, Carla Williams, and Derrick Eiland. "Depressive symptoms, stress, and social support among dental students at a historically black college and university." *Journal of American College Health*, 58 no. 1 (2009): 56–63.

Lee, John M. "An examination of the participation of African American students in graduate education without public HBCUs." In Palmer, Robert T., Adriel A. Hilton, and Tiffany P. Fountaine, *Black Graduate Education at Historically Black Colleges and Universities: Trends, Experiences, and Outcomes* (pp. 61–82). New York: IAP, 2012.

Marrast, Lyndonna M., Leah Zallman, Steffie Woolhandler, David H. Bor, and Danny McCormick. "Minority physicians' role in the care of underserved patients: Diversifying the physician workforce may be key in addressing health disparities." *JAMA Internal Medicine*, 174 no. 2 (2014): 289–291.

Mawhinney, Lynnette. "Othermothering: A personal narrative exploring relationships between black female faculty and students." *Negro Educational Review*, 62 no. 1–4 (2011): 213.

McGee Jr, Richard, Suman Saran, and Terry A. Krulwich. "Diversity in the biomedical research workforce: developing talent." *Mount Sinai Journal of Medicine: A Journal of Translational and Personalized Medicine*, 79 no. 3 (2012): 397–411.

Mobley, Steve D., and Jennifer M. Johnson. "The role of HBCUs in addressing the unique needs of LGBT students." *New Directions for Higher Education*, 2015 no. 170 (2015): 79–89.

National Research Council. *Measuring racial discrimination*. Washington, DC: National Academies Press, 2004.

Nichols, Joyce Coleman. "Unique characteristics, leadership styles, and management of historically black colleges and universities." *Innovative Higher Education*, 28 no. 3 (2004): 219–229.

Noonan, Allan, Ian Lindong, and Vijai N. Jaitley. "The role of historically black colleges and universities in training the health care workforce." *American Journal of Public Health*, 103 no. 3 (2013): 412–415.

Okoro, Ephraim A., and Melvin C. Washington. "Workforce diversity and organizational communication: Analysis of human capital performance and productivity." *Journal of Diversity Management (Online)*, 7 no. 1 (2012): 57.

Osanloo, Azadeh F., Christa Boske, and Whitney S. Newcomb. "Deconstructing macroaggressions, microaggressions, and structural racism in education: Developing a conceptual model for the intersection of social justice practice and intercultural education." *International Journal of Organizational Theory and Development*, 4 no. 1 (2016): 1–18.

Owens, Emiel W., Andrea J. Shelton, Collette M. Bloom, and J. Kenyatta Cavil. "The significance of HBCUs to the production of STEM graduates: Answering the call." *Educational Foundations*, 26 (2012): 33–47.

Palmer, Robert T., Adriel A. Hilton, and Tiffany P. Fountaine (Eds.). Black graduate education at historically Black colleges and universities: Trends, experiences, and outcomes. New York: IAP, 2012.

Palmer, Robert T., Dina C. Maramba, Taryn Ozuna Allen, and Ramon B. Goings. "From matriculation to engagement on campus: Delineating the experiences of Latino/a students at a public historically black university." *New Directions for Higher Education*, 2015 no. 170 (2015): 67–78.

Palmer, Robert T., and Dina C. Maramba. "The magnificent "MILE": Impacting black male retention and persistence at an HBCU." *Journal of College Student Retention*, 15 no. 1 (2013: 65–72.

Palmer, Robert T., Larry J. Walker, Ramon B. Goings, Charmaine Troy, Chaz T. Gipson, and Felecia Commodore (Eds.). *Graduate education at Historically Black Colleges and Universities (HBCUs): A student perspective*. New York: Routledge, 2016.

Palmer, Robert T., Ryan J. Davis, and Marybeth Gasman. "A matter of diversity, equity, and necessity: The tension between Maryland's higher education system and its historically black colleges and universities over the Office of Civil Rights Agreement." *The Journal of Negro Education*, 80 no. 2 (2011): 121–133.

Palmer, Robert T., Ryan J. Davis, and Tiffany Thompson. "Theory meets practice: HBCU initiatives that promote academic success among African Americans in STEM." *Journal of College Student Development*, 51 no. 4 (2010): 440–443.

Palmer, Robert, and Marybeth Gasman. "'It takes a village to raise a child': The role of social capital in promoting academic success for African American men at a black college." *Journal of College Student Development*, 49 no. 1 (2008): 52–70.

Patton, Lori D., and Symone L. Simmons. "Exploring complexities of multiple identities of lesbians in a black college environment." *Negro Educational Review*, 59 no. 3/4 (2008): 197.

Patton, Lori D. "Perspectives on identity, disclosure, and the campus environment among African American gay and bisexual men at one historically black college." *Journal of College Student Development*, 52 no. 1 (2011): 77–100.

Peters, Jr. Ronald J., Kentya Ford, Angela Meshack, Regina Jones Johnson, Mandy Hill, and Ronald J. Peters. "The relationship between perceived psychological distress, behavioral indicators and African-American female college student food insecurity." *American Journal of Health Studies*, 28 no. 3 (2013): 27–133.

Richards, David A. R, and Janet T. Awokoya. "Understanding HBCU retention and completion." *Frederick D. Patterson Research Institute*, UNCF, (2012): 1–24.

Ross, Dorene, Alyson Adams, Elizabeth Bondy, Nancy Dana, Stephanie Dodman, and Colleen Swain. "Preparing teacher leaders: Perceptions of the impact of a cohort-based, job embedded, blended teacher leadership program." *Teaching and Teacher Education*, 27 no. 8 (2011): 1213–1222.

Russell-Brown, Katheryn. "Black protectionism as a civil rights strategy." *Buffalo Law Review*, 53 (2005): 1.

Seymour, Sean, and Julie Ray. "Recent grads more likely to have had useful internships." *Gallup Latest News, Education*, 2014. Retrieved from www.gallup.com/poll/179201

Strayhorn, Terrell Lamont, and James Michael DeVita. "African American males' student engagement: A comparison of good practices by institutional type." *Journal of African American Studies*, 14 no. 1 (2010): 87–105.

Strayhorn, Terrell L., Michael Steven Williams, Derrick Tillman-Kelly, and Todd Suddeth. "Sex differences in graduate school choice for black HBCU bachelor's degree recipients: A national analysis." *Journal of African American Studies*, 17 no. 2 (2013): 174–188.

Sydnor, Kim Dobson, Anita Smith Hawkins, and Lorece V. Edwards. "Expanding research opportunities: Making the argument for the fit between HBCUs and community-based participatory research." *The Journal of Negro Education*, 79 no. 1 (2010): 79–86.

Thompson, Derek. "A world without work." *The Atlantic*, July/August issue.

Tweedy, Damon. "The case for black doctors." *The New York Times*, May 15, 2005.

Walker, Larry J. "We are family: How othermothering can increase mental health awareness among African-American males at HBCUs." In Lucian Yates (Eds.), *The role of non-cognitive factors in the success of African-American collegians* (in press).

Walker, Larry J. *Trauma, environmental stressors, and the African-American college student: Research, practice, and HBCUs*. Philadelphia, PA: Penn Center for Minority Serving Institutions, 2015. Retrieved from www2.gse.upenn.edu/cmsi/content/reports

Wilcox, Clyde, oVita Wells, George Haddad, and Judith K. Wilcox. "The changing democratic functions of historically Black colleges and universities." *New Political Science*, 36 no. 4 (2014): 556–572.

3 Securing the Future

Creating "Social Engineers" for Societal Change at Historically Black College and University Law Schools

Steve D. Mobley, Jr., Sunni L. Solomon II, and A.C. Johnson

Introduction

Historically Black Colleges and Universities (HBCUs) have long been at the fore of shifting and creating societal change. During critical Civil Rights efforts in the 1950s and 1960s, the Black Power movement of the 1970s, and even during the fight to end apartheid in South Africa in the 1980s and 1990s, these unique post-secondary contexts played pivotal roles in creating spaces for their campus communities to transgress and combat systemic societal oppression.[1] Many of the societal advancements that have been made by African Americans in the broader societal context can be credited to HBCUs and their graduates.[2] "Notwithstanding criticism and questions about their relevance in the twenty-first century, HBCUs have been, and continue to be at the forefront of critical issues confronting higher-education in America."[3] The contributions by these unique higher education contexts, and their law schools in particular, cannot be denied. In this chapter, we chronicle the histories of HBCU schools of law, offer a glimpse into how these unique professional programs provide access and myriad opportunities for underrepresented populations to gain entry into the legal field, and underscore their contemporary contributions to the society at large.

A Glimpse Into the Past

Since their founding, HBCU law schools[4] have consistently trained dynamic cohorts of social justice oriented change agents dedicated to advancing Black issues.[5] Though small in number, Historically Black College and University schools of law have long occupied the role of training social engineers in the nuances of legal practice, dating back to the late 1800s with the founding of the Howard University School of Law—the first HBCU law school.[6] The Howard University School of Law (HUSL) was founded as the Howard University Law Department on January 6, 1869 under the leadership of John Mercer Langston.[7] Howard's School of Law was established to prepare African American lawyers who would be committed to helping their communities protect their civil rights.[8] This was especially important during this time period, as Blacks were excluded by Jim Crow segregationist practices from pursuing law degrees at historically White institutions. Another HBCU law school would not be established until 70 years later.

The second HBCU law school to be founded was North Carolina Central University's (NCCU) School of Law. It was established in 1939 as the North Carolina College for Negroes Law School after the North Carolina General Assembly sanctioned House Bill 18.[9] House Bill 18 was endorsed 25 years after Shaw University, in Raleigh, North Carolina, closed its law school in 1914. The closing of Shaw's law school left no option for Blacks to attain a formal legal education in North Carolina, and the state wanted to avoid similar civil rights litigation that was occurring in other states where Blacks were suing to gain admission into public, all-White law schools.[10] The founding of the NCCU School of Law was in theory a prime example of the de facto segregation that was occurring in public education during this time period. The school was established as a "separate but equal" option for Black students who wanted to become lawyers without the state being forced to integrate the University of North Carolina at Chapel Hill's law school.[11]

The NCCU School of Law was not the only HBCU law school to be established as a result of legal intervention. During the 1940s, many professional schools began to emerge in the United States as Blacks who were being denied admission into graduate schools at segregated public universities brought several court cases.[12] "As a result of the lawsuits, legislators in these states opted to start publicly supporting HBCUs rather than integrating all-White schools."[13] This "support" led to the founding of several public HBCU law programs that included: Texas Southern University's Thurgood Marshall School of Law (1947), the Southern University Law Center (1947), and the Florida A&M School of Law (1949).

Like the NCCU School of Law, Texas Southern University's Thurgood Marshall School of Law was also born out of civil rights legislation. In 1947, the 50th Texas legislature passed Texas Senate Bill 140 to establish the Texas State University for Negroes for the primary purpose of creating a separate law school for Blacks[14]. This effort by the Texas legislature was a staunch effort to thwart Herman Sweatt (a Black applicant) from gaining admission into the University of Texas Law School.[15] During the time that Sweatt brought his lawsuit against the state of Texas, the state did not have a law school where Blacks could receive a legal education. Thus, the Texas State University for Negroes was established, and three years after it was founded, it became Texas Southern University[16].

The Southern University Law Center would also have similar beginnings. In 1946, as a response to a Black Louisiana resident seeking admission into Louisiana State University, the Louisiana State Board of Education granted $40,000 for The Southern University Law School to be established for Black law students[17]. The school would open its doors in September 1947. A few years later, in 1949, a similar civil rights case was filed in Florida that would later lead to the establishment of the Florida A&M School of Law. Virgil Darnell Hawkins, a Black student from Daytona Beach, Florida, sought admission into the University of Florida; at the time, this university had the only public law school in the state of Florida.[18] Hawkins was refused admission into the University of Florida College of Law, and in order to maintain a system of segregated schooling, the Florida Board of Control began graduate level programs in pharmacy, engineering, and law at Florida Agricultural and Mechanical College for Negroes, which would later be renamed Florida Agricultural and Mechanical University.[19]

The University of the District of Columbia David A. Clarke[20] School of Law (UDC-DCSL) evolved from two institutions: the Antioch School of Law and the District of Columbia School of Law. The UDC David A. Clarke School of Law is also the only law school in the US to be created as a result of a grassroots campaign and the only publicly funded urban land grant law school.[21] In 1986, when Antioch University decided it could no longer afford its law school and moved to close it down, thousands of DC residents heeded the call of students, alumni, and staff and rallied in support, overcoming objections by powerful Washington, DC institutions, including *The Washington Post Newspaper* and a number of elected city officials.[22] Eventually, The Antioch School of Law was approved to merge with the University of the District of Columbia in 1998; the UDC David A. Clarke School of Law was formally recognized as an HBCU in 1999[23].

As evidenced by their complex histories, HBCU law schools were often created with the purpose and duty to train generations of lawyers that are capable of ushering in social change to benefit African Americans, America, and the African diaspora.[24]

Access and Opportunity

> HBCUs have been leaders in providing higher education access to low-income students, have functioned as economic engines, have enhanced racial and ethnic diversity in higher education, and have prepared students for careers in education, business, politics, science, technology, medicine, and *law*.[25]

Though there are questions surrounding the relevance of HBCUs, these inquiries are ripe with misconceptions and should be squelched within higher education discourses. Today, there are still pervasive instances of systemic racism that pervade the American societal context. HBCUs have served as places of academic refuge to combat these societal ills, serving as rich and encouraging bastions of higher learning for Black students to thrive and excel[26]. This has been especially true for Black students at HBCU law schools. For African Americans who aspire to become lawyers, HBCUs often provide encouraging academic and social cultures that allow them access to positive educational experiences. It is widely known that there is a lack of diversity in law schools across the country. White students have consistently been admitted to law school at higher rates than students of color since the mid-1970s.[27] The extant literature on minority law school admissions also reveals that minorities are often admitted to give a façade of diversity.[28] Conversely, HBCU law schools serve a larger purpose in society by providing access to students of color who otherwise would not have the opportunity to study law.[29]

These exceptional professional programs also offer a professional education to Black students without the inclusion of additional stressors and microagressions that may include instances of institutional racism and tokenism that are often prevalent at historically White institutions. Instead, they focus on applied clinical experiences and teach culturally inclusive curricula that assist in molding future lawyers of color to later mentor and fight for social justice in their communities. HBCU law schools also deliver culturally engaging curricula and have found a way to strengthen their niche by crafting diverse and contemporarily relevant legal programs.[30] Staying true to their missions that focus on social justice, the deans of the six HBCU law schools have taken strides to offer academic and professional opportunities that make their students quite competitive in the legal realm upon graduation.[31] "These institutions provide a supportive social environment conducive to personal and academic development, as evidenced in high levels of student achievement, as measured by their student persistence, graduation rates, and student satisfaction."[32] These factors are vital especially in a law school context, which can be stressful and highly competitive in nature. HBCU law schools also provide an environment that breeds trustworthiness and encouragement because they "offer hope and opportunity to those who perform better in an environment created on the premise that they belong and have the potential to contribute fully to society."[33] HBCU law schools have been able to sustain positive and affirming cultures for their students, while also encouraging achievement and service to their communities upon graduation. Also, as a result of the diverse nature of HBCU law classes, minority students are able to minimize feelings of hypervisibility.

These educational environments are in direct contrast to PWI law schools. In HBCU law school environments, feelings of difference are lessened by the presence of more than a token number of minority peers.[34] Minority students desire a sense of community and the ability to express their issues with likeminded individuals who empathize with their experiences. This sense of belonging is critical to minority student success. HBCU law students are cultivated and provided with faculty of color who serve as role models and mentors. The nurturing atmosphere present at HBCU law schools creates an environment for Black students to excel in their studies and reach personal and professional goals.

Mission Driven and Student Centered

>The very mission statements of HBCU law schools give rise to a special duty to produce multitudes of effective social engineers for the betterment of the African American community. Indeed, this duty can be said to be essential to their reason for being.[35]

Another highly regarded vanguard of HBCU law school communities is their social justice oriented missions. It is emphasized in their mission statements to educate and produce lawyers who will be of service to their communities and society. The missions of these schools prominently underscore that their goals are not only to provide an education to minority students, but these institutions also wish to produce legal professionals who will contribute to society in myriad ways. For example, Howard University School of Law's mission explicitly underscores their desire for African Americans and other minorities to be in "active pursuit of solutions to domestic and international legal, social, economic and political problems that are of particular concern to minority groups."[36] Similarly, the Florida A&M University College of Law's mission places particular emphasis on their historical legacy of training Black students "to serve as a transformative force for the public good" while also serving "as a beacon of hope and catalyst for change by providing access to excellent educational training and opportunities to generations of students seeking to serve the needs of traditionally underserved people and communities locally, nationally and internationally."[37] HBCU law schools explicitly adopt a distinct duty to not only produce stellar legal professionals, but the desire for their graduates to provide leadership in teaching and public service, and solve the social, economic, and political problems of African Americans.[38] HBCU law school mission statements espouse a certain level of "duty" that is deeply embedded within an ethos of racial uplift.

While there are HBCU law schools that have mission statements that do not overtly mention Black or minority communities, they still contain a charge that connotes and calls for advocating for and serving underserved populations.[39] The mission of the North Carolina Central University School of Law states their desire to "foster in each student a deep sense of professional responsibility and personal integrity so as to produce competent and socially responsible members of the legal profession."[40] Furthermore, the University of the District of Columbia David A. Clarke School of Law's mission maintains that they are dedicated to the recruitment and enrollment of students traditionally underrepresented at the bar while also providing a "well-rounded theoretical and practical legal education that will enable students to be effective and ethical advocates."[41] Also, the Southern University Law Center's mission statement asserts that it strives to "provide access and opportunity to a diverse group of students from underrepresented racial, ethnic, and socioeconomic groups to obtain a high quality legal education."[42] HBCU law school mission statements provide a glimpse into the cultural fabrics of these historic institutions. These institutions are a part of the very fabric of the Black community and have, shall, and continue to assist in taking a concerted effort in advocating for the rights and needs of Black and minority communities.[43] The missions of HBCU law schools provide a key foundation into how these schools operate. They set the tone into how their students are treated *and* how they in turn aid in their evolution into fair and civil minded social justice oriented legal professionals.

From the Classroom to the Community

HBCU law programs place great emphasis on a particular brand of applied learning. The clinical and experiential learning opportunities embedded within HBCU law school curricula represent a significant departure from "traditional" styles of legal education, which not only makes their graduates more marketable by providing them with real-world experience, but also provides their students with the opportunity to better understand and relate to the populations they intend to serve once they enter the field.[44] Hinged upon the pre-existing commitment to social justice and racial uplift that underpins the missions, traditions, and value systems of all HBCUs, the legal clinics at these institutions serve as educational tools that transpose classroom knowledge into legal action on behalf of some of our nation's most vulnerable, underrepresented, and voiceless populations.[45] Upon review of the various HBCU law school clinical education programs, it is clear that a significant amount of thought and financial resources have been poured into creating an experience that both benefits and educates students, and also improves the lives of the institution's most vulnerable neighbors through legal assistance. These legal clinics focus on a number of different areas, including: criminal justice, juvenile justice, fair housing, veteran affairs, homelessness, family law, and civil rights. All clinics are pro bono (free of charge) and are supervised by licensed professors with extensive knowledge and experience in the area of legal focus for the clinic. A few examples of these community oriented learning initiatives are highlighted within this portion of the chapter.

Currently, Texas Southern University's Thurgood Marshall School of Law has one of the oldest clinical programs in the city of Houston, and it is among the oldest in the state of Texas.[46] The Earl Carl Institute for Legal and Social Policy at Texas Southern offers direct legal services and addresses issues that have a disproportionate impact on people of color as well as other populations that are disenfranchised on the local, state, and national levels.[47] "The program is built on a strong foundation of providing quality legal services to the underrepresented, while training the lawyers of the future."[48] Through academic and grassroots efforts, the Thurgood Marshall School of Law's law clinic offers legal services that focus on decriminalizing poverty, homelessness, human sex trafficking, and issues involving disproportionate minority contact in the juvenile system.[49] Professors and students also regularly host workshops and do community outreach where sound legal advice is provided to those who cannot afford legal counsel.

The University of the District of Columbia David A. Clarke School of Law also has an extensive clinical program. Currently, the UDC-DCSL has the nation's largest requirement of clinical engagement—currently 700 hours are required of their law students.[50] Also, in 2016, the institution was ranked seventh in the US by the *US News and World Report* for their extensive clinical legal training programming efforts.[51] A foremost goal of The University of the District of Columbia's clinical program is to provide legal services to DC residents who are not able to afford representation. All UDC-DCSL students participate in at least two clinics during their student tenures. Nine clinical options are available and include: criminal law, housing and consumer law, juvenile and special education law, immigration and human rights, and community development.[52]

Similarly, the North Carolina Central University School of Law has a clinical program that is also dedicated to its surrounding community. Their clinics are devoted to supporting the Durham community in which they are situated and have consistently served as a resource to countless community members and organizations. Of particular note is their Center for Child & Family Health (CCFH), which was founded in 1996 and is a partnership with Duke University, the University of North Carolina at Chapel Hill, and the greater Durham community. The mission of the CCFH is to support children and families that have been affected by neglect, abuse, and other forms of trauma.[53] Through its legal interventions, the CCFH strives to restore hope and stability to children and their families who have encountered unfortunate circumstances. Each year the center provides assistance to more than 2,000 children in Durham and its surrounding communities. This exemplary program has also provided national assistance to child evacuees from Hurricane Katrina and children who were traumatized by the 9–11 tragedy in New York City.[54] These notable acts of service are a direct result of the clinic's mission, which believes that "every child has the right to be loved, nurtured, and safe."[55]

Lastly, and equally important, the Florida A&M College of Law has two principal clinical opportunities that provide its law students with the valuable opportunity to serve traditionally underserved clients. The first is their Housing Clinic, which features community outreach projects that are designed to help underserved minority communities in the greater Tallahassee region attain critical information to avoid predatory home loans, avoid foreclosures, and buy their first home. Other services within this initiative include Section 8 assistance and avoiding termination of public housing.[56] Their second clinical initiative is the Homelessness and Legal Advocacy Clinic (HALAC). This intervention focuses on aiding and empowering low-income individuals. As a whole, the HALAC provides legal assistance in areas that include filing disability claims, support in applying for government benefits (e.g., Social Security, Medicare, Medicaid), and family law.[57] HBCU law schools have continued to implement cutting edge clinical programs that firmly ground their students in not only the practices of law but in the tradition of being of service to their communities while working on behalf of underrepresented populations and the public interest.[58] It is evident that they truly believe that this grounding should serve as an essential facet of legal practices across the nation.

Contemporary Contributions: Necessary Work for the Social Good

Overall, Historically Black Colleges and Universities have played vital roles in educating Black legal professionals. Roughly 50% of Black attorneys and 80% of Black judges in the United States have attained their baccalaureate or law degrees from HBCUs.[59] Furthermore, four of the top five producers of Blacks who attain law degrees are HBCU institutions. They include the Howard University School of Law, Texas Southern University's Thurgood Marshall School of Law, Florida A&M University's College of Law, and the Southern University Law Center.[60] Unfortunately, the legal profession is one of the least diverse professional endeavors within the American societal context. However, HBCU law schools have taken up the helm of being a tremendous resource in producing socially conscious minority leaders in law, government, and public service.

When discussing the contemporary role of historically Black law schools and the current landscape of African Americans in the legal profession, it is important to note that there has been little progress in increasing racial/ethnic representation within the field over the last 50 years.[61] While there have been some significant changes in society with regards to equal treatment and access to essential growth opportunities, including a "quality education," African Americans continue to suffer disproportionately in a number of areas, including mass incarceration.[62] With this in mind, the concept of racial representation and ethnic diversity within the legal profession becomes especially important in criminal justice cases, where an overwhelming majority of the defendants are from underrepresented populations.[63] But, even with the existence of six academically sound, accredited law schools at Historically Black Universities that have been in existence since the late 19th century, a tremendous racial representation gap remains within the legal profession. White law students outnumber their African American classmates at a rate of seven to one,[64] and 88% of currently licensed lawyers in the US are White, while African Americans represent only 5% of the profession.[65] The racial representation disparity increases drastically when considering that of the 30,000 state judges that preside over a majority of the cases that appear in court, only 2.5% are African American.[66]

This current predicament brings attention to the critical need for HBCU law schools, as they serve as fundamental points of access for Blacks who seek to enter the legal realm. Charles Hamilton Houston, former Dean of Howard University Law School, once stated:

> A lawyer's either a social engineer or . . . a parasite on society. . . . A social engineer [is] a highly skilled, perceptive, sensitive lawyer who [understands] the constitution of the United States and [knows] how to explore its uses in the solving of problems of local communities and in bettering the conditions of the underprivileged citizens.[67]

Houston's words were a call to action. It is impossible to acknowledge the contemporary lineage of social engineers that have been produced by historically Black law schools without first recognizing Thurgood Marshall, Robert Carter, Spottswood William Robinson III, Oliver Hill, and George E. C. Hayes—the Howard University School of Law graduates that were instrumental in successfully constructing and arguing the pivotal 1954 *Brown v. the Board of Education* school desegregation case.[68] The legacy these historic and pioneering legal minds created during the civil rights movement lives on in the institutions themselves, as they have now taken up the mantle of becoming the premier modern-day producers of social engineers by embedding experiential learning and clinical work in their core curriculums. Given the proper resources and agency, they will continue to play a significant role in the education of those who have been and are currently underrepresented in the legal field.[69]

Today, the existing six Historically Black University law schools continue to carry more than their share of the ethical and professional burden when it comes to producing the next wave of social engineers that Hamilton spoke of during his tenure as the Dean of Howard University Law School. These institutions currently account for the education and preparation of nearly 20% of all African American law students,[70] and between 2010 and 2015 they produced a pool of at least 3,303 unique first time law school applicants.[71] Over the past five years, Howard University, Spelman College, Florida Agricultural and Mechanical University, Hampton University, North Carolina Agricultural and Technical State University, Morehouse College, and North Carolina Central University have all maintained uninterrupted positions on the American Bar Association's list of the 240 top feeder schools in the US.[72] These significant contributions by HBCUs in the areas of supplying qualified applicants and admits are extremely important when considering that racial and gender identity, as well as the lived experiences and biases, of those who work in the legal profession can have a profound impact on the internal workings of the justice system.[73] The imbalance in representation can also impact the external perception of courts and judges, because the lack of cultural competency in judges can influence how they hear cases and make decisions.[74] In a nation where roughly four in ten people are individuals of color, historically Black law schools are essential to the goal of ensuring that our nation's courts are representative and able to fulfill their purposes. The structure of the justice system is based on the premise that our judges and attorneys are able to understand the circumstances of the communities in which they serve. The US judicial system depends on the general public's faith in a fair and unbiased interpretation of the law, and this will be very hard to achieve without the significant contributions of Historically Black University Law Schools and Historically Black Colleges and Universities.[75]

The impact that HBCU law school graduates have had on our society is also of considerable note. Their contributions have been recognized on local, national, and global levels. Prominent HBCU law school alumni include: Thurgood Marshall (Howard University), the first African American appointed to the US Supreme Court; Sharon Pratt Kelly (Howard University), the first female mayor of Washington, DC; Vernon E. Jordan, Jr. (Howard University), former executive director of the United Negro College Fund (UNCF) and past president of the National Urban League; L. Douglas Wilder (Howard), the first African American Governor of Virginia; H. Patrick Maynard Jackson (NCCU), the first African American mayor of Atlanta; Leroy R. Johnson (NCCU), the first African American member of the Georgia State Senate since reconstruction; Harry E. Johnson (Texas Southern), former National President of Alpha Phi Alpha Fraternity, Inc., and current President and CEO of the Washington, DC Martin Luther King, Jr. National Memorial Project Foundation, Inc.; Morris Overstreet (Texas Southern), the first African American elected to statewide office in Texas; Jesse N. Stone, Jr. (Southern University), Louisiana Supreme Court Associate Justice and former president of the Southern University System; Briana Westry-Robinson (Southern University), the youngest African American judge in the state of Alabama's history; Dwayne M. Murray (Southern University), past Grand Polemarch of Kappa Alpha Psi Fraternity, Inc.; Rick Gallot (Southern University), former Louisiana State senator and current president of Grambling State University; and Penny Willrich (UDC), the first African American woman Superior Court Judge in the state of Arizona. These renowned HBCU law school graduates are a testament to the manner in which these schools train their students to be leaders in myriad enterprises.

Equally impressive are the current student leaders at these particular schools, and the faculty and administrators that engage them in such a way that it awakens the spirit of grassroots leadership. Kezar and Lester described grassroots leaders as passionate individuals without any formal authority, who seek to initiate social change and challenge the status quo without the use of hierarchical or institutionalized structures.[76] The concept of HBCU law school students as grassroots leaders is further highlighted by their ability to develop an international network of civil and human rights activists that have and are currently contributing to society, including feeding into the creation of the now essential "Black Lives Matter" movement.

#BlackLivesMatter

Within American history, HBCUs have been the training grounds for some of our nation's most influential leaders and activists. Consider the North Carolina A&T students that integrated a Woolworth Counter on February 1, 1960 in Greensboro, North Carolina; there was also Diane Nash, a Fisk University student who was active in the "Freedom Riders" movement and a founding member of the Student Nonviolent Coordinating Committee (SNCC).[77] There are numerous examples of HBCU students who were and are activists in local and national settings.[78] These spirited activists and powerful leaders are still emerging today, especially within HBCU law school environments. In an era where many Black Americans feel under siege following the controversial deaths of Sandra Bland, Freddie Gray, Eric Garner, Alton Sterling, Michael Brown, and countless other unarmed Black Americans, Black communities are beginning to actively resist and respond to the toxic systemic racism that permeates our society.[79]

A little over a year before the creation of the now infamous "Black Lives Matter" movement's call to action in 2012, and approximately two weeks after the fatal shooting of 17-year-old Trayvon Martin by a neighborhood watch member in the suburban community of Sanford, Florida, the collective social consciousness of Howard University School of Law students and alumni erupted into what would become the very first US based social media human rights campaign. Howard Law School alumnus Kevin Cunningham was working as a social media coordinator for a Palestinian children's charity, and had been inspired by the social media presence of the Egyptian uprising that eventually toppled the government of Hosni Mubarak.[80] Wanting to get involved but not really knowing how he could, Cunningham remembered the "social engineer" concept of Charles Hamilton Houston that was instilled in him during his time as a Howard law student and stepped out into a new form of social media to create what would become one of the most supported www.change.org petitions in the history of the website, earning 2,271,988 signatures of support for the arrest and criminal prosecution of George Zimmerman.[81]

Courtney Scrubbs, a second-year Howard law student, had a similar moment where she realized her role as a social engineer, and this led her to contact several undergraduate, graduate, and alumni peers as the first step in creating the campus organization Howard University Students for Justice.[82] Also, having learned those unforgettable words uttered by Houston, Scrubbs and the students she was working with felt that at the core of the matter was the fact that racial profiling had led to Trayvon Martin's death, and in that moment, they decided that they needed to bring more attention to racial profiling by producing the "Do I Look Suspicious" YouTube video that eventually went viral.[83] When the Dean of Howard University Law School, Kurt Schmoke, became aware of the grassroots efforts that were being led by his students, he took it one step further by extending an offer to lead attorney Benjamin Crump to use Howard law students to assist with both investigating the incident and examining the laws surrounding it.[84] Speaking to Howard University students one year after Trayvon's killing, his mother, Sybrina Fulton, stated, "Whenever I'm asked about how all of this started, I mention that it started at Howard," referencing the media attention and public interest in the death of her son.[85] The contemporary activism that is conveyed within this section shows the power of social engineering, and the true essence of historically Black law school cultures. They train students in such a way that when society erupts and injustice tips the scales against our most vulnerable neighbors, these young men and women are moved to step in and provide competent, clear-headed legal counsel, service, and activism at a moment's notice.

Conclusion

It is clear that historically Black law schools remain a vital presence in the higher education realm, as they contribute greatly to the education of Blacks and other underrepresented populations who aspire to the legal profession. HBCU law schools do not just produce lawyers. Instead, they generate leaders who are primed and ready to advance the cause of civil rights with the same passion and commitment of previous generations of graduates, faculty, and administrators.[86] There is much to be learned from these exceptional institutions. Since the founding of the very first HBCU law school, more than 100 years ago, these institutions have produced thousands of graduates who have gone on to become leaders in America and the global community at large. For more than a century, they have operated not only as institutions dedicated to advancing their students, but as engines for the advancement of communities and populations whose progression has often been met with resistance and struggle.[87] HBCU law schools encourage social change through their mission statements, socially adept curricula, holistic practical experiences, and the mentorship opportunities that they offer their students. They have been places of "refuge and advancement for those weary from the battle of institutional racism and stereotypes that often plague the educational field for people of color."[88] As we look to the future, it will be imperative to look to these schools and their graduates as we as a society continue to battle various forms of systemic oppression that plague our nation.

Notes

1 Mobley and Johnson 2015
2 African American and Black are used interchangeably throughout this study to refer to persons whose ancestry denotes Black racial groups of Africa, as defined by the US Census Bureau.
3 Pierre and Welch 2009, p. 103
4 Currently, there are six law schools that are accredited by the American Bar Association (ABA) and officially designated as HBCUs. However, we would also

like to acknowledge Miles School of Law (MSL). Though MSL is not officially recognized as an HBCU law school, it does have historical ties to Miles College (private HBCU), though they are separate entities. Founded in 1974, Miles School of Law was established to provide Black students with access to a legal education when predominately White institutions still hindered their abilities to do so (J. Richet Pearson, Dean of Miles School of Law, personal communication, February 15, 2017). Due to the dearth of minority lawyers in the state of Alabama, MSL was developed as an evening law program to supply the greater Alabama region with more Black lawyers to serve the needs of the area and these grossly underserved communities. MSL's motto, "Striving for Balance," reflects this mentality. The law school was also founded to attract non-traditional students who wished to obtain law degrees. Notable alumni include: J. Richmond Pearson, first Black member of the Alabama state senate since Reconstruction; William A. Bell, Sr., current mayor of the city of Birmingham, AL; George T. French, Jr., current president of Miles College; Judge Lynneice Washington, first African American woman elected district attorney in Alabama; and Rodger M. Smitherman, Esq., Alabama State Senator.

5 Gasman and Williams 2012
6 Williams and Ashley 2004
7 Howard University School of Law Website 2016
8 Hilton et al. 2012
9 North Carolina Central University School of Law Website 2016
10 Hilton et al. 2012
11 North Carolina Central University School of Law Website 2016
12 Gannon 1996
13 Hilton, Gasman, Wood, and Williams 2012, p. 148
14 Butler 1997
15 Jones 1976
16 Butler 1997; Jones 1976
17 Southern University Law Center Website 2016
18 Hilton et al. 2012
19 Hilton et al. 2012
20 David A. Clarke was a prominent figure in Washington, DC during the Civil Rights Movement. He was legal counsel and director of the DC Bureau of the Southern Christian Leadership Conference (SCLC) and also served as a legal assistant to the NAACP Legal Defense Fund. Before his untimely death in 1997, Clarke was a fierce advocate and life-long champion for the rights of the disenfranchised and working people of DC. A Howard University School of Law graduate, he served as chair of the Washington, DC City Council, where he championed the conception of the District's public law school and its unique program of mandatory clinical service that now bears his name on the part of all law students (University of the District of Columbia David A. Clarke School of Law School Website, 2016).
21 Broderick 2009
22 Libertelli, personal communication, December 1, 2016
23 Mawakana 2010
24 Mawakana 2010
25 Pierre and Welch 2009, p. 104
26 Mobley in press
27 Kidder 2003
28 Hamlar, 1983; Hughes, Noblit, and Cleveland 2013
29 Gasman and Williams 2012
30 Oguntoyinbo 2012
31 Gasman and Commodore 2014
32 Toblowsky, Outcalt, and McDonough 2005, p. 63

33 Gasman and Williams 2012, p. 19
34 Hamlar 1983
35 Mawakana 2010, p. 693
36 Howard University School of Law Website 2016
37 Florida A&M University College of Law 2016
38 Mawakana 2010
39 Mawakana 2010
40 North Carolina Central University School of Law Website 2016
41 University of the District of Columbia David A. Clarke School of Law School Website 2016
42 Southern University Law Center Website 2016
43 Mawakana 2010
44 Mawakana 2010
45 Oguntoyinbo 2012
46 Cartwright and Harmon 2013
47 Texas Southern University Thurgood Marshall School of Law Website 2016
48 Cartwright and Harmon 2013, p. 223
49 Texas Southern University Thurgood Marshall School of Law Website 2016
50 Libertelli, personal communication, December 1, 2016
51 University of the District of Columbia David A. Clarke School of Law Website 2016
52 University of the District of Columbia David A. Clarke School of Law Website 2016
53 North Carolina Central University School of Law Center for Child & Family Health Website 2016
54 North Carolina Central University School of Law Center for Child & Family Health Website 2016
55 North Carolina Central University School of Law Center for Child & Family Health Website 2016
56 Florida A&M College of Law Website 2016
57 Florida A&M College of Law Website 2016
58 Broderick 2009
59 Gasman and Williams 2012
60 Pierre and Welch 2009
61 George and Yoon 2016
62 Mawakana 2010
63 George and Yoon 2016
64 American Bar Association Section of Legal Education and Admissions to the Bar 2016
65 Holley et al. 2016
66 United States Department of Justice 2013
67 Mawakana 2010, p. 679
68 Williams and Ashley 2004
69 Gasman and Williams 2012
70 American Bar Association Section of Legal Education and Admissions to the Bar 2016
71 Law School Admission Council 2016
72 Law School Admission Council 2016
73 George and Yoon 2016
74 George and Yoon 2016
75 George and Yoon 2016; Oguntoyinbo 2012; Mawakana 2010
76 Kezar and Lester 2011
77 Cohen, Snyder, and Carter 2013
78 Gasman and Commodore 2014
79 Black Lives Matter Website 2016
80 NBC News 2012
81 NBC News 2012

82 Rhodan 2012
83 Rhodan 2012
84 *The Baltimore Sun* Staff 2012
85 *The Jurist* 2013
86 Gasman and Williams 2012
87 Lomax 2007
88 Wolff 2010, p. 777

Bibliography

American Bar Association Section of Legal Education and Admissions to the Bar. *Compilation—All schools data: JD enrollment and ethnicity (academic year)* [Data file], 2016. Retrieved November 8, 2016, from www.abarequireddisclosures.org

Baltimore Sun Staff, March 22, 2012. "Baltimore efforts under way to rally support for Trayvon."

Black Lives Matter Website, 2016. Retrieved from http://blacklivesmatter.com/

Broderick, Katherine S. "The nation's urban land-grant law school: Ensuring justice in the 21st century." *University of Toledo Law Review*, 40 (2009): 305–325.

Butler, Marguerite. L. "The history of Texas Southern University, Thurgood Marshall School of Law: The house that Sweatt built." *Thurgood Marshall Law Review*, 23 (1997): 45–53.

Cartwright, Matina E., and Thelma Harmon, T. "Fifty plus years and counting: A history of experiential learning and clinical opportunities at Thurgood Marshall School of Law." *Thurgood Marshall Law Review*, 39 (2013): 187–223.

Cohen, Robert, and David Snyder. *Rebellion in black and white: Southern student activism in the 1960s*. Baltimore, MD: Johns Hopkins University Press, 2013.

Florida A & M University College of Law Website, 2016. Retrieved from http://law.famu.edu/about-us/mission/

Gannon, Michael. *The new history of Florida*. Gainesville, FL: University of Florida Press, 1996.

Gasman, Marybeth, and Felicia Commodore. "(HBCUs: A history and future of preparing activist leaders." *HBCU Lifestyle*, 2014. Retrieved from http://hbculifestyle.com/hbcu-activist-leaders/

Gasman, Marybeth and Michael S. Williams. "A short history of graduate and professional programs at historically black colleges and universities." In Robert T. Palmer, Adriel A. Hilton, and Tiffany Patrice Fountaine (Eds.), *Black graduate education at historically Black colleges and universities: Trends, experiences, and outcomes* (pp. 9–23). Charlotte, NC: Information Age Publishing, 2012.

Gasman, Marybeth, and Felicia Commodore. "The state of research on historically black colleges and universities." *Journal for Multicultural Education*, 8 no. 2 (2014): 89–111.

George, Tracey E., and Albert H. Yoon. *The gavel gap: Who sits in judgment on state courts?* Washington, DC: The American Constitution Society for Law and Policy, 2016.

Hamlar, Portia. "Minority tokenism in American Law Schools." *Howard Law Journal*, 26 no. (1983): 443–600.

Hilton, Adriel A., Marybeth Gasman, J. Luke Wood, and Michael Williams. "The relevance of Black Law Schools." *Southern University Law Review*, 40 no. 1 (2012): 145–156.

Holley, Dannye, Danielle Holley-Walker, John Pierre J., A. Felicia Epps, Phyliss V. Craig-Taylor, and James M. Douglas. "HBCU law deans say ABA bar-passage rule changes will hurt profession's diversity." *The National Law Journal*, (2016). Retrieved from www.nationallawjournal.com/id=1202770271784?keywords=HBCU+Law+Deans

"How one man helped spark online protest in Trayvon Martin case." *NBC News*, March 29, 2012. Retrieved from https://usnews.newsvine.com/_news/2012/03/29/10907662-how-one-man-helped-spark-online-protest-in-trayvon-martin-case

Howard University School of Law Website, 2016. Retrieved from www.law.howard.edu/19

Hughes, Sherick, George Noblit, and D. Cleveland. "Derrick Bell's post-Brown moves toward critical race theory." *Race Ethnicity and Education*, 16 no. 4 (2013): 442–469.

Jones, Vonceil. "Texas Southern University School of Law—The beginning." *Texas Southern Law Review*, 4 (1976): 197–208.

Kezar, Adrianna J., and Jaime Lester. *Enhancing campus capacity for leadership*. Stanford, CA: Stanford University Press, 2011.

Kidder, William C. "Struggle for access from Sweatt to Grutter: A history of African American, Latino, and American Indian Law School admissions, 1950–2000." *The Harvard BlackLetter Law Journal*, 19 (2003): 1–42.

Law School Admission Council Website, 2016. Retrieved from http://www.lsac.org/

Lomax, Michael L. "Historically black colleges and universities: Bringing a tradition of engagement into the twenty-first century." *Journal of Higher Education Outreach and Engagement*, 11 no. 3 (2007): 5–14.

Mawakana, Kemit A. "Historically black college and university law schools: Generating multitudes of effective social engineers." *The Journal of Gender, Race, & Justice*, 14 (2010): 679–702.

Mobley, Jr., Steve D. (in press). "Seeking sanctuary: (Re)Claiming the power of HBCUs as places of Black refuge." *International Journal of Qualitative Studies in Education*.

Mobley, Jr. Steve D., and Jennifer Johnson. "The role of HBCUs in addressing the unique needs of LGBT students." In Robert Palmer, Rob Shorette, and Marybeth Gasman (Eds.), *Exploring diversity at historically black colleges and universities: Implications for policy and practice*. (pp. 79–90). San Francisco: Jossey-Bass, 2015.

North Carolina Central University School of Law Center for Child & Family Health Website, 2016. Retrieved from http://law.nccu.edu/clinics/community/ccfh/

North Carolina Central University School of Law Website, 2016. Retrieved from http://law.nccu.edu/about/history/

Oguntoyinbo, Lekan. "Social justice." *Diverse Issues in Higher Education*, 29 no. 4 (2012): 12.

Pierre, John K., and Charity Welch. "Why historically black colleges and universities are needed in the 21st century." *The Journal of Race, Gender & Poverty*, 1 (2009): 101–115.

Rhodan, Maya. "'Do I look suspicious?' Howard students' video goes viral." *Ebony*, April 2, 2012. Retrieved from www.ebony.com/news-views/do-i-look-suspicious-howard-students-video-goes-viral#axzz4UHoJdTKf

"Sybrina Fulton one year later: Mother of Trayvon Martin visits Howard." *The Jurist: Howard University School of Law News Journal*, 22 no. 1 (2013). Retrieved from www.law.howard.edu/dictator/media/230/2013_jurist.pdf

Southern University Law Center Website, 2016. Retrieved from www.sulc.edu/Texas Southern University Thurgood Marshall School of Law Website, 2016. Retrieved from www.tsulaw.edu/centers/ECI/index.html

Tobolowsky, Babara F., Charles, Outcalt, and Patricia M. McDonough. "The role of HBCUs in the college choice process of African Americans in California." *The Journal of Negro Education*, 74 no. 1 (2005): 63–75.

United States Department of Justice, Office of Justice Programs, Bureau of Justice Statistics. *Special Report: State Court Organization, 2011* (NCJ 242850), 2013. Retrieved from www.bjs.gov/content/pub/pdf/sco11.pdf

University of the District of Columbia David A. Clarke School of Law Website, 2016. Retrieved from www.law.udc.edu/?page=History

Williams, Juan, and Dwayne Ashley. I'll find a way or make one: A tribute to historically Black colleges & universities. New York: Harper Collins, 2004.

Wolff, Kamille. "From pipeline to pipe dream: The HBCU effect on law school deans of color." *The Journal of Gender, Race & Justice*, 14 no. 1(2010): 765–796.

4 Factors for Effective Recruitment, Development, Mentorship, and Retention of Education Doctoral Students

Cheron H. Davis

Introduction

Historically Black Colleges and Universities (HBCUs) are defined as "Black academic institutions established prior to 1964, whose principal mission was, and still is, the education of Black Americans."[1] However, the National Association for Equal Opportunity in Higher Education has also designated some institutions that were established after 1964 as HBCUs.[2] The year of 1964 represents a historical marker because it was at this time that the *Civil Rights Act* was passed. Since the implementation of the *Civil Rights Act* of 1964, federal student aid programs, and affirmative action, there has been a shift in the number of African Americans attending HBCUs. Whereas previously a critical mass of African American students attended HBCUs, by 1973, three-fourths of Blacks were attending predominately White institutions (PWIs).[3] HBCUs represent roughly 4% (approximately 100 in total) of American universities and colleges, but enroll approximately 16% of all African Americans in four-year institutions and graduate 30% of African Americans earning bachelor's degrees.[4] Professional schools of education on HBCU campuses are especially significant, as they graduate 25% of African American teachers with bachelor's degrees.[5] Additionally, HBCUs with education preparation programs have consistently produced more African American graduates in the science, technology, engineering, and math (STEM) fields than any other type of institution. This is critical to note, as K-12 classrooms are continuously becoming more ethnically diverse; however, the teaching profession has not followed the same trend, as the majority of the American teaching profession is comprised of individuals from White middle-class backgrounds. It is imperative that educational leaders seek HBCU professional education programs as a source for making large-scale improvements among students of color in PK-12 schools. However, the downward trend in enrollment in teacher preparation programs nationwide has an even larger impact on graduate schools of education. With fewer teachers entering the profession, there are fewer master's and doctoral level students. This begs the question: how are we to more effectively recruit, mentor, develop, and retain African American doctoral level education students?

Review of Literature

The recruitment and development of talented future educators of color begins long before they enter the doors of the ivory tower. In fact, public P-12 education is the grooming room for many Black students in this country who later go on to earn graduate degrees. The US Department of Education's 1983 highly publicized report *A Nation at Risk* warned, even then, that America would lose its economic edge if it did not improve public education. President Trump's 2017 appointment of billionaire philanthropist Betsy DeVos to lead the Department of Education highlights the critical state of public education and the firestorm in which educators and policymakers currently find themselves. A strong proponent of school choice, DeVos has stated that "if a school is troubled, or unsafe, or not a good fit for a child . . . we should support a parent's right to enroll their child in a high-quality alternative."[6] Unfortunately, the schools where these problems exist are disproportionately educating students of color. Low-income families lack adequate support in securing affordable childcare, as well as high quality PreK programs. These issues compound what is already a struggling public education system. Teachers still lack adequate training that makes meaningful connections between research, practice, and policy. Additionally, teachers of color are an important resource in K-12 and higher education classrooms. However, the limited presence of African American teachers is an ever-increasing issue facing the educational climate. The National Center of Educational Statistics (2010) projects a significant increase in enrollment of culturally diverse school-aged students, while culturally diverse educators may not keep the same pace.[7] Thus, it is imperative to address the preparation of teachers, and especially teachers of color, to become effective, culturally competent elementary and secondary educators.[8] These teachers are the most likely to enter graduate degree programs and become teacher educators in the future.

Minority teachers who are trained properly and supported professionally make a significant impact on the minority students they teach. One study found that minority teachers can generate higher achievement gains among minority students than any other group of teachers.[9] School-age children need teachers with whom they can relate culturally and who have been trained on culturally conscious instruction. However, as professional education programs see decreases in enrollment nationwide, many African American students enrolling in HBCUs are opting for majors in STEM with plans for careers outside of academia. This trend presents a number of challenges for professional education programs in the areas of recruitment, development, mentorship, and retention, especially at the graduate level. In the following, the author discusses some of the challenges and offers practical considerations for addressing these issues.

Recruitment

For more than 150 years, HBCUs have played a significant role in providing access to postsecondary education for millions of first generation college students from low-income backgrounds. HBCUs are pressured to be accountable for favorable student outcomes, most often retention and graduation rates. These unique challenges are often overlooked in institutional evaluations by accreditation bodies focused on retaining and graduating students.

The number of minority faculty members at our nation's colleges and universities and the barriers faced in creating a more diverse professoriate are alarming.[10] According to a 2010 report by the National Center for Education Statistics, African Americans represent 6% of the faculty in higher education. Williams and Williams found that unsupportive work environments and indifferent attitudes make it difficult for faculty of color to develop solid working relationships with fellow faculty members.[11] Moreover, student level factors, such as pre-college preparation, socioeconomic background, status as a first-generation student, and a host of other factors often combine to hinder post-secondary success. HBCUs tend to enroll a large number of these students, whose backgrounds predict difficulty succeeding in college. Recruiting the brightest scholars of color to HBCUs has not traditionally been an issue as much as recruiting those students to the teaching profession. The median salary for teachers in the US in 2013 was approximately $58,064.[12] This average salary rises with advanced degrees and years of experience. However, for the average incoming salary, which is roughly $35,000, it is difficult to compete with professions like engineering, nursing, and computer science, whose starting salaries are at least double those of teachers. Convincing students of color that the cornerstone programs of many HBCUs, the professional education programs, are the pillars of the university and careers worthy of the four years of debt they will accrue in order to obtain degrees and certifications to teach seems unlikely and difficult to do.

HBCUs must utilize a number of initiatives and directed strategies in recruitment of scholars of color to doctoral education programs. A number of recruitment strategies must be in place, including making personal contact with prospective students and creating pipelines with local school districts and institutions of higher education. Many of the doctoral students in education majors are current K-12 teachers or administrators and make up more than half of the enrollment in these programs. There must also be an effort to target undergraduate minority students of color at their home institutions for recruitment. Black students enrolled in non-HBCUs are prime candidates for consideration of furthering their careers by attending an HBCU. Because they do not have these experiences, it is important for HBCUs to sponsor visits to campus by graduate programs, tour the facilities, and meet with faculty and students. Additionally, the availability and use of online materials, particularly social media sites, is an attractive way to get the attention of millennials who are shopping for graduate school options.

Mentorship

Mentoring is the act of providing guidance and support from the mentor to the mentee. Mentoring often involves career socialization, inspiration and belief in each other, and promoting excellence and passion for worth through guidance, support, and networking. It also typically involves taking interest in each other as human beings as well as supporting professional practice.[13] Most models of mentoring suggest that mentoring involves not only professional support, but also a strong interest in the individual person. As such, mentoring may have both instrumental and psychosocial functions.[14] The psychosocial function relates to uses of help and support of the individual. The instrumental functions are more career-related and can involve advocacy, assistance with negotiating institutional politics, and access to networks.

Graduate students benefit from mentorship in many ways. Among those are academic guidance, career development, personal guidance, and overall socialization in the political landscape of higher education. Graduate students benefit from the exposure that enhanced access to a professional network can provide. Students gain access to the ability to develop meaningful relationships with future colleagues in their profession. Honest feedback is also a benefit of positive mentorship. Students are able to navigate the doctoral process with more self-confidence, support, and sense of competence. However, given minority graduate students' historical exclusion from higher education, the persistent group stereotypes that relate to their academic abilities and competencies, as well as unique cultural perspectives, necessitate that more attention be given to the qualities needed to effectively mentor these students, factors that go beyond similar cultural backgrounds.

Austin's review of higher education literature on preparing next generation faculty members revealed that students often complain about the lack of support systems and mentorship and that they often have to make their own way through graduate programs.[15] Smith and Davidson surveyed Black graduate students and found that one third reported having no help with their development from faculty or other university staff.[16] Many mentors do not have a formal process for selecting student mentees; therefore the selection process gives rise to ethical concerns. Specifically, there is little discussion of the issue of equal access in regards to which faculty members choose to mentor informally. Therefore, mentors are more likely to select mentees based upon perceived potential for success and perceived similarities.[17]

However, barriers still exist when both the students and faculty share an ethnic minority status. The lack of minority faculty places minority students at a disadvantage, as diverse faculty are sorely underrepresented widely. More specifically, at HBCUs, minority faculty may be overloaded with course responsibilities, which limits their ability and time to be effective mentors.[18] Students with negative graduate school experiences are less likely to consider academic careers themselves.[19] Graduate education professional programs are often populated by adults already working in K-12 schools. In order to populate and diversify the professoriate, it is critical for these professionals to choose to further their educations by entering doctoral programs. Lack of positive mentoring relationships may be especially important to understanding how these negative mentoring relationships influence retention of graduate students in education.

Development

African American graduate students often come to higher education with deeply internalized beliefs and challenges regarding their potential for success.[20] Bonner (2010) stated that "much like grand bodies of water, comprising multiple and competing tributaries, so too, is achievement of [African American students] affected by a number of influences" (p. 66).[21] As a result of the low-socioeconomic and first generation college student backgrounds for some, many possess a desire to improve education for African American children, represent their needs and concerns, and be a voice for them. Knowing the financial strains of many students of color, it is important that these students receive adequate financial support. Freedom from undue financial stress has many benefits beyond stress relief. Travel grants allow for presentations at conferences and create opportunities for students to meet other students with similar research interests. Collaborative studies, writing groups, and peer support networks are all products of the institutional support of graduate students.

Graduate students also benefit from successful role models who have overcome stereotypes. It is beneficial for African American graduate students to have peer relationships with African American faculty, even from different institutions, in order to help mitigate social and intellectual isolation resulting from stereotype threat. African American graduate students also benefit from highly interactive and collaborative relationships with student peers. Similar interests, writing and research groups, and accountability are all benefits to formalizing and promoting these positive student relationships. The sense of solidarity with, rather than competition among, students and faculty of color is a positive outcome of positive collaborative relationships.

Teacher leadership holds great promise in closing achievement gaps for P-20 students. Teachers who transition from leadership roles in K-12 to higher education must recognize the importance of leadership as a framework for working with colleagues as well as future teachers (pre-service teachers). Muijs and Harris (2003) have stated, "While the quality of teaching most strongly influences levels of pupil motivation and achievement, it has been demonstrated that the quality of leadership matters in determining the motivation of teachers and the quality of teaching in the classroom,"[22] Teacher leaders are developed long before they enter the classroom. Professional development creates networks in which teachers may share new ideas and improvements in practice. Educational policymakers, influential educational organizations, and institutions of higher education have placed increasingly more emphasis on the recruitment and development of educational leaders. This grooming process also occurs in the trenches of the doctoral degree process.

Providing high-quality teachers for students, regardless of background, is crucial, as teacher quality is an important factor in improving student achievement.[23] However, Sleeter (2005) emphasized that teachers with limited multicultural experiences and low expectations of culturally diverse children may have fewer successes in decreasing the achievement disparity.[24] Research has shown that having a broader pool of well-qualified African American educators has the potential for shrinking the achievement gap between White and non-White students.[25] For this reason, and for HBCUs' ability to produce African American graduates, HBCUs are capable of addressing the disparity of African Americans in the teaching profession. However, the legitimacy and rigor of these institutions has consistently been under fire (Strayhorn, 2008). African American graduate students are overwhelmingly selecting non-traditional (online) programs in order to obtain doctoral degrees (Mervis, 2017).

Retention

Success in academia, including doctoral work, requires successful socialization into the culture. Formal orientation, information sharing, and overt instructions are all part of the acculturation process which is beneficial to the student.[26] This process, however, has been historically problematic for African Americans.[27] The process of socializing African American graduate students in higher education lacks the conceptual framework and research that seeks to understand the underlying reasons for the low retention rates of these students. HBCUs have a unique culture that lends them to a support model that differs from other types of institutions of higher learning. It is important to consider the framework of HBCUs when discussing overall student retention in these institutions: 1) the maintenance of the Black culture and historical traditions; 2) the creation and retention of Black leadership within the HBCU; 3) the commitment to begin an economic unit within the community in which each school respectively stands; 4) the creation of Black role models to interpret the dynamics that impact other Black people outside the college community; 5) the creation of leaders that are confident and competent in their dealing with issues that affect all people; and 6) the creation of change agents that can conduct research, training, and disseminate information benefiting everyday lives of all minority communities.[28] Understanding the fundamental characteristics of HBCUs serves as a framework of analysis of the role these institutions play in society and how they serve graduate students of color.

Retention, in large part, is dependent upon student resiliency. Students with a strong sense of self and cultural identity are less likely to be vulnerable in an environment that many not be as welcoming to them.[29] African American students that have a positive self-image and have confidence in their abilities have fewer self-doubts in their ability to attain their degrees.[30] The most important attributes that African American students need in order to persist in doctoral studies are a strong sense of confidence, pride, and determination. The challenge for many colleges of education has become instilling and fostering these attributes in students so that they persist in their doctoral studies. With greater responsibilities being placed on teachers and administrators and K-12 salaries not rising at comparable rates, it is difficult to recruit and retain the best and brightest African American students to pursue doctorate degrees in education.

Conclusion

HBCUs recognize and acknowledge the complexity of issues that impair the success of African American doctoral students. Persistence of minority students in graduate programs is dependent upon the level of support they receive socially, financially, and academically. African American students in doctoral education programs need formal and informal mentoring to overcome the barriers of marginalization, neglect, sexism, racism, and other forms of oppression within programs, in academic environments, and across institutions. Moreover, the recruitment, development, mentorship, and recruitment of African American doctoral HBCU students are critical to the success of P-12 educational systems. Enrollment in US public schools has become increasingly diverse, with projections suggesting that the majority of students in public schools will belong to ethnic minorities by the year 2020. In stark contrast, the teaching force is overwhelmingly comprised of White women. HBCUs have the capacity and potential to address the disparity of African Americans in the teaching profession and those who become teacher educators. Academic colleges and schools, such as schools of education on HBCU campuses, are especially critical in recruiting and developing future education faculty. Factors such as financial support, positive mentoring experiences, self-efficacy, and socialization play a large role in the resiliency and persistence of African American doctoral students, particularly those in educational fields. Education is the cornerstone of this country and, in the words of Horace Mann, the "great equalizer of the conditions of men, the balance-wheel of the social machinery." Until that balance is reached on the doctoral level, and students of color are afforded equitable opportunities to succeed in obtaining graduate degrees, the conditions of man will remain unequal.

Notes

1 Roebuck and Murty1993, p. 3
2 Roebuck and Murty 1993
3 Allen and Jewell 2002
4 Irvine and Fenwick 2011
5 National Association for Equal Opportunity in Higher Education 2008
6 Fox News January 17 2017
7 National Center of Educational Statistics 2010
8 Hussar and Bailey 2013
9 Dee 2004
10 Gainen and Boice 1993; Magner 1993; Miller 1991
11 Williams and Williams 2006
12 NCES 2016
13 Vance 2002
14 Thomas 2005
15 Austin's 2002
16 Smith and Davidson 1992
17 Thomas et al. 2005
18 Bowman et al. 1999
19 Ellis 2000
20 Astin 1982
21 Bonner 2010
22 Muijs and Harris 2003, p. 437
23 Irvine and Fenwick 2011
24 Sleeter 2005
25 Castenell 2002 as cited in Southern Education Foundation 2006; King 1993
26 Tierney and Bensimon 1996
27 Debord and Millner 1993; Turner and Thompson 1993
28 Brown and Davis 2001
29 Chavous et al. 2002
30 Ervin 2001; Gloria et al. 1999

Bibliography

Allen, Walter R., and Joseph O. Jewell. "A backward glance forward: Past, present, and future perspectives on historically black colleges and universities." *Review of Higher Education*, 25 no. 3 (2002): 241–261.

Astin, Alexander. *Minorities in American higher education.* (1st ed., pp. ix–263). San Francisco: Jossey-Bass Inc., Publishers, 1982.

Austin, Ann E. "Preparing the next generation of faculty: Graduate school as socialization to the academic career." *Journal of Higher Education*, 73 no. 1 (2002): 94–122.

Bonner, Fred A., II. "Focusing on achievement African American student persistence in the academy." In Terrell Strayhorn, and Melvin C. Terrell (Eds.), *The evolving challenges of black college students new insights for policy, practice, and research*. (1st ed., pp. 66–84). Sterling, VA: Stylus Publishing, LLC, 2010.

Bowman, S. R. et al. "Developmental relationships of Black American in the academy." In Audrey Murrell, Faye Crosby, and Robin Ely (Eds.), *Mentoring dilemmas: Developmental relationships within a multicultural world* (pp. 21–46). Englewood Cliffs, NJ: Lawrence Erlbaum and Associates, 1999.

Brown, M. Christopher, and James E. Davis. "The historically Black college as social contract, social capital, and social equalizer." *Peabody Journal of Education*, 76 no. 1 (2001): 31–49. doi:10.2307/1493004

Castenell, Louis. *Historically black colleges and universities: An opportunity for leadership in the twenty-first century*. Atlanta, GA: Southern Education Foundation, 2002.

Chavous, Tabbye, Deborah Rivas, Laurette Green, and Lumas Helaire. "Role of student background, perceptions of ethnic fit, and racial identification in the academic adjustment of African American students at a predominantly white university." *Journal of Black Psychology*, 28 no. 2 (2002): 234–260.

Debord, Larry W., and Steven Millner. "Educational experiences of African-American graduate students on a traditionally white campus: Succor, socialization, and success." *Equity and Excellence in Education*, 26 (1993): 60–71.

Dee, Thomas S. "Teachers, race, and student achievement in a randomized experiment." *The Review of Economics and Statistics*, 86 no. 1 (2004): 195–210.

Ellis, Evelynn M. *Race, gender, and the graduate student experience: Recent research*, 2000. Retrieved February 10, 2007, from www.diversityweb.org/Digest/F00/ graduate.html

Ervin, Kelly S. "Multiculturalism, diversity, and African American college students." *Journal of Black Studies*, 31 no. 6 (2001): 764–776.

Gainen, Joanne and Robert Boice. *Building a diverse faculty*. San Francisco: Jossey-Bass, 1993.

Gloria, Alberta M., Sharon E. Robinson Kurpius, Kimberly Hamilton, and Marcia Wilson. "African American students' persistence at a predominantly white university: Influences of social support, university comfort, and self-beliefs." *Journal of College Student Development*, 40 no. 3 (1999): 257–267.

Hussar, Williamd and Tabitha Bailey. "Projections of Education Statistics to 2021." NCES 2013–008. National Center for Education Statistics, 2013.

Irvine, Jacqueline J., and Leslie Fenwick. "Teachers and teaching for the new millennium: The role of HBCUs." *The Journal of Negro Education*, 80 no. 3 (2011): 197–208.

King, Sabrina H. "The limited presence of African-American teachers." *Review of Educational Research*, 63 no. 2 (1993): 115–149.

Magner, Denise K. "Duke University struggles to make good on pledge to hire black professors." *Chronicle of Higher Education*, 39 no. 29 (1993): 13–15.

Mervis, Jeffrey. *Online university leads United States in awarding doctorates to blacks*, 2017. Retrieved from http://www.sciencemag.org/news/2017/02/online-university-leads-united-states-awarding-doctorates-blacks

Miller, Keith. "Formula for success: A study of minorities in academe who are making it." *CUPA Journal*, 42 no. 1 (1991): 27–33.

Muijs, Daniel, and Alma Harris. "Teacher leadership-Improvement through empowerment? An overview of the literature." *Educational Management Administration & Leadership*, 31 no. 4 (2003): 437–448.

National Association for Equal Opportunity in Higher Education. *The state of America's black colleges*. Silver Spring, MD: Beckham Publications Group, 2008.

National Center for Education Statistics. *Digest of education statistics: 2009*, 2010. Retrieved from http://nces.ed.gov/programs/digest/d09/tables/dt09_250.asp?referrer=list

National Center for Education Statistics. *Digest of education statistics: 2016*, 2016. Retrieved from https://nces.ed.gov/programs/digest/d16/tables/dt16_211.50.asp

Roebuck, Julian and Komanduri Murty. *Historically black colleges and universities: Their place in American higher education*: ERIC, 1993. Retrieved from https://eric.ed.gov/?id=ED363683

Sleeter, Christine. Un-standardizing curriculum: Multicultural teaching in the standards-based classroom. New York: Teachers College Press.

Smith, Emilie P., and William Davidson. "Mentoring and the development of African American graduate students." *Journal of College Student Development*, 33 (1992): 531–539.

Strayhorn, Terrell. "Influences on labor market outcomes of African American college graduates: A national study." *The Journal of Higher Education*, 79 no 1 (2008): 29–57.

Thomas, Kecia M. *Diversity dynamics in the workplace*. San Francisco: Wadsworth-Thomson, 2005.

Thomas, Kecia M., Changya Hu, Amanda G. Gewin, Kecia Bingham, and Nancy Yanchus. "The roles of protégé, race, gender, and proactive socialization attempts on peer mentoring." *Advances in Human Resource Development*, 7 no. 1 (2005): 540–555.

Tierney, William and Estela Bensimon. *Promotion and tenure: Community and socialization in academe*. Albany, NY: SUNY Press, 1996.

Turner, Caroline, Sotello Viernes, and Judith Rann Thompson. "Socializing women doctoral students: Minority and majority experiences." *Review of Higher Education*, 16 no. 3 (1993): 355–370.

Vance, Connie. "Mentoring at the edge of chaos." *Creative Nursing*, 8 no. 3 (2002): 7.

Williams, Brian, and Sheneka Williams. "Perceptions of African American male junior faculty on promotion and tenure: Implications for community building and social capital." *Teachers College Record*, 108 no. 2 (2006): 287–315.

5 Historically Black Medical Schools

Addressing the Minority Health Professional Pipeline and the Public Mission of Care for Vulnerable Populations

Nycal Anthony-Townsend, Bettina M. Beech, and Keith C. Norris

Introduction

Historically Black Colleges and Universities (HBCUs) are unique institutions of higher learning that have played a significant role in educating African Americans in the US.[1] Officially designated by the *Higher Education Act* of 1965, these institutions emerged after the Civil War, when with rare exception freed slaves were not permitted to attend White colleges and universities. HBCUs were founded with the principal mission of educating African Americans, primarily in liberal arts, vocational and religious education, and manual trades.[2] Historically Black Health Professional Schools have grown over time and include professions such as nursing, social work, public health, pharmacy, veterinary medicine, dentistry, and medicine. This chapter will focus on Historically Black Medical Schools (HBMS) as an exemplar of Historically Black Health Professional Schools.

At the turn of the 20th century, there were ten Black medical schools, but only two (Howard University School of Medicine and Meharry Medical College) survived the 1910 recommendations of Dr. Flexner's evaluation of American and Canadian Medical Schools.[3] In the 1970s two new medical schools were created (Morehouse School of Medicine and Charles R. Drew University of Medicine and Science), bringing the present number to four.[4] Currently, 107 institutions are classified as HBCUs, representing 3% of all colleges and universities in the US.[5] Approximately 9% of African American college students attend HBCUs; however, graduates of these institutions now represent 17%, 31%, and 31% of the bachelor's degrees awarded to African Americans in the health professions, biological sciences, and mathematics, respectively.[6] Collectively, faculty at HBCUs have considerable potential to diversify the biomedical and health professions workforce, as they are in a unique position to provide critical role models and educate, impact, and encourage more than 330,000 students who may consider and are ultimately prepared for careers in the biomedical/bio-behavioral and health professional fields. In 2015, 5.7% of US medical school graduates were African American, and of this group, 18.1% graduated from the four Black medical schools; thus, 3% of US medical schools produced nearly 20% of Black medical school graduates in 2015.[7] These findings highlight HBMS as an important resource for ensuring the health of racial and ethnic minorities. Ample research demonstrates the linkage between population health outcomes and the cultural competence of healthcare professionals.[8] As evidenced by these data, Black medical school graduates are vital contributors to our nation's health.

HBCUs and Health

The presence of racial and ethnic inequities in health in the US has been well documented dating back to the late 19th century.[9] Indeed, in 1899 W. E. B. Du Bois noted, "there have been few other cases in the history of civilized peoples where human suffering has been viewed with such peculiar indifference."[10] With rare exception, post emancipation minority physicians were not allowed to train in, nor were minority patients allowed to receive care in, most White educational/medical facilities until the Civil Rights Movement and the associated legislative changes to end segregation laws.[11] In today's context, nearly 64 million individuals, who are disproportionately minorities, live in over 6,500 designated primary care shortage areas in the United States.[12] By definition, individuals in these urban and rural communities face a deficit of primary care providers in four primary care specialties: general or family practice, general internal medicine, pediatrics, and obstetrics and gynecology.[13] The residents of these communities often face economic, cultural, or linguistic barriers to healthcare.[14] As part of their mission, Historically Black Medical Schools (HBMS) have prioritized the need to increase primary care providers, and in particular minority providers, highlighting the critical role HBMS provide in contributing to health professional training that remains as important today as it was more than 100 years ago.[15]

The origin of HBMS and other Historically Black Health Professional Schools was grounded in a vision of preparing high quality minority health providers;[16] however, it was not shared by all.[17] In fact, Abraham Flexner in his 1910 report on US and Canadian Medical education stated, "The Negro must be educated not only for his sake, but for ours. The pioneer work in educating the race to know and to practice fundamental hygienic principles must be done largely by the Negro doctor and the Negro nurse. A well taught Negro sanitarian will be immensely useful; an essentially untrained Negro wearing an M.D. degree is dangerous."[18] As noted earlier, at the time of the 1910 Flexner Report, there were ten Black medical schools, but with limited financial support for Black medical schools, eight were soon discontinued.[19] Andrew Carnegie, one of a few sources of support for

African American medical colleges in the early 20th century, stated, "If we start helping medical colleges for colored people, we cannot discontinue." He felt their needs were too great and their allies who might help in the funding, too few.[20] Thus only Howard University College of Medicine and Meharry Medical School remained, a situation that did not change until the 1970s with the creation of Morehouse School of Medicine and Charles R. Drew University of Medicine and Science.[21] The precarious nature of these early Historically Black Medical Schools' financial arrangements, whether overseen by White missionary groups or by enterprising independent Black physician proprietors, put them in a vulnerable position. Unfortunately, the relatively low level of funding and vulnerability has not changed much since.[22] While the financial viability of these institutions to support physicians of color remains essential, there are other significant public health equity issues that also weigh into the importance and continued need for Historically Black Medical Schools.

Impact of Health Equity/Social Determinants of Health

Historically Black Health Professional Schools and programs embrace a mission of educating and training culturally competent healthcare providers that aim to reduce health disparities among minority populations. Despite these efforts, substantial racial and ethnic disparities in health and healthcare still remain in the United States.[23] Health disparities continue to occur in the quality of care received even when income, health insurance, and access to care are taken into account.[24] Patients from racial and ethnic minorities often fare far worse than their White counterparts on a range of health indicators: life expectancy, infant mortality, prevalence of chronic diseases, and insurance coverage, among others.[25] These disparities have been linked to conditions such as poverty, unequal access to healthcare, lack of education, stigma, and racism as well as the places where people live, learn, work, and play, collectively known as social determinants of health.[26] Health equity has also been defined as "the absence of systematic disparities in health between and within social groups that have different levels of underlying social advantages or disadvantages—that is, different positions in a social hierarchy."[27] Addressing social determinants of health is a primary approach to achieving health equity, "when everyone has the opportunity to 'attain their full health potential' and no one is 'disadvantaged from achieving this potential because of their social position or other socially determined circumstance.'"[28]

HBCUs offer a unique opportunity to bridge the health disparities gap and social determinants of health through healthcare workforce diversity. A 2002 article by Cohen and colleagues introduced the notion that greater diversity in the workforce can advance cultural competency by allowing individuals from varied racial/ethnic backgrounds to interact with each other.[29] By helping to establish a firm understanding of how and why culturally determined factors affect illness, medical adherence, and response to treatment, diversity can, in turn, translate to improved health for patients.[30] Healthcare professional students who are exposed to underserved populations during education and training are more likely to care for this same population once in practice;[31] this may strengthen the healthcare infrastructure in underserved communities.[32] In fact, primary care physicians who complete residency training in community health centers (safety-net providers for the uninsured and other vulnerable populations) are significantly more likely to practice in medically underserved areas,[33] as are medical students who train in HBMS.[34] Finally, medical students who train with underserved populations are thought to learn and rediscover social responsibility and further understand the social determinants of health.[35]

Research as a Foundation for Advancing Education

While student education continues to be the principal mission of HBCUs, research and health professions activities have grown to become an integral and important component of their respective missions.[36] Despite an interest in expanding their research portfolios, resources needed for viable research infrastructure investments at HBCUs are threatened by economic factors such as fiscal shortfalls in funds needed for daily operations, capital expenditures to update facilities, and increasing competition for shrinking philanthropic donations and dwindling endowments.[37] Building collaborations with more research-active HBCUs or research-intensive majority institutions is one approach that has shown promise to be an effective model for engaging biomedical and health professional students and faculty in research training and collaborations.[38] Unfortunately, there are often few training opportunities for faculty through these collaborations that are specifically designed to address most HBCU faculty members' unique context, (e.g., heavy teaching loads, limited research training, minimal research infrastructure/graduate research programs, and lack of a critical mass of research peers and mentors).[39] In order to more fully realize and build upon the full potential that resides within HBCUs, effective models of research training and mentoring for faculty are critically needed. By virtue of infusing additional research infrastructure into HBCUs, faculty will create new and emerging knowledge that they integrate with external research findings, with the end result being even more relevant teaching being provided to students and greater exposure for university excellence.

Challenges in Faculty Development

Unfortunately, there are numerous contextual disadvantages faced by underrepresented minorities (URM) health professionals or research faculty at HBMS, such as constrained resources, lack of available mentors owing to heavy teaching or administrative responsibilities, and relatively few experienced researchers with a funding track record,[40] greater likelihood of having limited research training experience after receiving terminal degrees,[41] and lesser likelihood to receive quality mentoring from experienced senior researchers regardless of institutional affiliation.[42] The lack of advanced research-focused graduate programs at HBCUs precludes the availability of a critical mass of research peers. Also, factors such as academic pedigree can create "invisible endorsements" that advantage their peers and contribute to differences in rates of funding success.[43]

Indeed, an NIH-commissioned study titled "Race, Ethnicity, and NIH Research Awards" documented a significantly lower likelihood of *peer-reviewed* NIH R01 grant funding (a national metric of research excellence) between African American (13.2 points less likely) and White applicants, even after multiple adjustments.[44] Further, large differences were found between the number of applicants and applications from underrepresented minority (URM) faculty compared to Whites, and URM, who represent over 35% of the US population, accounted for only 5% of NIH awarded research grants as principal investigator.[45] At an institutional level, investigators at the 30 most highly NIH-funded institutions were more likely to be successful in being awarded NIH R01 grant funding.[46] Collectively, results from this study suggest that African American faculty at HBCUs tend to be at a "triple disadvantage," as these individual, institutional, and system level factors combine to undermine the probability of an HBCU faculty having a successful research career. Common barriers to successful training of health professions faculty at Historically Black Colleges and Universities included:

- Limited research infrastructure and constrained resources for research;
- Heavy teaching or administrative responsibilities;
- Limited faculty development programs;
- Relatively few experienced researchers with a funding track record or formal research training;
- Limited administrative support;
- Limited formal research training for many faculty;
- Limited funding and protected time for many faculty participating in research or mentoring;
- Changing duties of the faculty during the course of a training period; and
- Limited resources to support implementation of some training program recommendations.

Data from the study also detailed that NIH grant applications from individuals with post-degree research training experiences (e.g., postdoctoral fellowships) were more likely to be funded, and as noted earlier, faculty at HBCUs typically have limited research training experience after receiving terminal degrees. Health professions and research training as well as mentoring programs for underrepresented minority faculty in HBCUs are particularly valuable because of potential "ripple effects" that extend beyond individual faculty members' careers to their students, peers, and institutional environments, thereby opening the "health profession and biomedical research workforce pipeline." Without a significant investment in faculty training and mentoring, the US is unlikely to achieve the nation's goals for increasing the health and biomedical research workforce diversity.[47] The importance of proficiency in biomedical science education and professional development for biomedical science teachers, particularly at HBCU institutions, cannot be overlooked.[48]

Since a greater percentage of URM scholars are more likely to conduct health disparities research than non-URM scholars, increasing diversity in the biomedical research and health professions is recognized as a major national strategy to reduce racial/ethnic health disparities.[49] This effect underscores the urgent need to increase the quantity and quality of URM researchers working in areas of importance to minority health, such as obesity, hypertension, diabetes, and mental health. Expanding the pool of minority investigators is essential to eliminating health disparities, a major objective of Healthy People 2020 that has yet to be met.[50] Regardless of institutional affiliation, too few URM faculty receive quality mentoring from experienced senior researchers.[51] The NIH Biomedical Research Workforce Pipeline report highlighted three issues as impediments to URM research career success: i) mentee transition points, ii) mentorship, and iii) conscious and unconscious factors.[52] These are highly relevant for HBCU students and faculty as well. In addition to the report's focus on students and faculty, it also touched upon the importance of institutional transformation. Key to the success of institutional transformation is the vision and buy-in of institutional leadership.

Tradition of Leadership

Historically Black Health Professional Schools (from beginning to now), like many other institutions, are experiencing substantial challenges in recruiting, developing, and retaining effective and consistent leadership. Many health professional institutions are seeing a much more rapid turnover in leadership, in large part based on pressure from the Board of Trustees for rapid changes in performance outcomes across multiple domains, which are often, but not always, longstanding, institutionalized issues for which rapid change is often unrealistic. As an institution, most if not all, HBCUs in many respects are still maturing and require close attention to developing sustainable and well-designed systems and structures that are flexible enough to meet the changing demands of our society. This may necessitate significant changes, but these need to be done in a very deliberate manner, leveraging the collective insights and will of students, faculty, administrators, and stakeholders in the context of the shifting marketplace of higher education. This will also require strategic investments. For example, in the 1930s–40s, Howard University made investments in select faculty development under the College of Medicine Dean, Dr. Numa P. G. Adams, who obtained grants from the General Education Board established by the Rockefeller Foundation to support two years of advanced training for 25 promising young Black faculty to attend prestigious universities and hospitals around the country, such as Dr. Charles Drew, who earned the D.Sc. degree from Columbia University.[53] More recently, the Robert Wood Johnson Harold Amos Medical Faculty Development Program[54] and others have provided similar opportunities for minority trainees at both research-intensive institutions and HBCUs.[55] Taking advantage of programs like these will be crucial for the continuing success of Historically Black Health Professional Schools.

Historically Black Medical Schools in the Educational Marketplace

Accounting for less than 3% of US colleges and universities, yet graduating nearly 20% of all African American students in the nation, HBCUs are a unique subset of federally designated postsecondary institutions.[56] Given the significant role these institutions play in American higher education, it is important that they serve students well, run efficiently, and provide a positive return on investment for stakeholders. The role and use of affirmative action in higher education have created an increased demand for clarifying the significance of HBCUs.[57] According to the *Brown v. Board of Education* decision, the primary goal of integration was not to make students smarter, get them better jobs, or improve their civic values. Rather, the goal was primarily to eliminate the racialized nature of our schools that was "harmful to the educational, social, and psychological development of [Black] children."[58] However, HBCUs have a diverse student and faculty body and are actually leading the push for diversity while still providing crucial opportunities for Black students and students from low-income families to be educated in a supportive environment where they are valued, similar to religious-based higher education programs such as Catholic, Seventh-day Adventist, and Jewish based institutions.[59]

HBCUs are facing a looming shift in the college student demographics. According to a National Center for Education Statistics (NCES) report, college enrollment will slow dramatically over the next decade, with most growth occurring among traditionally underserved, minority populations. It projects a 25% increase of African American students and a massive 42% increase of Hispanic students by 2021.[60] From this data, we can infer that college students will increasingly come from underserved and lower income communities and families, and many of these students are likely to be first generation college students who in turn are significantly more likely to drop out than those whose parents have college degrees. In addition, more college students are "non-traditional," which could range from part-time attendees to older and working. This trend is likely to grow, with enrollment of students 25 and older projected to be nearly double of that of younger students through 2020.[61] Similarly to minority students, non-traditional students are more than twice as likely to be low-income as "traditional" students, with all of the challenges to degree attainment that accompany low-income students.[62] These trends will require HBCUs to examine and retool program designs to accommodate the needs of the college student of the future. Even more important is assessing the readiness of these students and how to create or maintain an advantage in recruiting, retaining, and graduating promising minority students and non-traditional students.

Over the past decades, the federal courts have overturned several school systems' policies that attempted to integrate and diversify their student bodies by using race as a factor in admissions or class placement.[63] Even those programs that have not been overturned often have been heavily scrutinized.[64] These decisions have left universities, colleges, and elementary and secondary schools struggling to develop ways to justify their race-conscious and affirmative action programs,[65] and have led to the implementation of a holistic assessment of health professional students through the admissions process.[66] The Supreme Court has come to view programs that specifically benefit racial minorities in the same way that it views practices that intentionally discriminate against minorities,[67] and educators often cannot find any justification other than that of remedying past discrimination, as persisting racial discrimination is more difficult to prove since it is no longer codified in policies or laws.[68] Despite promises and rhetoric of equality, progress has been slow. In 1977, Arnold S. Relman, then editor-in-chief of the *New England Journal of Medicine*, remarked how little had changed since the Supreme Court ruled segregation unconstitutional and stated: "The legal and philosophical subtleties of quotas, goals, reverse discrimination, " etc. have been exhaustively explored and the problem is not to be resolved merely by tinkering with admissions policies, and noted the social, economic, and cultural problems that are responsible for the underrepresentation of minorities in medical schools cannot be solved by the courts.[69] He suggested we look beyond the courts to the actual educational handicaps faced by poor and minority children in this country.[70] While there have been improvements since 1977 in the diversity of the health professional workforce, the advances continue to be slow and unfortunately, more recent data suggests stagnation.[71]

Enhanced access for racial/ethnic minorities at traditional medical schools has become a major threat to HBMS, as there is now increasing outreach for minority students occurring at larger research intensive medical schools in an effort to increase the diversity of their student body. These research-intensive medical schools have substantially more resources, allowing them to provide major scholarships and other support services to help recruit students that traditionally would matriculate at an HBMS. While the number of African American students at these institutions is still relatively small, usually approximately 8%, many of these schools have much larger class sizes and thus they can now create a critical mass of minority students that can provide the type of social network many seek in considering attending research-intensive medical schools.

Another challenge is the model of institutional financing. Unlike many educational institutions, which derive core funding from tuition, most Health Professional schools generate the majority of their revenue from clinical income, research funding, and philanthropy, and for many a smaller portion from tuition. Some research-intensive schools receive state funding support, and fortunately some HBMS also receive limited state or federal support. The clinical care programs and associated faculty practice plans that are a significant source of revenue for many research intensive institutions are not available to HBMS, which are commonly linked to systems providing indigent care, county safety-net programs, and low revenue private hospitals, which provide training opportunities but limited revenue. HBMS affiliated hospitals and clinics care for a disproportionately higher percentage of indigent patients that not only do not allow for the types of clinical revenue streams that are generated by many of their peer research-intensive medical schools, but are much less likely to care for persons able to provide philanthropic support. With the full implementation of the *Affordable Care Act*, the rates of uninsured patients has decreased, yet the rates of reimbursements for these facilities has not significantly impacted HBMS.

The increasing cost of tuition over the last 30 years has risen much more rapidly than most working salaries, leading to tuition now being one of the major cost burdens on families, and particularly families with lower levels of annual income. In our society these are predominately racial and ethnic minorities' families—many of the families whose children are likely to matriculate at HBCUs. Conversely, many large research-intensive institutions have now amassed substantive endowments to provide major scholarships to many students from low-income families, allowing them to defray the burden of tuition on their students and their families. Unfortunately, this occurs primarily in those institutions that have the combination of clinical revenue, research, and philanthropic funding streams that have occurred in a much more limited manner at HBMS. Thus, HBMS must carefully balance tuition increases needed to support the provision of quality institutional resources and faculty ratios, possibly pricing out many of the students who might otherwise attend.

Another major challenge for Historically Black Health Professional Schools is creating a clear identity. They differ from most recognized private universities with large endowments and often a mission of research excellence. Historically Black Health Professional Schools by tradition have a public mission,[72] but this often puts them at a disadvantage when trying to generate financial support and inherently leads them to be compared with and compete with many large public institutions that have strategically placed alumni, substantial state funding, and associated plethora of other state resources. It is now more critical than ever that Historically Black

Health Professional School leadership articulate clear and compelling messages that capture their unique contributions to society.[73]

Leadership Strategies

Presidential and executive team leadership at HBCUs in general and Professional Health Schools/Colleges specifically require a unique set of skills, perspectives, and resources to successfully meet the mission of these institutions. These include:

- Creation of a leadership learning community with mentors experienced in leading universities or colleges (HBCUs and non HBCUs);
- Creation of an administrative and educational leadership pipeline (HBCUs and non HBCUs);
- Development of administrative and educational leadership partnerships at both HBCUs and non HBCUs;
- Cultivation of present student body to develop the passion and commitment to the ongoing success of the institution as part of alumni relations;
- Development and maintenance of a strong alumni network; and
- Compelling articulation for the value and need for HBCUs going forward.

The American Council on Education (ACE) Leadership Academy provides a series of training programs designed to support new and aspiring University Presidents to better serve and lead complex institutions by being able to anticipate critical leadership issues and imperatives. This and related programs for senior leaders can be important for both incumbent leadership teams and for succession planning. For example, the ACE Institute for New Presidents addresses issues such as: i) insights and lessons about the leadership challenges faced by new presidents; ii) knowledge and skills for dealings with high-visibility, high-exposure, and unexpected challenges and opportunities; iii) practical advice on working effectively with the media; iv) increased understanding of how to assess and manage campus culture and change processes; v) practical advice on how to form and manage a highly effective executive team; vi) an extended professional network of fellow presidents from a cross-section of institutions; and vii) a low-risk setting to test ideas.[74]

One report reinforced the importance in leadership of learning and doing to move leadership beyond the acquisition of administrative and management skills to the cultivation and sharing of leadership throughout the institution, as well as the need to better understand leadership roles (e.g., leadership vs. management) and organizational culture.[75] This will be essential to effectively address emerging issues such as the effect of globalization, the impact of e-learning on shifts in education and training modalities, and the cost of education and strategies for institutional sustainability.[76] Attention will also need to be given to including new partnerships with state institutions and community colleges, especially federal efforts to minimize or even eliminate their tuition costs, with a likely major change over the next few years in the number of quality students seeking further training from the community colleges pathway.[77]

Conclusion

The role for Historically Black Health Professional Schools remains clear and compelling, but market forces are pressuring most Historically Black educational institutions. Several key questions for Historically Black Health Professional Leadership to reflect on might include: i) what is the future role of Historically Black Health Professional Schools in maintaining quality healthcare and quality teaching programs to address minority and low resource communities; ii) how to effectively partner with research-intensive institutions or uniquely matched HBCUs to optimize their mission to improve the health of those less fortunate and eliminate disparities in health and; iii) how do Historically Black Health Professional Schools create and maintain a culture of excellence and accountability?[78] Historically Black Health Professional Schools will need to be cognizant of, and develop new models of, sustainability, and the opportunity or need to partner should be strategic and proactive, rather than reactive. The traditional approach to leadership selection, which has too often been internal and relationship driven, needs to balance retention of institutional memory with bringing in personnel with new experiences and concepts of innovation in a rapidly changing world. Creating novel partnerships with research intensive institutions, such as partnerships developed by Emory University/Morehouse School of Medicine in Atlanta, Georgia; Georgetown University/Howard University in Washington, DC; Vanderbilt University/Meharry Medical College in Nashville, Tennessee; University of California, Los Angeles/Charles Drew University in Los Angeles, California; and Weill Cornell Medical College/Hunter College in New York, New York may be models for future consideration.[79] There will continue to be struggles grounded in both institutional and persisting individual racism, but leading with excellence and not echoes of past injustices will be critical. In the words of the late Dr. Charles Drew, "Excellence of performance transcends artificial barriers created by man."

Notes

1 Baskerville, Berger, and Smith, 2008; Brown II and Ricard 2007
2 Allen and Jewell 2002; Lee and Keys 2013; Roebuck and Murty 1993; Wolanin 1998
3 Flexner, Pritchet, and Henry 1910; Savitt 2006
4 Norris et al. 2009
5 Gasman 2013
6 Lee and Keys 2013

7 Sullivan 2016
8 Smedley, Stith, and Nelson 2009
9 Chase 1903; Du Bois and Eaton 1899
10 Du Bois and Eaton 1899
11 Baker et al. 2008
12 HRSA 2016
13 HRSA 2016
14 HRSA 2016
15 Norris et al. 2009; Savitt 2006; Smedley 2004; Sullivan 2004
16 Savitt 2010
17 Flexner et al. 1910; Savitt 2006
18 Flexner 2013
19 Flexner 2013
20 Savitt 2006
21 Norris et al. 2009
22 Norris et al. 2009
23 Forum 2017
24 Smedley, Stith, and Nelson 2009
25 Smedley, Stith, and Nelson 2009
26 Braveman and Gruskin 2003; DHHS 2013; Povall et al. 2013
27 DHHS, 2013
28 Brennan Ramirez, Baker, and Metzler 2008
29 Cohen, Gabriel, and Terrell 2002
30 Cohen, Gabriel, and Terrell 2002
31 Tavernier et al. 2003
32 Vanderbilt et al. 2013
33 Ferguson et al. 2009
34 Ko et al. 2005; Ko et al. 2007; Mullan et al. 2010
35 Fournier, Perez-Stable, and Greer 1993
36 Brown II and Ricard 2007
37 Gasman 2013
38 Clewell 2006; Ofili et al. 2013
39 Boyington et al. 2016; Fabris et al. 2016
40 Waller and Shofoluwe 2013
41 Norris et al. 2009; Ofili et al. 2013
42 Shavers et al. 2005
43 NIH 2012
44 Ginther et al. 2011
45 Ginther et al. 2011
46 Ginther et al. 2011
47 NIH 2012; Sullivan 2004
48 Pellegrino 2013; Wilson 2013
49 Valantine and Collins 2015
50 DHHS 2013
51 NIH 2012
52 NIH 2012
53 Cobb 1951
54 Ardery, Krol, and Wilkes 2014
55 Palermo et al. 2008
56 Conrad and Gasman 2015; Gasman and Conrad 2013; Gasman, Baez, and Turner 2008
57 Killenbeck 1999
58 Killenbeck 1999
59 Sullivan 2016
60 Hussar and Bailey 2013

61 Hussar and Bailey 2013
62 Chen and DesJardins 2010
63 Moses, Yun, and Marin 2009; Orfield 2001
64 Black 2002
65 Killenbeck 1999
66 Kirch and Nivet 2013; Scott and Zerwic 2015; Witzburg and Sondheimer 2013
67 Blake 2012
68 Black 2002
69 Relman 1977
70 Relman 1977
71 Sullivan 2016
72 Mullan et al. 2010
73 Arnett 2014
74 ACE 2016
75 Amey 2006
76 Stinson 2015
77 Stinson 2015
78 Norris et al. 2009; Treadwell et al. 2009
79 Ofili et al. 2013

Bibliography

ACE. *The American Council on Education (ACE) Leadership Academy*, 2016. Retrieved from www.acenet.edu/leadership/programs/Pages/default.aspx

Allen, Walter R., and Joseph O. Jewell. "A backward glance forward: Past, present, and future perspectives on historically black colleges and universities." *Review of Higher Education*, 25 no. 3 (2002): 241–261.

Amey, Marilyn J. "Leadership in higher education." *Change: The Magazine of Higher Learning*, 38 no. 6 (2006): 55–58.

Ardery, Nina L., David M. Krol, and David S. Wilkes. "Leveraging diversity in American academic medicine: The Harold Amos medical faculty development program." *Annals of the American Thoracic Society*, 11 no. 4 (2014): 600–602. doi:10.1513/AnnalsATS.201402-064PS

Arnett, Autumn. "State of HBCUs." *Diverse Issues in Higher Education*, 31 no. 23 (2014): 18.

Baker, Robert B., Harriet A. Washington, Ololade Olakanmi et al. "African American physicians and organized medicine, 1846–1968: Origins of a racial divide." *JAMA*, 300 no. 3(2008): 306–313. doi:10.1001/jama.300.3.306

Baskerville, Lezli et al. "The role of historically black colleges and universities in faculty diversity." *American Academic*, 4 no. 1 (2008): 11–31.

Black, Derek W. "The case for the new compelling government interest: Improving educational outcomes." *North Carolina Law Review*, 80 no. 3 (2002): 923–974.

Blake, Valarie. "Affirmative action and medical school admissions." *Virtual Mentor*, 14 no. 12 (2012): 1003–1007. doi:10.1001/virtualmentor.2012.14.12.hlaw1-1212

Boyington, Josephine E. et al. "A perspective on promoting diversity in the biomedical research workforce." *Ethnicity and Disease*, 26 no. 3 (2016): 379–386.

Braveman, Paula, and Sofia Gruskin. "Defining equity in health." *Journal of the Epidemiology and Community Health*, 57 no. 4 (2003): 254–258.

Brennan Ramirez, Laura K., Elizabeth A. Baker, and Marilyn Metzler. *Promoting health equity: A resource to help communities address social determinants of health*. Atlanta, GA: Centers for Disease Control and Prevention, 2008.

Brown II, M. Christopher., and Ronyelle Bertrand Ricard. "The honorable past and uncertain future of the nation's HBCUs." *The NEA Higher Education Journal* Fall (2007): 117–130.

Chase, Thomas. Mortality among Negroes in cities: Proceedings of the conference for investigations of city problems held at Atlanta university, May 26–27, 1896. Atlanta, GA: Atlanta University Press, 1903.

Chen, Rong, and Stephen L. DesJardins. "Investigating the impact of financial aid on student dropout risks: Racial and ethnic differences." *Journal of Higher Educatiom*, 81 no. 2 (2010): 179–208.

Clewell, Beatriz, Clemencia Consentino de Cohen, Nicole Deterding, and Lisa Tsui Final report on the evaluation of the National Science Foundation Louis Stokes Alliances for Minority Participation program: Full technical report and appendices. Washington, DC: The Urban Institute, 2006.

Conrad, Clifton and Marybeth Gasman. *Educating a Diverse Nation*. Cambridge, MA: Harvard University Press, 2015.

Conrad, Clifton and Marybeth Gasman. *Minority serving institutions: Educating all students*. Philadelphia: Penn Center for Minority Serving Institutions, University of Pennsylvania, 2013.

Cobb, W. Montague. "Numa P. G. Adams, M.D., 1885–1940." *Journal of National Medical Association*, 43 no. 1(1951): 42–54.

Cohen, Jordan J., Barbara A. Gabriel, and Charles Terrell. "The case for diversity in the health care workforce." *Health Affairs*, 21 no. 5 (2002): 90–102.

Department of Health and Human Services. US department of health human services office of disease prevention health promotion: Healthy people 2020. Washington, DC, 2013.

Du Bois, W. E. B., and Isabel Eaton. *The Philadelphia Negro: A social study*. Published for the University, 1899.

Fabris, F. et al. "Junior faculty career development through an NHLBI program to increase diversity in cardiovascular health-related research." *Journal of the American College of Cardiliogy*, 67 no. 19 (2016): 2312–2313.

Ferguson, Warren, Suzanne Cashman, Judith Savageau, and Daniel H. Lasser. "Family medicine residency characteristics associated with practice in a health professions shortage area." *Residency Education*, 41 no. 6 (2009): 405–410.

Flexner, Abraham. Medical education in the United states and Canada: A report to the Carnegie foundation for the advancement of teaching. New York: Carnegie Foundation, 2013.

Flexner, Abraham et al. *Medical education in the United States and Canada bulletin number four (The Flexner Report)*. New York: The Carnegie Foundation for the Advancement of Teaching, 1910.

Fournier, Arthur. M., Alina Perez-Stable, and Pedro Greer. "Lessons from a clinic for the homeless: The Camillus health concern." *Journal of the American Medical Association*, 270 no. 22 (1993): 2721–2724.

Gasman, Marybeth. *The changing face of historically Black colleges and universities*. Penn Center for Minority Serving Institutions, 2013 http://repository.upenn.edu/gse_pubs/335

Gasman, Marybeth, Benjamin Baez, and Caroline Sotello Viernes Turner. *Understanding minority-serving institutions*. New York: SUNY Press, 2008.

Ginther, Donna K. et al. "Race, ethnicity, and NIH research awards." *Science*, 333 no. 6045 (2011): 1015–1019. doi:10.1126/science.1196783

Health Resources & Services Administration. *Health professional shortage areas & medically underserved areas/populations.* US Department of Health and Human Services Health Resources and Services Administration, 2016. Retrieved from https://datawarehouse.hrsa.gov/topics/shortageAreas.aspx

Hussar, Williamd and Tabitha Bailey. "Projections of Education Statistics to 2021." NCES 2013–008. National Center for Education Statistics, 2013.

Killenbeck, Mark. "Pushing things up to their first principles: Reflections on the values of affirmative action." *California Law Review*, 87 no. 6 (1999): 1299–1407.

Kirch, Darrell G., and March Nivet. "Increasing diversity and inclusion in medical school to improve the health of all." *Journal of Healthccare Management*, 58 no. 5 (2013): 311–313.

Ko, Michelle, Kevin Heslin, Ronald Edelstein, and Kevin Grumbach. "The role of medical education in reducing health care disparities: The first ten years of the UCLA/Drew Medical Education Program." *Journal of General Internal Medicine*, 22 no. 5 (2007): 625–631.

Ko, Michell, Ronald Edelstein, Kevin Heslin, Shobita Rajagopalan, LuAnn Wilkerson, Lois Colburn, and Kevin Grumbach. "Impact of the University of California, Los Angeles/Charles R. Drew University Medical Education Program on medical students' intentions to practice in underserved areas." *Academic Medicine*, 80 no. 9 (2005): 803–808.

Lee Jr., John Michael, and Samaad Wes Keys. Repositioning HBCUs for the future: Access, success, research & innovation. APLU Office of Access and Success Discussion Paper, 1, 2013.

Moses, Michelle S., John T. Yun, and Patricia Marin. "Affirmative action's fate: Are 20 more years enough?" *Education Policy Analysis Archives*, 17 no. 17 (2009). Retrieved from http://epaa.asu.edu/epaa/v17n17/.

Mullan, Fitzhugh, Candace Chen, Spehen Petterson, Gretchen Kolsky, and Michael Spagnola. "The social mission of medical education: Ranking the schools." *Annals of Internal Medicine*, 152 no. 12, (2010): 804–811.

National Quality Forum. "Disparities in healthcare and health outcomes in selected conditions." *National Quality Forum*, 2017. Retrieved from www.qualityforum.org/Publications/2017/01/Disparities_in_Healthcare_and_Health_Outcomes_in_Selected_Conditions.aspx

National Institites of Health. Draft report of the Advisory Committee to the Director Working Group on Diversity in the Biomedical Research Workforce. Bethesda, MD: The National Institutes of Health, 2012.

Norris, Keith C. et al. "Historically black medical schools: Addressing the minority health professional pipeline and the public mission of care for vulnerable populations." *Journal of the National Medical Association*, 101 no. 9 (2009): 864–872.

Ofili, Elizabeth O. et al. "Models of interinstitutional partnerships between research intensive universities and Minority Serving Institutions (MSI) across the Clinical Translational Science Award (CTSA) Consortium." *Clinical and Translational Science*, (2013), 435–443. doi:10.1111/cts.12118

Orfield, Gary. *Schools more separate: Consequences of a decade of resegregation.* Cambridge, MA: The Civil Rights Project Harvard University, 2001.

Palermo, Ann-Gel et al. "Diversity in academic medicine no. 5 successful programs in minority faculty development: Overview." *Mount Sinai Journal of Medicine*, 75 no. 6 (2008): 523–532. doi:10.1002/msj.20083

Pellegrino, James W. "Proficiency in science: Assessment challenges and opportunities." *Science*, 340 no. 6130 (2013): 320–323. doi:10.1126/science.1232065

Povall, Susan L., Fiona A Haigh, Debbie Abrahams, and Alex Scott-Samuel. "Health equity impact assessment." *Health Promotions International*, (2013). doi:10.1093/heapro/dat012

Relman, Arnold S. "Minority admissions: Beyond bakke." *New England Journal of Medicine*, 297 no. 21 (1977) doi:10.1056/nejm197711242972110

Roebuck, Julian and Komanduri Murty. *Historically black colleges and universities: Their place in American higher education*: ERIC, 1993. Retrieved from https://eric.ed.gov/?id=ED363683

Savitt, Todd. "Abraham Flexner and the black medical schools. 1992." *Journal of the National Medical Association*, 98 no. 9 (2006): 1415–1424.

Savitt, Todd. "The journal of the national medical association 100 years ago: A new voice of and for African American physicians." *Journal of the National Medical Association*, 102 no. 8 (2010): 734–744.

Scott, L. D., and Zerwic, Julie. "Holistic review in admissions: A strategy to diversify the nursing workforce." *Nursing Outlook*, 63 no. 4: 488–495. doi:10.1016/j.outlook.2015.01.001

Shavers, Vickie L. et al. "Barriers to racial/ethnic minority application and competition for NIH research funding." *Journal of the National Medical Association*, 97 no. 8 (2005): 1063–1077.

Smedley, Brian et al. Unequal treatment: Confronting racial and ethnic disparities in health care (with CD). Washington, DC: National Academies Press, 2009.

Smedley, Brian D. "Committee on institutional and policy-level strategies for increasing the diversity of the US health care workforce." In board on health sciences policy and Brian D. Smedley, Adrienne Stith, Butler Lonnie R. Bistow (Eds.), *The nation's compelling interest: Ensuring diversity in the health-care workforce*. Washington, DC: The National Academies Press, 2004.

Stinson, Sonya. "America's college promise." *Community College Journal*, 85 no. 4 (2015): 10.

Sullivan, Louis. "Diversity and higher education for the health care professions." *The Milbank Quarterly*, 94 no. 3 (2016): 448–451. doi:10.1111/1468–0009.12203

Sullivan, Louis W. "Missing persons: Minorities in the health professions, A report of the Sullivan Commission on Diversity in the Healthcare Workforce." 2004.

Tavernier, Laura A. et al. "Does exposure to medically underserved areas during training influence eventual choice of practice location?" *Medical Education*, 37 no. 4 (2003): 299–304.

Treadwell, Henrie, Ronald Braithwaite, Kisha Braithwaite, Desiree Oliver, and Rhonda Holliday. "Leadership development for health researchers at historically black colleges and universities." *American Journal of Public Health*, 99 no. Suppl 1 (2009): S53–S57. doi:10.2105/ajph.2008.136069

Valantine, Hannah A., and Francis S. Collins. "National institutes of health addresses the science of diversity." *Proceedings of National Academy of Sciences U S A*, 112 no. 40 (2015): 12240–12242. doi:10.1073/pnas.1515612112

Vanderbilt, Allison. A. et al. "Health disparities among highly vulnerable populations in the United States: A call to action for medical and oral health care." *Medical Education Online*, 18 (2013): 1–3.

Waller, Lewis S., and Musibau Shofoluwe. "A qualitative case study of junior faculty mentoring practices at selected minority higher educational institutions." *Journal of Technology, Management & Applied Engineering*, 29 no. 3 (2013): 1–11.

Wilson, Suzanne M. "Professional development for science teachers." *Science*, 340 no. 6130 (2013): 310–313. doi:10.1126/science.1230725

Witzburg, Robert A., and Henry M. "Sondheimer. Holistic review—Shaping the medical profession one applicant at a time." *New England Journal of Medicine*, 368 no. 17 (2013): 1565–1567.

Wolanin, Thomas R. "The federal investment in minority-serving institutions." *New Directions for Higher Education*, 102 (1998): 17–32.

6 Staying in Focus

Research Self-Efficacy and Mentoring Among HBCU Professional Doctorates

Nadielka Bishop, Comfort Okpala, and C. Dean Campbell

Introduction

Mentoring is an important agent of graduate student success in university settings.[1] The approach to guiding doctoral graduate students plays a critical role in academic and professional development. Positive attitudes and behaviors that are developed due to such guidance can increase the likelihood of engaging in research activities. And while Historically Black Colleges and Universities (HBCUs) have been lauded for their ability to create positive faculty-student relationships, an existing gap in academic discourse has yet to explore doctoral students' perceptions that affect research productivity. Training and supervising the work of doctoral students is integral to their development and has direct relationships to their research attitudes and behaviors. This is not solely related to PhDs but professional doctorates as well.

The purpose of this chapter is to elaborate on the attitudes of professional doctoral students at Historically Black Colleges and Universities (HBCUs) as a preliminary discussion to improvements in research training in HBCU professional doctoral programs. This information will add to the body of knowledge on faculty-student mentoring and provide more discourse in support for graduate student research training to help diversify research and higher education.[2] This chapter also hopes to explore opportunities that expand solution-oriented research to cultural issues that cause a variety of imbalances in many social institutions.

Purpose and Significance of this Exploration

With racial and ethnic disparities occurring in economics, healthcare, education, and law enforcement, there is a need for an even more diverse pool of professionals across disciplines. The overall progress of further diversifying this selection bank of scholars has increased; but, consistent progress has been made in neither disparities nor professional diversification.[3] Since HBCU degree recipients are fundamentally a part of the professional pipeline from college to the work force, it's important to examine knowledge around the research mentoring efforts of HBCU graduate programs.[4]

Beyond tallying degrees awarded, literature has failed to evaluate the research experiences of HBCU professional doctorate recipients. But with HBCUs awarding more Black doctoral degrees than any other institution in 2006, these doctoral-granting institutions have the potential to use research to become the "decoder of disparities."[5]

Rationale

Historically Black Colleges and Universities (HBCUs) make up approximately 3% of colleges in the Unites States yet manage to award 9% of doctoral degrees earned by African Americans.[6] Statistics are impressive, despite the comparatively weak support given to research personnel at such institutions compared to predominantly White universities (PWIs).[7] In fact, the lack of support is credited for the underrepresentation of minorities in various educational populations, including faculty and tenured positions in higher education and institutional and individual research funding recipients.[8]

Research further suggests that HBCUs are notorious for their ability to retain Black students and increase their sense of self-worth more than predominantly White colleges.[9] This suggests that HBCUs have a superb capacity for student development through "nurturing," mentoring, interpersonal relationships, and emotional support.[10] But, concerns surrounding adequate mentoring, or lack thereof, have been credited with a decreased ability in placing people of color in supervisory or training positions.[11]

In addition to benefitting the professional doctorates, a university's culture can be influenced by the production of research.[12] Research modeling by experts who value ethical execution of systematic inquiry should be nurtured, and additional development should be considered a priority to ensure that reputation remains positive. Mentoring experiences and socialization practices should do more than trickle down: there should be broad strokes of moral behavior that start with the mentors (faculty, staff, and administration) and sweep across all other impressionable mentees. Whether formal or informal, it is important for socialization to take place in order to satisfy the social pressure element of social cognition. The Ferguson, Masur, Olson, Ramirez, Robyn, and Schamling study stresses that mentoring behaviors should be investigated since behaviors influence the research climate of a university.[13] Furthermore, the means by which the research is completed is just as important as the outcome itself.[14] Training is discussed in the content of socializing trainees toward morality in addition to generally understanding the significance of research. Naturally, this creates a favorable reputation for both the university and the doctoral student.

Not only can training and mentoring improve diverse scholars' research abilities, non-mainstream topics affecting specific cultural communities are more likely to be addressed.[15] Deficiencies exist in the literature because few studies take into account the specialized mission at HBCUs (to educate

Blacks in particular, but not exclusively). The strength of nurturing for which HBCUs are commonly lauded has not been directly addressed in conjunction with research training. Particular consideration should be given to the implication that non-Whites rely on vicarious experiences and social pressures to build academic efficacy.[16] Minority-serving institutions with professional doctorate programs, graduate students seeking professional doctorates, and higher education officials dedicated to diversity would benefit from this study.

The emotions toward ability and actions of developing those skills are impacted by one's perception of self-efficacy.[17] Considering that social pressure and vicarious experiences (mentoring) contribute to attitudes and behaviors, it can be predicted that mentoring should be examined. According to Gelso's research training environment theory subscales, training opportunities may include research modeling by faculty, providing graduate researchers occasions to conduct research without subjection to severe risks, and teaching various aspects of research and scientific method (including encouraging students to develop their own research ideas based on students' interest).[18] By examining the students' perceptions of experiences as a mentee based on RTE theory and Allen's list of the purpose of HBCUs, students are able to discuss the influences of their environment and provide explication of faculty-student relationships. Mentoring relationships can include faculty-student relationships, advisors, and other members of the department that students consider to be academic coaches.[19]

Although professional disparities persist among Blacks in America, the HBCU is well documented for its unwavering ability to line the ranks of Black professionals with its undergraduate alumni as well as the development of a Black middle class population in America.[20] The inclusion of conversation aimed at research production by professional doctorate recipients attending Historically Black Colleges and Universities is simply another opportunity to create discourse with both academic and culturally specific focus. From there, the academic narrative can enter empirical space and introduce more opportunities to move beyond identifying disparities and into providing solutions, particularly considering how broad and vast discourse disparities in the Black community can be.

The benefits of mentoring to improve research interests and behaviors are not solely awarded to the student and the institution. The students do gain the social cognition aspects of vicarious experiences and social pressure, but faculty members can benefit from these experiences as well. Studies show faculty who encouraged research with mentees actually refined research ideas that went on to flourish into obtainable systematic studies.[21]

Framework and Methodology

A call for a qualitative approach to the perceptions of students' academic mentoring has emerged.[22] Exploring the perceptions of doctoral students' research training by evaluating faculty-student mentoring experiences within respective departments can provide insight to students' perceptions of their mentoring relationships, training environment, and the assumed effects on their abilities. These feelings toward the task impact execution, dedication, and interest in tasks.[23] It is therefore relevant to uncover HBCU students' perception of how faculty-student mentoring impacts their research training. This serves to begin conversations, assisting in an even stronger pipeline of underrepresented groups in professional and research doctoral programs. It also serves to uncover where or not a practitioner's identity finds its way into research or what degree identity plays in distributing research ideas.

According to Walter Allen, HBCUs are such institutions, however, charged with six specific responsibilities:[24]

1. Maintaining the legacy and cultural tradition of HBCUs;
2. Ensuring there is relevant leadership for the cultural needs of the African American community;
3. Making sure the Black community functions economically;
4. Providing role models of African descent;
5. Ensuring those who graduate from such institutions are capable of addressing the needs of the Black community;
6. Creating Black agents capable of researching, teaching, and distributing findings that address all minority populations.

Brown and Davis continue highlighting HBCUs as agents of social capital. Since social capital includes formal and informal relationships and linkages, and HBCUs are responsible for the production of scholars capable of identifying needs as well as disseminating solutions, it is fitting for mentoring experiences to be collected to discover themes that may be specific to special missions at HBCUs.[25]

The role of efficacy and identity among underrepresented students is important to production. Another study depicts the necessity of research experiences and self-efficacy.[26] There are further claims that research efficacy has a relationship to the development of scientific careers. This provided a foundation to search for particular variables in the interviews: (a) the self-efficacy of the practitioner interviewed, (b) her/his perception of their department's mentoring, and (c) the interviewees' perception of her/his ultimate identity as a practitioner as a result of mentoring experiences. This study finds further evidence that points to self-efficacy as an enhancer of academic development with a dependency on the identity of the student body being taken into account.[27] With this existence of an empirically justified link between identity and self-efficacy development, the exploration is further rationalized.

While substantial literature exists to examine mentoring experiences,[28] as well as quantitative studies on research attitudes, there stand few qualitative accounts of the perceived expectations of mentorship in relation to research training and self-efficacy from a professional doctoral students' experience.[29]

The strength of this framework will lie in the merging of the theories surrounding the benefits of self-efficacy, the importance of identifying and improving environments that create self-efficacy, and how all of this relates to the responsibility of HBCUs, particularly reason number six listed above by Walter Allen: creating research, teaching, and sharing of information to the Black community.

Thus this exploration not only uses research training environment ideas for the formulations of questions, but also aims to uncover what level of responsibility the professional doctorate recipient feels to place a cultural lens on her/his practice and sharing whatever findings may benefits the Black community. This practice can lead to research specific enough to alleviate disparities that may often be found in predominately Black communities.[30]

While professional degrees do not require a peer review, the responsibility of HBCUs, as outlined by Walter Allen, does not exclude professional degree recipients from participating in the duty of HBCUs. The responsibility of the institutions for "creating Black agents capable of researching, teaching, and distributing findings that address all minority populations" is as relevant to professional degree recipients as it is to HBCU graduates who are required to create knowledge by writing a dissertation. In order to do so, the University should create environments in which students understand and accept the challenge of research implementation during and after matriculation.

This responsibility is perpendicular to the global notion that faculty should create an environment which favorably promotes these capabilities by "instructing research execution in a practice setting, reinforcing research activity, and stressing the relationship between research and industry."

The importance of students' self-efficacy in research, their perceptions of a research training environment, and the responsibility of HBCUs to create research agents have led to the formulation of the following interview questions.

1. How have your mentoring relationships prepared you for using research?
2. Do you feel compelled or responsible for conducting or continuing research after graduation?
3. Do you feel prepared to engage in conferences, publications, and presentations if you desired?
4. Please describe any relationship with a mentor or advisor.
5. Were research behaviors appropriately modeled by your department's faculty?
6. Are there any other comments or experiences you would like to share?

One-on-one interviews were conducted via telephone or face-to-face at a location of the participant's choosing. Pseudonyms were used by each participant and created by the researchers to protect the identity of the participants. Snowball sampling was also used, as the researchers encouraged participants to recommend classmates who may be interested in participating in the survey.

All participants were solicited by the researchers based on the criteria that they attended an HBCU for a professional doctorate degree. Three participants earned a juris doctorate. One participant earned a doctorate in physical therapy. The final participant is completing a doctorate in dental surgery.

Participant Responses

Participants came from two Historically Black Universities: one private medically focused university and the other a public university.

When asked about research training, Thomas responded,

> It's not emphasized. Because we're a professional school it's not needed. But they do expect you to know. They give us assignments and topics . . . dealing with scholarly articles. Every class has a research component.

Lisa, with a juris doctorate degree, echoed the sentiment that research occurs in class and in mentoring situations but is not applicable in her day-to-day activities. "Your mentors often help you to hone in on what are the particular issues that you're having so that you can address that."

She describes research as "going down the rabbit hole." And while she feels prepared for conferences and presentations that include research, she applies it to best practice but does not intend to add to the body of knowledge through research. But she values research and the sharing of ideas. She purports about her experiences presenting at conferences:

> And when I think about how I present to different audiences, if I'm at a conference doing something on child support or father's rights I also to tend to follow her method of teaching but with an open dialogue. I like for people to interrupt me and ask me particular questions that might be more particular so that they can understand what it is that they need to understand. Because in law school we were all taught that your interpretation of the law might not be what the person sitting next to you's interpretation of the law is. But you'll need to constantly question what's going on. I think that's why I like a lot of dialogue.

While she's not particularly committed to engaging in research, she feels strongly about her mentoring experience:

> [My mentor] was the person who taught me how to be a lawyer fresh out of law school. Because at that time that was like right when the recession hit. And so there weren't jobs for any lawyers coming out.

So you had to start your own practice on your own. And law school doesn't necessarily teach you how to do solo practice. She was my safe space that I could go to. . . . She did the same kind of law that I did or that I wanted to do. So she was able to give me the templates, the advice from more seasoned council. She really at the end of the day was the person that taught me how to be a working lawyer. Her capacity, she was a clinic professor. Part of her job was to be a mentor to students who were in her clinic. And she ran the domestic violence clinic. Part of her job entails her to do that. When I look at other clinical professors in that same clinic, they would have a teacher student relationship. But she would treat like one professional to another soon-to-be professional. She recognized that we weren't babies. She treated us like "you're all through the door. So I'm going to give you more respect that maybe other teachers may have given."

When discussing professors as mentors, juris doctorate Thomas gave a definition but indicated that there was no formal or informal individual that encouraged research behavior. He called mentoring guidance. "They [professors] can guide you to a certain path . . . what you could do, the possibilities, based on what they know," he stated. But, in terms of finding an individual to provide that, he stated:

It's not mandatory or provided. Mentors are someone in the field outside the school. It doesn't affect how well you were before or where you wind up after . . . there's no one I apply to as a mentor.

However, there are models of research behaviors in his department. "All professors are practitioners who are trained to educate . . . professors publish and have contributions in books and articles."

Additional questions that arose during the interview concerned the interest level that being at an HBCU had given the participants. Thomas responded,

Possibly. I want to practice, more so. But I do want to keep in touch with what's going on because things are always changing . . . certain procedures and some techniques are improved on or discredited.

The encouragement to consume research was a sentiment that repeated itself throughout interviews. Kyle stated, "Because the law is so fluid that stuff is ever changing. So you always have to be mindful of updates." Though the participants engaged in different fields of study, the idea that research keeps them current on best practices was repeated. But in terms of his interest in conducting research outside of practice, Kyle stated:

If it's something criminal or something civil attorneys use that's research in practice. But if it uses research to help serve the purpose of the case

> I'm in the area of law where I very seldom have to do legal research. I do real estate transactions so it's transactional. So I never actually [call on] legal research.... I have had to do legal research for that [a specific case] and that was refreshing to try to remember all of that.

And when prompted to discuss his research interests, Kyle purported, "But I haven't done it to this point. I honestly haven't been interested in it. I'm fine staying in my lane." While research is introduced, practitioners lack interest in using those skills beyond identifying best practice in their discipline.

The creation of knowledge and the distribution of new ideas are not examined, according to participants. Research training is mentioned and opportunities are presented, but focus remains on industry and practice. In terms of mentoring, respondents did not identify a specific advisor. When discussing who mentored him most concerning research, Kyle replied:

> In law, it's actually funny because the law librarians are actually, like, gods. Because they know so much about the law and how to find different and various research. So they were probably the biggest tools we had.

As far as other research opportunities in his law program, he continues:

> ... [the law department] had an advanced legal research course, which I actually did take as well. And that one was for people who were really serious about legal research. It took what we kinda touched on [in the introductory legal research class] and took that to a whole other level. And this professor was more geared and focused towards legal research so he had a way larger knowledge base. It was beneficial. There are tools to use to verify that that research is the most current research.

To summarize his answer on having a specific mentor for researching, he discussed the department's proclivity to provide research guidance for the purpose of practical application. "Because the law is so fluid the answer to your question will be different for almost any lawyer."

Kyle often returned to the idea that research was something he consumed for his practice and not something that he executed to add to a body of knowledge. His mentoring experiences reflect that. He stated:

> There are attorneys that attend conferences and do education courses. There wasn't a go-to person that I would go to for that kind of stuff. Whoever was available at that time would try to help. With us [law students] they're just like, "we are going to train for the law. We're going to get you ready to take the bar and pass the bar." People who were teaching assistants for professors ... would brush up on those skills.

Thomas had additional exposure to research opportunities and spoke specifically about attending and presenting at a conference, where best practice and new ideas are prevalent.

> The few [conferences] I've attended . . . I think professors and practitioners at conferences know the importance of research. . . . I feel like it could be beneficial to have a mentor who was saying that you could do both. I know what opened my eyes is knowing that there is clinical research and that you could do both.

Other research opportunities were available to Thomas that gave him additional perspective on research's potential role in his career as a practitioner.

> I've done clinical research because I've had the backing of the school or a grant backing me. Having to take that track on my own would be a challenge. In order to be successful at it [research] you'd have to work in a school environment.

According to Gelso's RTE theory, modeling appropriate research behavior can improve research self-efficacy. Respondents confirm that research modeling exists, but as students, they were never drawn in to low-risk opportunities for research, which is also relevant to research training.

Ultimately, participants were asked to summarize research mentoring at HBCUs and how the cultural lenses affected their educational experience. Thomas stated:

> As a minority student we do get reminded that we are going into a field where we are overwhelming the minority. So while you'd feel it at a majority school, you have a backing to remind you [at HBCUs]. So while currently I'm in a program where most people look like me, that won't be the case when I got out to the "real world." Professors and other colleagues do remind you that things are going to be different . . . so it's important to be a good practitioner because things are against you. Stuff like that. And it's a good contrast when you do go to conferences and you do see the true population of certain professors.

He continued and discussed his potential aspiration to be a future mentor to doctoral students and how it influenced him as a practitioner, saying that his HBCU experience

> has shaped it a lot . . . I can say this as far as who I would service: maybe more of a community service, focusing on serving a community. I do think the message is important because there is always a shortage of professionals especially professionals of color. And I think these schools do a good job of making sure there are still some being produced.

Kyle made similar comments about his HBCU experience and why he focuses on practicing more than research at this point in his career.

> Coming from an HBCU, I always want to show them the quality of education we received and that we're just as competent as our colleagues at other, bigger named schools. But as far as research and stuff prolly [sic] not [compelled to culturally research]. We kind of feel like we're underdogs to begin with based on that.

He explains how he uses research by stating:

> With my area of law, a lot of it is driven by set statutes. Most real estate laws go back to England and the British common law and the granter/grantee system. I've been in the register of deeds office. You could go back as far as seeing in some cases where the queen granted the land and you saw how we adopted that from English as a way of doing things.

Staying true to his claim that he was properly trained in research and has chosen not to make his skills part of his personal practice, Kyle says, "the knowledge base and the times that I had had to do research, the skill set that I was given was definitely adequate." However, there were no apparent plans or desires to create culturally specific research that could be distributed for the purpose of addressing specific cultural issues.

Discussion

Focused discussion of mentors' influence in creating an environment for research training at HBCUs was confined to mostly informal relationships or in the development of research training outside of the department. Role modeling, coaching, counseling, and advising are the ways in which mentoring relationships can be manifested.[31] And while appropriate behavior was modeled in the departments, the participants seemed disconnected from opportunities to present research or create new knowledge for distribution. These relationships may also satisfy the vicarious and social aspects of self-efficacy building and subsequently influence interest in research, research productivity, and research attitudes and behaviors.[32] To capture professional doctorates' experiences in settings with specialized cultural missions creates discourse that is currently missing and begins dialogue on how leaders can aim to affect the neophyte researchers to carry the specialized mission through their careers as practitioners.

Ultimately these experiences are demonstrative of creating spaces that stress existing opportunities that HBCU graduates have in pursuing research ideas within a variety of profession industries. Research training is not a primary focus in these degree programs; participants agree that they employ research when necessary, and all participants feel adequately trained to engage in research if necessary and give verbal confirmation that their research self-efficacy is sufficient. Most participants recognize the value in research, but demonstrate no desire to engage. Furthermore, the participants varied on having mentors who exhibited positive research behaviors.

Implications for Future Research, Policy, and Practice

The participants in this study admitted to using research to aid their professional development. Participants were confident in their ability to find research that was critical to implementing best practice when it comes to the day-to-day challenges of work. And while participants engaged in research and used it to develop best practices, they weren't convinced that publishing research based on their findings was a part of their responsibilities as HBCU graduates. Regional and nationwide studies should be conducted that examine HBCU professional doctorates' perceptions concerning the importance of publishing and presenting.

In terms of implications for practice, faculty who are engaging with students pursuing professional doctorates should consider labeling the use of stored information in problem solving as research in a direct and strategic way. Policy could be created to showcase curriculum modified to draw similarities between the teaching and the use of research among students in PhD programs and students in professional doctorate programs. By identifying the departmental atmosphere as one that is teaching research, graduates' self-efficacy could improve, which could lead to increased desire to publish and present.

Conclusion

Research self-efficacy can be found in the interviews, and some respondents felt confident that they would eventually engage in research activities. However, respondents considered research in the context of seeking information and applying it to their practice. Respondents showed little interest in creating and adding to the body of knowledge in their field (as previously discussed in Allen's six responsibilities of Historically Black Colleges and Universities list). And while there were some training opportunities in the programs, ultimately being a practitioner took precedence over finding the relationship between research and practice. This is an integral part of research surrounding research training environments. Finding such a connection is important to research self-efficacy and performance. Tenets of the theory that were found included the habit of instructing students on a variety of approaches to research. Respondents showed that classroom activity did provide opportunities for such instruction. However, the RTE idea of stressing the relationship between research and industry was not easily found. Participants were trained to be practitioners and to utilize research to stay current and increase the abilities to execute best practices in the field.

Participants felt confident in their abilities but did not see much of their work as research, could not identify a particular research mentor, knew of research opportunities, but did not find them relevant to their pursuit of professional degrees, and were not compelled to distribute research findings even though they identified opportunities to place a cultural lens in their personal practice.

Compared to a study using similar constructs, professional doctoral recipients perceive themselves to be capable of research more often than research doctoral recipients. Not surprisingly, the instruction that was provided in the professional doctoral programs granted the majority of participants with adequate self-efficacy when it came to research.

Notes

1. Quarterman 2008
2. Cohen, Friedman, and Zier 2008
3. Noonan, Lindong, and Jaitley 2013
4. Nealy 2009
5. Noonan, Lindong, and Jaitley 2013; Palmer, Davis, and Thompson 2010; Nealy 2009, p. 18
6. Brown and Davis, 2001; Palmer, Davis, and Thompson 2010
7. Stuart 2012
8. Davidson and Foster-Johnson 2001; Evans and Cokley 2008; Sibulkin and Butler 2011; Stahl 2005; Treadwell et al. 2009
9. Treadwell et al. 2009
10. Fountaine 2012; Palmer, Davis, and Thompson 2010; Treadwell et al. 2009
11. Dutta, Kundu, and Chan 2010
12. Rip 2011
13. Ferguson et al. 2007
14. Ferguson et al. 2007
15. Love et al. 2007; Dutta, Kundu, and Chan 2010; Stuart 2012
16. Usher 2009
17. Bandura 1989
18. Gelso's 1996
19. Melanson 2009
20. Stahl 2005; Brown and Yates 2005
21. van Dinther, Dochy, and Segers, 2011.
22. Lev, Kolassa, and Bakken 2010.
23. Bandura 1997
24. Brown and Davis, 2001
25. Brown and Davis 2001
26. Chemers et al. 2011
27. Chemers et al. 2011
28. Eby et al. 2010; Ortiz-Walters and Gilson 2005; Wang et al. 2009
29. Baltes et al. 2010; Chemers et al. 2011; Lev, Kolassa, and Bakken, 2010; Love et al. 2007

30 Brown and Davis, 2001; Nealy 2009
31 Melanson 2009
32 Knight 2012

References

Baltes, Beatte, Peter Hoffman-Kipp, Laura Lynn, and Lisa Weltzer-Ward. "Students' research self-efficacy during online doctoral research courses." *Contemporary Issues in Education Research*, 3 no. 3 (2010): 51–57.
Bandura, Albert. "Regulation of cognitive processes through perceived self-efficacy." *Developmental Psychology*, 25 no. 5 (1989): 729–735.
Bandura, Albert. *Self-efficacy: The exercise of control*. New York: Freeman, 1997.
Brown, M. Christopher., and Trimika Yates. "Toward an empirical corpus of literature on historically black colleges and universities." *American Journal of Education*, 112 no. 1 (2005): 129–134.
Brown, M. Christopher, and James E. Davis. "The historically black college as social contract, social capital, and social equalizer." *Peabody Journal of Education*, 76 no. 1 (2001): 31–49. doi:10.2307/1493004
Chemers, Martin M., Eilieen Zurbriggen, Moin Syed, Barbara Goza, and Steve Bearman. "The role of efficacy and identity in science career commitment among underrepresented minority students." *Journal of Social Issues*, 67 no. 3 (2011): 469–491. doi:10.1111/j.1540-4560.2011.01710.x
Cohen, Benjamin, Erica Friedman., and Karen Zier. "Publications by students doing a year of full-time research: What are realistic expectations?" *The American Journal of Medicine*, 121 no. 6 (2008): 545–548.
Davidson, Martin N., and Lynn Foster-Johnson. "Mentoring in the preparation of graduate researchers of color." *Review of Educational Research*, 71 no. 4 (2001): 549–574. doi:10.2307/3516098
Dutta, Alo, Madan Kundu, and Fong Chan. "The conduct of socially valid investigation by culturally diverse researchers: A Delphi study." *Rehabilitation Education*, 24 no. 3–4 (2010): 113–122.
Eby, Lillian T., Marcus M. Butts, Jaime Durley, and Belle Rose Ragins. "Are bad experiences stronger than good ones in mentoring relationships? Evidence from the protégé and mentor perspective." *Journal of Vocational Behavior*, 77 no. 1 (2010): 81–92.
Evans, Gina L., and Kevin Cokley. "African American women and the academy: Using career mentoring to increase research Productivity." *Training and Education in Psychology*, 2 no. 1 (2008): 50–57.
Ferguson, Kryste, Sandra Masur, Lynne Olson, Julio Ramirez, Elisa Robyn, and Karen Schmaling. "Enhancing the culture of research ethics on university campuses." *Journal of Academic Ethics*, 5 no. 2–4 (2007): 189–198. doi:10.1007/s10805-007-9033-9
Fountaine, Tiffany Patrice. "The impact of faculty-student interaction on black doctoral students attending historically black institutions." *The Journal of Negro Education*, 81 no. 2 (2012): 136–147.
Gelso, Charles J. "On the making of a scientist-practitioner: A theory of research training in professional psychology." *Training and Education in Professional Psychology*, S no. 1 (2006): 3–16. doi:10.1037/1931-3918.s.1.3

Gelso, Charles J. "Research training environment, attitudes toward research, and research self-efficacy: The revised research training environment scale." *Counseling Psychologist*, 24 no. 2 (1996): 304–322.

Knight, Donald Edward. "Examining the role of research mentoring in predicting research self-efficacy among minority professional psychology doctoral students." PhD diss., Ann Arbor: Western Michigan University, 2012.

Lev, Elise L., John Kolassa, and Lori L. Bakken. "Faculty mentors' and students' perceptions of students' research self-efficacy." *Nurse Education Today*, 30 no. 2 (2010): 169–174.

Love, Keisha M., Angela D. Bahner, Leslie N. Jones, and Johanna E. Nilsson, J. E. "An investigation of early research experience and research self-efficacy." *Professional Psychology: Research and Practice*, 38 no. 3 (2007): 314–320. doi:10.1037/0735-7028.38.3.314

Melanson, Mark A. "The mentoring spectrum." *U.S. Army Medical Department Journal*, (2009): 37–39.

Nealy, Michelle J. "Pride and peril: Historically black colleges and universities." *Diverse Issues in Higher Education*, 26 no. 14 (2009): 18–19.

Noonan, Alan, Ian Lindong, and Vijai N. Jaitley. "The role of historically black colleges and universities in training the health care workforce." *American Journal of Public Health*, 103 no. 3 (2013): 412–415.

Ortiz-Walters, Rowena, and Lucy Gilson. "Mentoring in academia: An examination of the experiences of protégés of color." *Journal of Vocational Behavior*, 67 no. 3 (2005): 459–475.

Palmer, Robert T., Ryan J. Davis, and Tiffany Thompson. "Theory meets practice: HBCU initiatives that promote academic success among African Americans in STEM." *Journal of College Student Development*, 51 no. 4 (2010): 440–443.

Quarterman, Jerome. "An assessment of barriers and strategies for recruitment and retention of a diverse graduate student population." *College Student Journal*, 42 no. 4 (2008): 443–453. doi: 10.1080/08109028.2011.639566

Rip, Arie. "The future of research universities." *Prometheus*, 29 no. 4 (2011): 443–453. doi:10.1080/08109028.2011.639566

Sibulkin, Amy E., and J. S. Butler, J. S. "Diverse colleges of origin of African American doctoral recipients, 2001–2005: Historically black colleges and universities and beyond." *Research in Higher Education*, 52 no. 8 (2011): 830–852.

Stahl, Jeanne M. "Research is for everyone: Perspectives from teaching at historically black colleges and universities." *Journal of Social and Clinical Psychology*, 24 no. 1 (2005): 85–96.

Stuart, Reginald. "Playing fair? Minority research institutions call for NIH to address funding disparities." *Diverse Issues in Higher Education*, 29 no. 19 (2012): 18–23.

Treadwell, Henrie M., Ronald L. Braithwaite, Kisha Braithwaite, Desiree Oliver, D., and Rhonda Holliday. "Leadership development for health researchers at historically black colleges and universities." *American Journal of Public Health*, 99 no. S (2009): 53–57.

Usher, Ellen L. "Sources of middle school students' self-efficacy in mathematics: A qualitative investigation." *American Educational Research Journal*, 46 no. 1 (2009): 275–314. doi:10.2307/27667179

van Dinther, Mart, Flip Dochy, and Mien Segers. "Factors affecting students' self-efficacy in higher education." *Educational Research Review*, 6 no. 2 (2011): 95–108.

Wang, Sheng, Raymond A. Noeb, Zhong-Ming Wang, and David B. Greenberger. "What affects willingness to mentor in the future? An investigation of attachment styles and mentoring experiences." *Journal of Vocational Behavior*, 74 no. 3 (2009): 245–256.

Yin, Robert K. *Applications of case study research*. Thousand Oaks, CA: Sage, 2003.

Young, K. J. "Research mentoring: Suggestions and encouragement from a reflection exercise." *Journal of Chiropractic Education*, 28 no. 2 (2014): 168–172. doi:10.7899/JCE-14-7

7 Social Work Education and Cultural Competence
The Role of Historically Black Colleges and Universities

Jennifer M. Johnson and Zuleka Henderson

Introduction

Social work professionals struggle with meeting the mental, behavioral, and emotional needs of individuals from ethnically and linguistically diverse populations.[1] Current and projected demographic shifts in the United States call for an already diverse nation to prepare social workers who can work effectively in increasingly diverse and multicultural settings.[2] The US Bureau of Labor Statistics (BLS) reports that social work is one of the fastest growing careers in the United States, with a projected growth of 19% between 2012 and 2022. Given these trends, it is increasingly important that this expansion of social workers includes individuals trained in culturally responsive ways. Cultural competence refers to "the integration and transformation of knowledge about individuals and groups of people into specific standards, policies, practices, and attitudes used in appropriate cultural settings to increase the quality of services, thereby producing better outcomes."[3] This concept emerged as an approach to ensuring that those in helping professions, such as social work professionals, can effectively meet the needs of all members of the community. A historical review of social work education reveals that the concept of "cultural competence" was embedded within the curriculum of social work programs at Historically Black Colleges and Universities (HBCUs) well before the profession embraced this philosophy, yet few are aware of the role HBCUs have played in training culturally competent social work professionals. In this chapter, we provide an overview of the history and development of social work programs designed for Black students attending HBCUs and show how these programs can serve as effective educational models for graduate level social work programs at Traditionally White Institutions (TWIs).

Social Work Education Through the 20th century

Professional social workers "help individuals, families, and groups restore or enhance their capacity for social functioning, and work to create societal conditions that support communities in need."[4] While social work was designed to systematically address human need, historically, the profession did not readily acknowledge the experiences and struggles of African Americans as a priority.[5] The National Conference on Social Welfare began in 1874 as a forum for discussing social welfare efforts in the United States and Canada. It would take three years before there was any mention of the challenges faced by Black Americans at the conference, and ten years before exclusive attention was paid to the Black experience in conference proceedings papers. According to Platt and Chandler, ". . . leading intellectuals enthusiastically constructed elaborate theories of racial differentiation to legitimize social inequality and to justify new policies of racial discrimination."[6] For Lide, the failure to recognize the plight of Black Americans and "the tacit acceptance of racial inferiority in many of the early papers suggests that racism was already being woven into the fabric of the emerging profession of social work."[7]

Despite this lack of national attention, African American social work leaders were early voices in the field advocating for a more deliberate focus on the needs of Black Americans across the nation. During the early 20th century, there were a multitude of social and economic problems that impacted the Black community. For example, migrant Blacks were subject to a myriad of undesirable social conditions and problems, including ". . . prejudice and discrimination; lynching; violence and race riots; the concentration of vice in Black areas; slum housing; inferior education; lack of police protection; inadequate sanitation; unequal employment opportunities; inadequate health care; lack of wholesome recreation; crime and delinquency; and poor protective services for women and children."[8] These problems were only exacerbated by the Great Depression (1929–1939), which had a tremendous impact on employment opportunities for African Americans.[9]

To address these and other issues, social work pioneers argued for the specialized training of Black Americans who were competent in "Black social problems."[10] Acclaimed sociologist Dr. E. Franklin Frazier remarked at the National Conference on Charities and Corrections that "the condition among Negroes in cities can best be improved by those of their own group whose latent capacity has had superior training directed toward social service."[11] Moreover, Dr. Frazier believed "social workers would never fully grasp the situation of Black migrants until these social workers had some basic understanding of Black culture."[12] This philosophy, shared by several other Black scholars of his day, was embedded in the development of social work programs at HBCUs.

HBCUs and the Education of Black Social Workers

Racist and discriminatory practices in education during the early 20th century contributed to the lack of trained social workers of color available to serve Black communities.[13] Black students interested in social work initially had to travel to northern schools and institutes for formal training and rarely returned to work in the south.[14] Within these northern institutions, the prevailing paradigm focused on a mono-cultural and generalist approach to social work education.[15] To stem this "brain drain" and ensure the needs of Black Americans were being met, a number of programs were created between 1910 and the early 1940s that were available to Black students. This included programs at Fisk University, the Atlanta School of Social Work, the Bishop Tuttle Memorial School of Social Work at St. Augustine College, and the Howard University School of Social Work, as well as specialized training programs offered by community partners such as the National League on Urban Conditions Among Negroes (National Urban League).[16] An examination of the history and development of these programs shows a distinct emphasis on meeting the needs of the population through following a philosophy guided by the principles that shape the emergent standards around "cultural competence."

One well-documented example was that of the leadership and vision of Dr. Inabel Burns Lindsay (1900–1983). Dr. Lindsay served as the founding dean of the Howard University School of Social Work, and is recognized as one of the first African American women to serve in an academic leadership position during the 1940s, 1950s, and 1960s.[17] She has been described as a child of the post-Reconstruction era, who grew up within a racially conscious household with early exposure to prominent Black figures such as Booker T. Washington and W. E. B. Dubois. As a student, it was documented that she was a founder of the Women's Suffrage League, Howard University Chapter, and during her studies at the New York School of Social Work (New York University) she advocated for the inclusion of a cultural perspective in the practice of social work.[18] While most of her graduate courses were based in Freudian psychology, she used this perspective to begin to understand how self-awareness of race is reflected in the accurate assessment of clients. Historians have documented her deliberate efforts to incorporate an understanding of race, class, and gender in the social work profession. According to documents of her work, "her vision for the School included a curriculum that reflected understanding of the impact of racial, social, and cultural factors on human beings and their importance in shaping human behavior and developed the needs of all people, but especially Black people."[19] Thus, from the very beginning, the development of the program curriculum was grounded in cultural consciousness and challenged the profession to understand the impact of racial oppression and other systemic forces on African Americans in the United States.[20] At Howard University, Dr. Lindsay's ecological approach differed somewhat from those social work educators and practitioners at TWIs who addressed culture but did not link their understanding of culture directly with socioeconomic power differentials, class, or institutional racism.

Forrester Blanchard Washington (1887–1963), at the Atlanta School of Social Work (now the Whitney Young Jr. School of Social Work at Clark Atlanta University), created a social work program committed to cultural competence through an emphasis on community organization, group work, casework, fieldwork, and research.[21] Washington's policy work and advocacy on behalf of Black Americans reflected his deep ties to the Black community, not just in theory, but through his daily practice. Washington, educated at Tufts College (now Tufts University), Harvard University, and Columbia University before receiving training at the New York School of Social Work, held several positions with the Urban League in Detroit and on the national level prior to becoming the director at the Atlanta School of Social Work where he served for 25 years. Historians of his life note his activism on issues such as employment and safe housing opportunities for members of the African American community as ways to help stem some of the social problems of the era. He also advocated for social workers to be involved in the design and expansion of social welfare systems that emerged during the Franklin D. Roosevelt administration.[22] For Washington, "the existence of the Negro group in a predominantly unsympathetic, hostile world is sufficient justification for specialized training for social work among Negroes."[23] Adopting a philosophy similar to one that informed Jewish social work education programs, the specialized training program offered at the Atlanta School of Social Work and the devices for social work among African Americans were apart from, and in additions to, the fundamental techniques commonly used for social work among all groups. Washington developed and implemented a curriculum "that contained courses to equip African American social workers with the specialized knowledge he believed to be essential to effect intervention with African Americans."[24]

Dr. George Edmund Haynes (1880–1960) established the first professional social work training program at Fisk University in 1910 as a "department of Social Science and Social Work."[25] Dr. Haynes is also recognized as a co-founder of the National Urban League (formerly National League on Urban Conditions Among Negroes), the nation's oldest community-based organization, initially focused on counseling Black migrants from the south, training Black social workers, and researching the problems faced by Blacks in America.[26] The Arkansas native was keenly aware of the challenges faced by Black Americans in the rural south. His writings reflect an understanding that race is not the only factor that mattered in the profession, as he was concerned with how Black social workers from the south would be prepared to work within Black communities in the north. The "Black Migrants" traveling north for "freedom and opportunity" experienced a great deal of racial discrimination that dampened opportunity for Black Americans. With this context in mind, when building his program he believed that Black social workers must have both a knowledge base as well as lived experience reflecting those situated within the community. Not only would students take courses in history, economics, and sociology, and the methods of social work, their senior year lectures were devoted to "special problems relating to Negroes."[27] As part of the program, students would work closely within the Nashville community, and then select students would travel to New

York and other large cities to continue supervised training within Black urban environments for extended periods of time. He called for all "Negro Schools" to follow their example if they truly wanted to support the betterment of the condition of Black Americans.

Culturally and Socially Responsive Curricula at HBCUs

As of 2015, there are 65 HBCUs that offer social work programs on the baccalaureate, master's, and doctoral levels. The most common degree offered is the bachelor's degree, offered by 58 HBCUs, followed by 26 HBCUs that offer master's degrees. Currently six HBCUs offer doctoral degrees: Clark Atlanta University, Howard University, Jackson State University, Morgan State University, Norfolk State University, and Southern University and A&M College. An examination of mission statements and graduate-level social work curricula across graduate-level social work programs at HBCUs reflects a deeply embedded focus on culturally and socially responsive curricula. Common curricula themes include: generalist training (formal curriculum in social work), Black-experience-specific oriented courses, field training, and interdisciplinary knowledge. Many of these schools addressed the basic or generalist student training through the provision of courses including: casework, child welfare, psychology, research, and community focused courses,[28] but their development of social work professionals for work in Black communities is mostly reflected in the Black-experience-based, field training, and interdisciplinary approaches to instruction.

Formal Curriculum in Social Work

The Council on Social Work Education (CSWE) Office of Social Work Accreditation is responsible for developing the accreditation standards, policies, and procedures for bachelor's and master's programs in social work. While the generalist training curricula in social work is regulated today across programs, it is important to note it was not until 1986 that CSWE mandated that all accredited programs "make special, continued efforts to enrich its program by providing racial, ethnic, and cultural diversity in its study body and at all levels of instruction and research personnel, and by providing corresponding educational supports."[29] This "diversity" mandate came about during a time when the profession was becoming more involved in social justice and civil rights issues. Students and practitioners began to call for more classes and faculty in social work programs (particularly within TWIs) that reflected the needs of the Black community.[30] The format of these training programs appeared to suggest that a generalist curriculum provided basic introduction to social work and sociology, but a Black-experience-based curriculum equipped social work students with the skills to return to Black communities as prepared and effective social work practitioners.

Black-Focused Curriculum

The primary focus of social work education programs at HBCUs historically and today was to create courses that reflected issues prevalent within the Black community. Black oriented courses explored specific issues, including: delinquency and probation; housing, recreational, and industrial problems in Black communities; as well as strategies for community work and conducting research with Black organizations and participants.[31] Additionally, curricula addressed problems with specific sub-populations, including the experiences of Black women and children. As indicated by Frazier, the rationale behind including many of these courses was to acquaint helping professionals with fundamental knowledge of human behavior and the causes of specific challenges impacting Black communities, including poverty and the dissolution of families.[32]

Across the social work programs reviewed, there are several examples of HBCUs' explicit emphasis on "Black social problems" through coursework. For instance, the School of Social Work at Jackson State University, established in 1994, offers a "Black Experience" course to introduce students to "Black-experience-based social work," offering specific strategies and skills for working with African American families. Other courses prepare BSW students for addressing issues such as teen sexuality and parenting in urban communities. These offerings reflect their mission to "produce graduates who will apply their knowledge and skills to improve the Urban quality of life in Mississippi, the nation, and the world."[33]

Field Training

The field training requirement of social work programs is intended to provide future social workers with opportunities to integrate theory and practice, and apply the lessons learned through coursework in real-world settings. Early examples of field training grounded in the Black experience can be found at the Bishop Tuttle Memorial School of Social Work at St. Augustine College. Located in Raleigh, North Carolina, the Tuttle school operated a special inner-city community center within Raleigh where students ran recreational and educational programs for neighborhood residents under the supervision of faculty.[34] Additionally, as a part of the program, "students were also expected to do field work in rural areas, where poverty was extensive and health and welfare services for Black people were almost nonexistent."[35]

The Ethelyn R. Strong School of Social Work at Norfolk State University houses baccalaureate, master's, doctoral, and continuing education programs in social work. The school's mission is: "to provide social work education programs which prepare students with competence to develop and deliver services that strengthen and/or empower individuals, families, groups, organizations, and communities." Norfolk State University has over 100 distinct partnerships in the Hampton-Roads area to facilitate the completion of the field training requirement for students at the BSW, MSW, and PhD levels. On the MSW level, their 24-credit Field Practicum requirement of the program provides opportunities for students to "develop advanced practice skills in clinical or community development social work practice."[36] At Morgan State University, students have the opportunity to choose a specific concentration for their advanced field experience in 1) children, youth, and families; 2) gerontology; 3) school social work; or 4) public health social work, and are assigned a field placement in an "urban social work service setting" accordingly.[37] The stated objectives of the field education requirements at Morgan State University include students' ability to "demonstrate a well-developed understanding of cultural diversity and be able to conduct culturally effective practice interventions at the micro, mezzo, and macro levels." Their field experience requirement is reflective of their mission. Morgan State University's School of Social Work was originally established in 1969 as the "Undergraduate Social Welfare Program." Designated as a department in 1975, the mission is "to fully prepare urban social work leaders who are committed to the alleviation of human suffering, social justice, and the improvement of the quality of life for diverse urban populations."

Interdisciplinary Knowledge

HBCUs also prepare social work students for culturally competent practice through their interdisciplinary approach to the curriculum. At the Bishop Tuttle Memorial School of Social Work, "the inclusion of nursing training was specifically included into the Tuttle School curriculum in order to provide its students with the skills to help poor rural families in meeting basic health care needs."[38] Students at Bishop Tuttle and Fisk University also enrolled in religion, biology, and sociology courses to explore the intersections of these topic areas and to develop knowledge that could be instrumental to helping efforts with their population of interest.

Additionally, HBCUs have historically included economics as part of their social work education curriculum. Several Black social work pioneers like Sarah Collins Fernandis historically addressed Black poverty by incorporating approaches that put tools and frameworks for economic success into the hands of Black people. Today, social work students at Howard University concentrating in Community, Administration, and Policy Practice take a required Resource Development course which "provides students with knowledge and skills in strategic planning for resource development, program planning, grant proposal writing, financial management, entrepreneurship, and community and institutional capacity building and multi-level fundraising ... [with] special attention given to the unique experiences and challenges faced by organizations in African American communities and other communities of color."[39]

Taken together, much can be learned from the culturally and socially responsive curricula offered at HBCUs. Modified strategies can help not only the Black community, but also the increasingly diverse population of the United States. Specific strategies that can be gleaned from HBCUs' approaches to developing a social work workforce of color include: identify the problem, recruit future social workers from various populations, update their curricular content to reflect the current needs of society, and ensure that field experience opportunities are reflective of the different areas where social workers can get involved, including opportunities to forge an interdisciplinary agenda with other professions as well as opportunities to work in policy and other areas.

Lessons Learned from HBCUs

During the early 20th century, African American social work leaders and educators defined a multidimensional problem: Black communities were plagued by a number of social, economic, and structural issues that challenged their wellbeing and opportunities for success; the available social welfare system was not efficiently or effectively addressing Black need; there was an insufficient social work workforce of color with the training and skills that could address these Black social problems; and educated Black social workers trained in northern institutions and were not returning to southern communities to practice where outstanding needs prevailed. This clear enumeration of the problem served as the foundation for the development and implementation of an agenda that could directly provide solutions to the professional and social dilemmas outlined. HBCUs established programs that not only made education and training available to Black students, but also developed a curriculum that would make them specifically knowledgeable and competent in Black issues. HBCUs also situated fieldwork opportunities directly within the urban and rural Black communities they hoped to serve.

This approach produced a number of outcomes, including an increase in the Black and competent social work workforce and community initiatives and partnerships that provided direct relief to Blacks across the nation. HBCUs have continued in this vein through sustaining curricular focus on Black-experience-based social work and offering courses and training that specifically orient students to Black history, culture, and social problems and to the strengths and community-based resources that can facilitate ongoing, mutually beneficial partnerships to better understand and ameliorate the social issues of our time. Empirical evidence suggests that this work has produced HBCU educated social work scholars whose competence in culturally responsive practice is significantly greater than students at traditional White institutions.[40] Thus, developing solutions for addressing the needs of an increasingly diverse America need not reinvent the wheel. The work of Historically Black institutions provides a useful template for how the social work profession can make good on its intentions to "promote human and community well-being . . . through its quest for social and economic justice, the prevention of conditions that limit human rights, the elimination of poverty, and the enhancement of the quality of life for all persons, locally and globally."[41] If the lack of trained social workers of color in communities of color is one of the articulated problems, then focused strategies for recruitment and training of a diverse workforce are a potential and feasible solution.[42] Addressing barriers to achieving this goal would need to include authentic efforts to address issues of cultural mistrust in the profession; debunking myths about what social work actually involves; making education and training affordable to students from diverse backgrounds; and ensuring that there is competitive compensation or other financial incentives to engage in social work on the graduate level.[43]

Furthermore, leaders at HBCUs were clear that the work of addressing Black social welfare issues could not be accomplished by well-intentioned individuals. Tam and Kwok defined gatekeeping in social work as "a professional responsibility to identify those students who are adequately prepared to [practice] and those not adequately prepared to practice."[44] They argue that gatekeeping serves "to protect public safety and the reputation of the profession" by only passing through those individuals who demonstrate preparation for practice.[45] Current and projected demographic shifts call for an already diverse nation to prepare social workers who can work effectively in increasingly diverse and multicultural settings. In addition to core social work knowledge and skills training, culturally specific training was imperative. Therefore, efforts to prepare a social work workforce that can address the needs of increasingly diverse communities must include more than cursory discussion of diversity and difference in social work courses. The development of culturally relevant curriculum should parallel the efforts of HBCUs and educate students from historical and contemporary perspectives on the specific challenges, dynamics, and strengths of individuals representing diverse identities.

Conclusion

Since the early 20th century, African American social work leaders have been instrumental in developing social work professionals who can directly work to address the needs of individuals and communities historically disregarded, marginalized, and oppressed. Few are aware of the role Historically Black Colleges and Universities have played in shaping the profession into what it is today. Born out of a time of tremendous struggle, HBCUs' social work programs historically have been committed to the core perspectives and values highlighted by the current CSWE mission as evidenced by their program curriculum. Today, HBCUs' social work programs remain committed to these core perspectives and values in their mission statements and program curriculum.

Notes

1 Furman et al. 2009
2 Bowie, Hall, and Johnson 2011
3 National Association of Social Workers 2017
4 National Association of Social Workers 2017
5 Lide 1973
6 Platt and Chandler 1988; Gary and Gary 1994
7 Lide 1973
8 Gary and Gary 1994
9 Barrow 2007
10 Frazier 1923
11 Frazier 1923, p. 384
12 Martin and Martin 1995
13 Frazier 1923
14 Frazier 1923
15 Washington 1935
16 Martin and Martin 1995
17 Brown, Gourdine, and Crewe 2011
18 Brown, Gourdine, and Crewe 2011
19 Howard University 2017
20 Brown, Gourdine, and Crewe 2011
21 Aubrey et al. 2016
22 Barrow 2007
23 Washington 1943, p. 89
24 Barrow 2007, p. 183
25 Haynes 1911
26 National Urban League 2017
27 Haynes 1911.
28 Gary and Gary 1994
29 Bowie, Hall, and Johnson 2011
30 Brown, Gourdine, and Crewe 2011
31 Gary and Gary 1994
32 Frazier 1923
33 Jackson State University 2017
34 Gary and Gary 1994
35 Kayser 2004, p. 112
36 Norfolk State University 2017
37 Morgan State University 2017
38 Kayser 2004
39 Howard University 2017
40 Bowie, Hall, Johnson 2011.
41 CSWE 2017
42 Zastrow and Bremner 2004
43 Karger and Stoesz 2003
44 Tam and Kwok 2007, p. 195
45 Tam and Kwok 2007, p. 195

Bibliography

Aubrey, Hal, Tina Jordan, Andre P. Stevenson, Rena Boss-Victoria, James Haynes, Anthony Estreet, Jahmaine Smith, Elijah Cameron, and Quotasze Williams. "Doctoral study programs in social work at HBCUs: Origin and program development." *Journal of Social Work Education*, 52 no. 1 (2016): 58–68.

Barrow, Frederica H. "Forrester Blanchard Washington and his advocacy for African Americans in the new deal." *Social Work*, 52 no. 3 (2007): 201–208.

Bowie, Stan L., J. Camille Hall, and Oliver J. Johnson. "Integrating diversity into graduate social work: A 30-year retrospective view by MSW-level African American social workers." *Journal of Black Studies*, 42 no. 7 (2011): 1080–1105.

Brown, Annie W., Ruby M. Gourdine, and Sandra E. Crewe. "Inabel Burns Lindsay: Social work pioneer contributor to practice and education through a sociocultural perspective." *Journal of Sociology & Social Welfare*, 38 no. 1 (2011): 143–161.

Clark Atlanta University. *School of Social Work*. Retrieved February 10, 2017, from www.cau.edu/school-of-social-work/index.html

Council on Social Work Education. *Council on Social Work Education*. Retrieved January 25, 2017, from www.cswe.org/Home.aspx

Frazier, Edward F. "Training colored social workers in the south." *The Journal of Social Forces*, 1 no. 4 (1923): 445–446.

Furman, Rick, Nalini J. Negi, Derek K. Iwamoto, Diana Rowan, Alison Shukraft, and Jennifer Gragg. "Social work practice with Latinos: Key issues for social workers." *Social Work*, 54 no. 2 (2009): 167–174.

Gary, Robenia B., and Lawrence E. Gary. "The history of social work education for black people 1900–1930." *Journal of Sociology and Social Welfare*, 21 (1994): 67–82.

Haynes, George. E. Cooperation with Colleges in Securing and Training Negro Social Workers for Urban Centers. *Proceedings of the National Conference of Charities and Correction*. Fort Wayne: IN: The Fort Wayne Printing Company, 1911.

Howard University School of Social Work. *Strengthening diverse families and communities: Vision & Mission*. Retrieved January 29, 2017, from www.howard.edu/schoolsocialwork/about/default.html

Howard University. *Howard University School of Social Work*. Retrieved January 10, 2017, from www.howard.edu/schoolsocialwork/about/default.htm

Jackson State University. *School of Social Work*. Retrieved February 21, 2017, from www.jsums.edu/socialwork/

Karger, Howard J., and David Stoesz. "The growth of social work education programs, 1985–1999: Its impact on economic and educational factors related to the profession of social work." *Journal of Social Work Education*, 39, no. 2 (2003): 279–295.

Kayser, John A. "The Bishop Tuttle School of Social Work and the life of Fannie Jeffery: An oral history." *Reflections*, (2004): 111–126.

Lide, Pauline. "The national conference on social welfare and the black historical perspective." *Social Service Review*, 47 no. 2 (1973): 171–207.

Platt, Tony and Chandler, Susan. "Constant struggle: E. Franklin Frazier and Black social work in the 20s." *Social Work*, 33 (1988): 293–297.

Martin, Elmer P., and Joanne M. Martin. *Social work and the black experience*. Washington, DC: NASW Press, 1995.

Morgan State University. *School of Social Work*. Retrieved February 21, 2017, from www.morgan.edu/ssw

National Association of Social Workers. About NASW. www.naswdc.org/nasw/default.asp National Association of Social Workers. Standards and indicators for cultural competence. www.socialworkers.org/practice/standards/standards_and_indicators_for_cultural_competence.asp

National Urban League. Mission and History. Retrieved February 20, 2017 from nul.iamempowered.com/who-we-are/mission-and-history.

Norfolk State University. *Social Work*. Retrieved February 21, 2017, from www.nsu.edu/social-work/

Southern University and A & M College. About the Department of Social Work. Retrieved February 21, 2017, from www.subr.edu/index.cfm/page/191/n/297

Tam, Dora MY and Siu-Ming Kwok. "Controversy debate on gatekeeping in social work education." *The International Journal of Learning*, 14, no. 1 (2007): 195–203.

Zastrow, Charles, and Judith Bremner. "Social work education responds to the shortage of persons with a doctorate and a professional social work degree." *Journal of Social Work Education*, 40 no. 2 (2004): 351–358.

8 Mentoring Experiences of Graduate Students in HBCU Professional Programs

Sean Robinson and Charmaine Troy

Introduction

In the past few decades, a number of researchers have paid close attention to graduate student experiences, including students' attrition and completion rates,[1] socialization processes,[2] advising relationships,[3] disciplinary differences,[4] and concerns involving the dissertation.[5] However, there remains minimal research on Black students' experiences in graduate and professional programs.[6] The lack of emphasis on Black students is problematic given that there is a long history of significant disparity in terminal degree completion between African American and White students in the United States.[7] Blacks comprised over 12% of the United States population in 2010, yet only earned 6% of the nation's conferred doctorates in 2010.[8] In comparison, Whites comprised approximately 72% of the population, and earned 74% of the doctorates during the same year.[9] For those Black students who do earn doctoral and professional degrees, they are increasingly likely to have graduated from a Historically Black College or University (HBCU) than a predominantly White institution (PWI).[10] According to the 2013 Survey of Earned Doctorates, between 2009–2013, of the 10,228 doctorates awarded to African American students, 2,836 doctorates were conferred by 20 individual institutions; within the top 20, three HBCUs (Howard University, Morgan State University, and Jackson State University) accounted for 21% (N=613) of the doctorates awarded. Furthermore, out of the 103 HBCUs in the US, there are currently 21 that award doctorates in a multitude of fields.

Thompson (2009) described HBCU culture as an "academically rigorous and socially conscious environment that challenges and shapes students' intellectual as well as their social, political and spiritual lives" (p. 30).[11] Although the purpose, nature, and overall experiences of undergraduate education are different than those of graduate education, the actual needs of graduate students may not be that dramatically different from those of undergraduates, including a need to be engaged with faculty and peers and having a sense of belonging. Although a number of scholars have provided solid discussions over the past 30 years of the ways that HBCUs impact undergraduate students in meaningful ways, a thorough examination of the essential support structures for African American graduate students at both PWIs and HBCUs is generally lacking in the empirical literature.[12] Given that mentoring is one key support mechanism that has been shown to impact engagement, retention, and completion for Black graduate students at PWIs, the purpose of this research was to extend this line of inquiry through an exploration of the socialization and mentoring experiences of graduate students attending an HBCU and who were enrolled in professional, practitioner-oriented terminal degree programs.[13]

Review of Literature on Mentoring

Much of the literature on the experiences of graduate students of color has emphasized increased recruitment efforts, financial and academic support, the presence of faculty and administrators of color, and the need to address race and culture in coursework.[14] What is missing is an exploration of the socialization process of Black graduate students; little empirical research has captured those systems, structures, or relationships that can be deemed as supportive, or of barriers to success and degree attainment. Gasman, Gerstl-Pepin, Anderson-Thompkin, Rasheed, and Hathaway reported that Black graduate students experience a lack of mentorship and opportunities for professional development, a devaluation of scholarship on Black history and culture, and the exclusion of Blacks from discourse on various mainstream topics.[15] Mentoring is generally thought of as a mechanism that could ideally enhance personal and professional satisfaction.

Research on the socialization experiences, professional development, and success of doctoral students and faculty has generally emphasized the importance and role of advisors as the support mechanism for students rather than the role of mentors.[16] King (2003) defined mentoring as a relationship that "suggests a level of personal interaction, nurture, and guidance that exceeds the requirements of 'good enough' research advising" (p. 15). King further states that "rather than being concerned solely with the student's completing the dissertation or developing technical competence, the mentor is concerned with promoting a broader range of psychosocial, intellectual, and professional development" (p. 15). If we assume that entering a graduate program occurs for both personal and professional reasons, then it stands to reason that providing a different level of support and mentoring should also enhance both the personal and the professional aspects of the academic experience for those involved in the mentoring relationship. Thus, the one tool that could have lasting and profound effects for the academic success of minority graduate students that clearly seems to be lacking is mentoring.

Within the educational arena, the concept of mentoring was first introduced through the research of Levinson, Darrow, Klein, Levinson, and McKee (1978). Their longitudinal study highlighted the importance of mentoring relationships in young men's adulthood. Mentoring was viewed as crucial for enhancing an individual's skills and intellectual development; for welcoming the individual into a new occupational and social world; for acquainting the individual to the norms, values, resources, and key players; and for role modeling certain types of behavior. According to Levinson et al. (1978), the most important function of the mentoring relationship was to "facilitate and support the realization of the Dream" (p. 98). Several studies have also highlighted the significance of mentoring for women at various stages of their undergraduate academic career, thereby allowing them to also "realize the dream."[17] Yet, it has only been in the past few years that we have seen a surge in the number of studies exploring the role of mentoring for graduate students, a relationship that is both separate and distinct from that of advising. Despite the evidence that mentoring can have a positive impact on the personal and professional development of graduate students,[18] a number of studies have described just how little faculty mentoring actually exists for students of color.[19] Blanchett and Clarke-Yapi contended that it is the lack of representative faculty across the country that results in inadequate and insufficient mentoring for these students.[20] One could also argue that mentoring does not occur as a result of lack of training, and the fact that faculty are rarely rewarded for mentoring of students, i.e., mentoring does not usually factor into one's promotion or tenure application.

The exploration of the mentoring effects of recent sociology doctoral recipients by Dixon-Reeves (2003) clearly demonstrated how mentoring can enhance the opportunities of Black students. In her study, Dixon-Reeves revealed that Black male faculty consistently provided Black graduate students with more support and guidance than other racial or gender combinations. Black students overall ranked Black women fourth in line as their mentors, falling behind both White men and White women. This can be seen as a low representation on the faculty, rather than a disinterest in serving these students, echoing earlier findings of Blanchett and Clarke-Yapi.

In a later study, Johnson-Bailey, Valentine, Cervero, and Bolwes surveyed all 2,287 Black students who graduated between 1962 and 2003 with a graduate or professional degree from a southern research-oriented PWI.[21] Their mixed methods study yielded 586 participants who responded to both closed-ended and open-ended survey questions. The quantitative analysis indicated that both Black professors and students provided more support for the Black students. In addition, the White faculty also provided support for the Black students, although much less so than their Black colleagues. The qualitative responses by the students supported the quantitative data. Responses to the open-ended questions revealed that support to the Black students occurred in five distinct ways: support by Black faculty, support by Black students, self-support, support by family, and support within their religious/faith communities. Nonetheless, the Black respondents consistently described their academic experiences as one of struggle and survival. Across the board, when asked what did or would have made their experiences better, 32% said having more Black faculty, and 24% said more Black students did make or would have made for a better overall experience. While not specifically looking at the intersection of race and gender, it is clear that this study by Johnson-Bailey et al., covering four decades of student graduates, indicates an overall lack of, and a greater need for, support and mentoring for Black graduate students. What these studies suggest is that there are simply not enough mentoring or appropriate socialization experiences taking place in the academy, nor are there enough Black faculty to support the academic success of students. Mentoring can be, and should be, personally espoused, personally rewarded, and personally valued. If the academy truly believes in promoting successful Black students through the pipeline, then faculty and administrators should seek to better understand the expectations, needs, and actual experiences of this growing population. Drawing on Kram's seminal work on mentoring within organizational and workplace contexts, we outline the general components of a successful faculty-student mentoring relationship, along with the two key functions of mentoring, those pertaining to career aspects, and those related to psychosocial wellbeing, as a framework for this study.[22]

Overview of Student-Faculty Mentoring

According to Jacobi, student-faculty mentoring exemplifies what in graduate education is considered the apprenticeship model.[23] Such a relationship is considered to be a necessary part of the student's educational experience because this type of interaction provides a means of learning beyond the classroom. In this context, the faculty member imparts knowledge, provides support, and offers guidance on both academic and nonacademic issues.[24] The mentoring relationship can thus help a student develop a sense of belonging within the institution as well as the discipline.[25] Graduate school mentoring relationships are highly variable and idiosyncratic, since guidelines do not typically exist for student-faculty relationships, and faculty have wide latitude in how they interact with their students. Student-faculty mentoring relationships have been characterized as either formal, such as various Undergraduate Research Opportunity Programs and the McNair Post-baccalaureate Achievement program, or informal.[26] Formal programs are intentional and structured, and are mainly found at the undergraduate level and usually rely on a third-party to pair up a mentor and a protégé; informal mentoring occurs almost spontaneously between a student and a faculty member, and lacks the organization and structure of formal mentoring relationships.

Mentor Functions

In her groundbreaking book *Mentoring at Work: Developmental Relationships in Organizational Life*, Kathy Kram outlined two important functions of the mentor, career-related and psychosocial. Career functions aid in the career development of protégés, while psychosocial functions enhance a protégé's sense of psychological wellbeing, competence, and identity.[27] In effect, career development functions assist the protégé in career advancement not only while in a graduate program but in post-graduation early career stages, whereas the psychosocial functions help a protégé's personal development by relating to the individual on a personal level. Kram suggested that the greater the number and depth of functions by the mentor, the more beneficial the relationship will be to the protégé. Waldeck et al. believed that "taken together, these personal and professional tools assist in the career advancement of protégés" (p. 89).[28] But as Ragins and Cotton contended, mentoring is not an all or nothing phenomenon; a mentor may address any number of the specific domains within a specific function.[29]

Career-related functions involve particular activities that aid in career development and advancement, and include sponsorship, exposure and visibility, coaching, protection, and challenging assignments. Sponsorship refers to nominating the protégé for an award or for particular programs aimed at graduate students (e.g., an emerging scholars workshop, public policy seminar, research grants, fellowships), or in providing necessary letters of recommendation. Exposure and visibility involve creating opportunities for the protégé to interact with senior faculty, scholars, or researchers who might also provide developmental opportunities. Coaching involves suggesting strategies for accomplishing specific career or academic related goals, or working through issues and challenges that serve as barriers to success for the protégé. Sometimes the mentor is called upon to protect the protégé from other individuals, politics, or situations that might prove harmful or derail the protégé. Finally, assigning challenging projects can help the protégé develop the skills and knowledge needed to succeed both during the academic program and into one's next professional job.

Psychosocial functions are more personal aspects and include role modeling, acceptance and confirmation, counseling and friendship. Unlike the career functions, which are more dependent on the mentor's ability to create opportunities for the protégé, psychosocial functions depend upon the relationship between the mentor and the protégé. In general, a mentor serves as a role model when the protégé emulates the values, behaviors, and attitudes of the mentor. When the mentor provides support, encouragement, and nurturance, this creates a safe environment in which the protégé can learn and take risks. Offering counseling is another way that a mentor can provide a safe environment, since the protégé is able to explore personal concerns and issues that might serve as obstacles to one's personal and professional growth. The last dimension, friendship, typically develops over a longer period of time, and involves the mutual liking and personal enjoyment between mentor and protégé, and may extend out of the academic context into more personal domains. It is this framework that served as the guide for this study, allowing us to explore the nature of mentoring for the professional program students attending several HBCUs.

Methodology

An exploratory, phenomenological qualitative research design was employed as a result of the purpose of this research and the fact that experiences can best be shared through the use of storytelling.[30] According to Gay and Airasian, qualitative research seeks to probe deeply into why things are the way they are and how participants perceive things.[31] Pugach emphasized the importance of sharing stories, particularly those in which the voices belong to individuals from marginalized and traditionally oppressed groups.[32] The primary research question we sought to answer was: how do graduate students attending an HBCU characterize current mentoring/advising relationships? What do these students say they need, versus what they are actually receiving? This study was designed to specifically explore the following aspects of the socialization and mentoring experiences of Black doctoral students attending HBCUs: a) prior mentoring relationships and support structures as an undergraduate student; b) current mentoring relationships, support structures, and socialization experiences; and c) the role of prior experiences in shaping the expectations of future mentoring relationships.

Participants

Both purposeful sampling and snowball sampling were utilized to identify participants for this study. According to Patton, "Purposeful sampling focuses on selecting information-rich cases whose study will illuminate the questions under study" (p. 230).[33] The lead author of this study initially solicited students from individual department chairs at those 21 HBCUs that award doctoral degrees, as well as graduate program coordinators affiliated with professional, practitioner-oriented degree programs (e.g., medicine, law, business, etc.). Given that a majority of professional degrees and doctorates awarded to Blacks hail from Howard University, Morgan State University, and Jackson State University, additional emphasis was placed on recruiting students from these institutions. Using snowball sampling, students who were interviewed were also asked to identify any peers that they believed would be willing to participate in the study. In total, 14 graduate students from the three targeted HBCUs (Howard University, Jackson State University, and Morgan State University) were interviewed. Of the 14 participants initially interviewed, only seven were in a professional, practitioner-oriented doctoral degree program, representing journalism, educational leadership, educational psychology, school psychology, and social work; the remaining students represent humanities disciplines and were not included for the purposes of this particular study. All of the participants were either actively working on their dissertations or had recently defended. One of the seven participants was male; six were female. All of the participants identified as either Black or African American. In our study, we utilized pseudonyms for the students to maintain confidentiality.

Data Collection and Analysis

Semi-structured interviews were conducted, lasting on average 90 minutes. Since the lead researcher (Robinson) on this project is a White male, all of the interviews were conducted by the second researcher (Troy) on this project, who is a Black woman, and was in the process of writing her dissertation in a practitioner-scholar field (educational leadership). The assumption behind this choice was that this would produce a richer, deeper interview, since there were more similarities and commonalities between the participants and the interviewer as doctoral students attending an HBCU; in this way, the interviewer could capitalize on her implicit understanding of the realities of being a Black doctoral student to uncover nuances and additional meanings within the interview. In doing so, she offered an authentic space for our participants to share their stories and experiences.

The interviews were transcribed by a third party with no knowledge of any of the participants. Interviews were coded based on the primary functions outlined above—career and psychosocial—using holistic coding, open coding, and *in vivo* coding to identify themes and patterns in the data.[34] Holistic coding was used to consider the meaning behind larger individual experiences or narratives that held a single unifying theme or idea. In open coding, the transcripts were coded line by line to uncover deeper nuances and meanings within the themes identified by holistic coding. *In vivo* coding was employed when the own words of a participant best captured the essence of an idea. All of these coding schemes led to larger categorical and thematic development, using the aforementioned career and psychosocial aspects of mentoring as reference points to frame the analysis. Peer debriefing and continuous reflections of our own biases, values, and judgments related to the data through research memos were utilized during the research to ensure the analysis and resulting interpretations were trustworthy.[35]

Findings

Many students in this study seemed to have embodied this very notion of mentoring for success. Using *career functions* and *psychosocial functions* of mentoring as departure points, we offer key findings exploring the role of mentoring within faculty-graduate student relationships in doctoral level, professional/practitioner-oriented programs at select HBCUs. Although not every faculty member engages in mentoring experiences, many faculty in graduate education do promote the benefits and importance of mentoring as a core component of the educational experience. Henry Ellis's (1992) widely read piece is still representative of the thinking among educators who engage in a mentoring relationship:

> I am convinced that the success of graduate education depends on a student-faculty relationship based on integrity, trust, and support. I believe that

quality graduate programs have some sort of faculty mentor system in which students can obtain advice, counseling, and helpful direction in their training. . . . Good mentoring represents one of the important factors in graduate training, fosters long-term competence, and promotes effectiveness for both scientists and professionals.

(p. 575)

As the narratives and excerpts in our study highlight, those students with mentors engaged in relationships in which they were able to grow and develop both personally and professionally. As our findings indicate, our participants discussed the ways in which faculty mentors helped them develop key skills related to completing their academic requirements, networking, scholarly productivity, and ultimately in the job search process, all primary career functions. Our participants also provided insight into how their mentors helped them psychosocially, working with them through particular personal, academic, or professional challenges. Many of our participants talked about how their mentors served as a friend, coach, counselor, and trusted advocate; in this way the mentors all held a vested interest in the overall wellbeing of their students.

Career Functions of Mentoring

Mentors are often credited with providing protégés the opportunities to develop the skills and abilities necessary for a chosen profession. Mentors act as role models, and can offer counseling, coaching, advising, and insider information as a way to help protégés learn the ropes of a given discipline and profession. Furthermore, mentors can also be supportive in helping protégés develop critical thinking and writing skills and particular habits of the mind. For many students, these particular skills were built up particularly during the dissertation phase of their programs. Janie summed it up this way:

> My mentor just stayed the course with me until, you know, until I got [my research] where it needed to be in order for me to go onto the next phase. At each phase he offered a lot of constructive criticism. He was real honest with me about what I needed to do and he didn't really give me a lot of answers but that helped me to basically kind of think it through to the point that I figured it out on my own. I would say that I appreciated that because I think I found more value in completing my work because I felt like I could own it myself.

Janie demonstrates the role of a faculty mentor in scaffolding her ability to work independently, to have the confidence in her work, and ultimately to make it her own. Noel takes that one step further as she describes her relationship with her mentor:

> She's been very impactful. I feel like, since she's been with the department and just the time I've spent working with her, I've gotten refocused

on research and figuring out like the end goal, so after year three, kind of knowing where I need to be and what I need to be doing. She's very good at just allowing things, making sure you see the bigger picture. And she'll also get on you to finish your work, to do what it is you said that you will do.

For Noel, her mentor served as a mechanism to keep her focused, and to make sure she stayed on track. Noel also sees her mentor not only as a role model but as someone that she wants to be like, when she exclaims, "Everything that she's done or is currently doing I would like; I could see myself doing the same things! I see a lot of who I want to be in her, and she's able to kind of use her resources or provide her resources with students like me who want to do more."

The sentiments by Janie and Noel about the relationship with their mentors were echoed by all six of the graduate students who had a mentor. The one student who did not have a mentor, Kendra, recognized that something was indeed missing from her experience, and also implicitly seemed to understand the power that a mentoring relationship could have:

I try to do a lot of things on my own just because I don't know, I just don't feel like, I don't know why I just feel like I have to do a lot of things on my own. . . . And I like I said before, it could be that I do have [a mentor] but I don't realize I have one just because of how I define 'mentor.' To me a mentor is somebody who calls and checks on you. Nobody calls and checks on me.

Kendra's overall experience appeared to frustrate her more than many others, simply because she did not have a mentor who "called and checked in" on a regular basis. In this respect, Kendra also missed out on the other benefits of having a mentor. We should also note that Kendra seemed to have a series of issues and obstacles with her dissertation that extended her process that those with a mentor experienced in a less challenging fashion.

One aspect of developing professional skills is that of networking, which in itself is a skill to be learned and practiced. Good mentors seek opportunities to introduce protégés to other faculty, researchers, and scholars outside of the institution, most often at professional conferences.[36] Clarice understood that the connections that her mentor provided her with would not have happened otherwise, and in fact these connections were not something that other faculty in her department had ever attempted to provide for her:

Our relationship looks like that because of the support that he gives towards not just your dissertation but also making sure you are active in the field itself. I think it's really important to be active in the field and going to conferences. Oh man, I would say he's a mentor because I don't think I've ever had a professor that says at a conference, 'Okay let's meet up and go to the bar and have some drinks and talk about workshops you've been to and who you've met' and things like that. I have never had that with any of my other professors I would have to say. So to me that's different, and shows that he is interested in your success and what you're learning that contributes to your overall knowledge of the field, and who you're meeting because it's very important to network. He will take you around and introduce you to people that you don't know and it's kind of cool because now I'm like, in all the books I've been reading, I know the names! I know these people; I know who they are. . . . My relationship with him has been different than anybody in the department because again the other department members are not really active in the field and in associations. But again he doesn't have to do all of that. He doesn't have to make sure that you know you have to go to certain workshops, or ask about what workshops you plan on attending, and giving debriefings and making sure you meet people and attend things that again. That's been different for me.

Not only did Cynthia's mentor provide her with an important professional opportunity, she worked to make sure that her protégé took advantage of it. Cynthia's experience with one conference exemplifies this:

I've had quite a few opportunities in graduate school that I wouldn't have had, had I not known my mentor because she introduced me—not only introduced me—but made sure I got there. I remember one time in particular, there was a conference in Atlanta and she put my name on a list; she actually nominated me and did all the things she needed to, and you know, told me to follow up and I didn't. When I didn't, she got on it and next thing I knew I was getting a phone call and an invitation to come to the conference. At that point didn't have enough time, energy and desire to do what I was supposed to do, but she recognized it as something I needed to do so she made sure I got there.

In this scenario, like Clarice's mentor, Cynthia's mentor was showing how deeply she was invested in the overall success of her student; this is a key aspect that a number of students in this study talked about when asked why they selected an HBCU for their terminal degrees. This shows up in a multiple conversations as students discussed their mentoring relationships.

When a mentor's circle of influence includes the protégé, she can benefit from greater professional influence, access to senior leaders/scholars/researchers, and ideally greater access to important resources, such as fellowships, grants, research opportunities, or even career opportunities. Within graduate programs, students such as Cynthia and Clarice, who are part of a mentoring dyad, often report feeling more connected and engaged with faculty at their institution as well as with other scholars in their field.[37] On the other hand, Kendra, who lacked a mentor, often felt disconnected and forced to figure things out on her own.

Beyond networking, learning the art of research and professional writing—for conferences, for publication, or even for more technical reports—is a key aspect for graduate students. Clarice put it succinctly when she stated, "The whole submitting proposals and things like that I did not learn that until I met [my mentor]. So I didn't know how to submit proposals for conferences or any of that stuff. I didn't know how that worked or the importance of any of that. I just learned all of that from him."

A majority of the students we spoke to lamented the fact that their programs overall did not provide many opportunities to work with faculty directly in preparing conference proposals or to collaborate on research projects. It was only via mentoring relationships that this happened for most of these graduate students, as in Clarice's case. Research and scholarly productivity is perhaps the most consistently demonstrated outcome of mentorship in graduate school. Hollingsworth and Fassinger found having a mentor is directly related to presenting papers at conferences, publishing, and securing grants or fellowships.[38] In addition, Hollingsworth and Fassinger posited that mentorship helps to provide the necessary relationship and environment that supports and encourages a high level of productivity; this notion was indeed highlighted in a number of our interviews. The impact of mentoring for graduate students regarding such productivity includes not only time in a graduate program, but extends well past one's exit from the program.

The last career-oriented benefit of mentoring relationships, and one that is certainly related to the aforementioned ones, concerns career opportunities following graduation. For many students, their mentors served as a resource and coach during the job search process. Sam's mentor had over 40 years of experience in the field and was able to be a significant resource for him as he considered multiple options as an academic administrator:

> I can consult with her about various positions that I am anticipating applying to. She provides letters of recommendation, she tells me about her academic experiences as she has served in almost every administrator capacity that you can think of in education from a faculty member to vice president, president, you know she's done it all. So she is just a walking HBCU knowledge book.

Clarice offers similar reflections about her mentor:

> He has coached me professionally, if you will, as far as, you know, with the job search and interviewing and things of that nature, which I've appreciated. I don't see faculty as having to really do that, but he does.

In general, the research suggests that protégés with strong mentors and who are satisfied with their program, exhibit a high level of professional competence, are confident and have a professional identity, and who have a portfolio of experiences will fare better on the job market. The students interviewed were certainly poised for success in terms of their job search, their opportunities, and their overall preparation.

Psychosocial Functions of Mentoring

One of the more important, but least tangible, aspects of mentorship is the enhancement of professional confidence and identity.[39] An additional area of potential benefit to protégés is that of personal wellbeing.[40] A number of students in this study discussed several aspects related to psychosocial health and general wellbeing. As a result of the close, trusting relationship with her mentor, Cynthia has learned a lot about herself:

> It's more than an academic mentorship. We talk about everything from academic to life in general. Like I said, we've broken bread on several occasions. We've done community service projects together as well as some travel together, that's why it goes beyond, I guess. I've learned to seek out opportunity, and to give more. I've learned that I can work with people from all backgrounds. Like I said, she and I are fairly different but we're able to come together and do some pretty good things. I've learned my areas that I need to work on because when we do bump heads she lets me know about myself and being that it comes from a trusted friend or a trusted mentor it's easier to swallow if it's something I need to work on. Because she's so close with me and understands a lot of my process again that just kind of validates her position as a trusted advisor and friend.

Cynthia is willing to engage in self-reflection because of her mentoring relationship, and is thus able to grow as a professional. For Roberta, her mentor's support and encouragement was truly the key to her personal wellbeing:

> To be honest, I love her dearly. She will probably retire within the next year or two, and she is . . . I don't know. . . . I just find her amazing and I'm fond of her, and having her on my committee, it really didn't matter what anybody else said to me, except for the fact that she said she was proud of me, and that I started strong and I finished strong, and that meant more to me than anything, than any words anyone else could have said to me.

As mentioned earlier, a number of students sought to continue their education at an HBCU specifically because they believed faculty would almost always have their best interest at heart, as captured by Sam's comment about both his mentor and his faculty overall:

> I'll tell you, she pretty much was like a mother figure or a grandmother figure; I mean she would call me early in the morning, almost like

calling me out, if I had not gotten something to her when I told her I was going to get it to her. She would say, "You plan on graduating? Because if you do you need to get busy. . . ." So it was more like a caring, nurturing, and kinda chastising relationship. So I do not think, matter of fact I almost know, you don't get that outside of the HBCU experience. That's exactly what I was looking for because I needed that. I needed somebody or a group of people who were interested in my wellbeing who were actually interested in seeing me as a Black man get my PhD. . . . In some ways I think she saw more in me than I saw in myself. I think what attributed to that was the fact that as I first stated they [the general faculty] had a vested interest in my success because it's an HBCU and that's what they do. So I think that attributes a lot to them seeing more in me than I actually saw in myself.

Roberta echoed Sam's feelings about the experience of attending an HBCU and what that did for her personally and professionally:

On a personal note, I feel better prepared. And it's very true to me that you don't leave here or probably any other HBCU without knowing who you are, and that experience to me was invaluable, it was worth every headache I ever had to be able to learn that for myself, to learn to distinguish when I'm listening to other people speak, if they're talking to be talking, or if there's any substances behind what they're saying, that they can speak to that makes them better advocates.

With regard to the experience of attending an HBCU, several interviewees noted how important it was to be able to have conversations with both their mentors and other faculty about navigating their professional worlds as African Americans, and for the women in our study, understanding the intersectionality of race and gender in the workplace. Roberta summed it up this way: "Every single one of the faculty led by example and didn't hesitate to share the experience and the challenge of being othered in the professional world, and they were very honest about it and very open with regard to the approaches that they took, and it was incredibly rewarding to see them progress. I mean, every single one of them has awesome accolades, and they're highly successful." Similarly, Sam's mentor would offer perspectives about working in PWIs: "I was just in a conversation with my mentor yesterday. . . . And we talked about the difficulties that African American men face who do have a doctoral degree in a predominantly White environment and how to navigate through that and what are the pros and cons of actually working in these environments. So you know he provides a good source of inspiration, particularly right now, because I'm working in a predominantly White environment. I need that support until I can get out of there and into an HBCU."

As the participants in our study suggest, faculty relationships, in the form of mentoring, can be vital for success. It's clear that in all of the mentoring dyads, the students saw their mentors as advisors, coaches, allies, friends, and family. This certainly harkens back to King's idea of mentoring as supporting the full range of intellectual, career, and psychosocial needs of a protégé, and going well beyond that of just a "research advisor."[41] The depth of interactions allowed the mentor to have authentic conversations with their protégé about personal, academic, and professional areas for growth and development. Even those few graduate students that maintained stricter, more formal boundaries sought opportunities for feedback and reflection from their mentors.

Discussion and Conclusions

As previously mentioned, doctoral education can be conceptualized as a socialization process between the faculty member and a graduate student. Building relationships with faculty, receiving adequate levels of social, psychological, and intellectual support, and feeling cared for are important components of this socialization process. The climate and culture at HBCUs is likely to facilitate doctoral student socialization by creating a sense of belonging, fostering ongoing relationships, and ultimately creating a culture that leads to academic engagement and success; certainly several of the students in this study alluded to this as part of their decision to attend an HBCU for their terminal degrees. Scholarship focused on the organizational perspective of the doctoral experience tends to contextualize socialization to highlight the role of academic environments (i.e., departments) as an important way to make distinctions among the ways in which students are socialized in a variety of contexts.[42] As our research suggests, much of this socialization can be accomplished through the development of mentoring relationships between doctoral students and faculty within departmental and disciplinary environments.

Although there is a significant body of research on the process of undergraduate education and retention, in comparison less such research exists as it relates to the doctoral experience, and very few studies explicitly address the role of mentoring for minority students. Given the high cost of doctoral education, the commitments necessary on the part of students, faculty, and institutions, and the increasing demands for institutional accountability, we need to develop a better understanding of the process of doctoral education, and the programs, tools, and services to better serve our students in the pipeline. In addition, understanding students' experiences may ultimately aid in retention and persistence, better organizational fit, appropriate career decisions, and better expenditure of individual and institutional resources.

The results of this research corroborate much of what is prevalent in the literature on the experiences of graduate students and faculty of color in higher education.[43] Several key attributes of mentoring were presented, generally by our participants, that provide a common frame, and that serve to reinforce the narratives presented. First, mentoring reflects a unique relationship between individuals.[44] Second, mentoring is a learning partnership.[45] Lastly, mentoring is a process, defined by the types of support provided by the mentor, and includes emotional, psychosocial, instrumental, and career-related aspects.[46] The experiences of the graduate students in this study offer further insights into how the mentor relationship can greatly impact them, both personally and professionally. The findings of this study offer a renewed call for faculty, administrators, departments, and HBCUs themselves to give additional weight to the role that mentoring plays in graduate student success. Furthermore, institutions need to consider formal programs that offer opportunities to train and orient faculty toward a "mentoring mindset," and to consider how best to reward faculty for mentoring activities.

This research is not without its limitations, however; this chapter draws upon interview data from a larger study exploring the socialization experiences of Black students pursuing PhDs in a multitude of fields, including social sciences, humanities, and professionally oriented programs. Neither the larger study, nor this particular study, included students in more traditional professional schools (e.g., law, medicine, business, dentistry, veterinary, engineering, etc.), thus the results here should be considered with this in mind. This is not to say that mentoring relationships in traditional professional schools would not function in the same way; those relationships, however, might have nuances to them not captured in more research-oriented professional programs. Likewise, the experiences of those enrolled in a master's terminal degree program (e.g., MBA, MFA, MPH) might have different expectations and experiences from those enrolled in doctoral terminal degree programs. Additional research could explore the mentoring experiences across all of these permutations. Finally, while this research explicitly looked at the socialization experiences of graduate students, and delved down into the specific ways that mentoring supported this development of students, understanding the experiences, including the challenges and obstacles, of those graduate students without mentors would be equally as beneficial for faculty, departments, and administrators who continue to seek to shorten the time to degree, and to strengthen the learning experiences of graduate students.

Notes

1 Bowen and Rudenstine 1992; Golde 2005; Lovitts 2001
2 Antony 2002; Austin 2002; Ellis 2001; Gardener 2007
3 Baird 1995; Sweitzer 2009
4 Gardener 2007; Golde 2005; Golde and Walker 2006
5 Boote and Beile 2005; Nettles and Millette 2006
6 Howard-Hamilton, Moerlon-Quainoo, Winkle-Wagner, Johnson and Santiague 2009
7 Thomas 1992
8 National Science Foundation 2013; US Census Bureau 2010
9 National Science Foundation 2011; US Census Bureau 2010

10 Gasman, Baez, Drezner, Sedgwick, Tudico and Schmid 2007
11 Thompson 2009
12 Fleming 1984; Flowers 2002; Nelson Laird et al. 2007; Palmer and Gasman 2008; Siefert, Drummond, and Pascarella 2006
13 Griffin et al. 2010; Herzig 2006; Milner, Husband, and Jackson, 2002; Patton and Harper 2003
14 Daniel 2007; Johnson-Bailey 2004
15 Gasman et al. 2004
16 Baird 1995; Bargar and Mayo-Chamberlain 1983; Gardner 2009; Golde 2001; Lovitts 2001; Tinto 1993; Zhao, Golde and McCormick 2005
17 Cheatham and Phelps 1995; Jacobi 1991; Robertson and Frier 1994
18 Blackwell 1983; Faison 1996; Willie, Grady, and Hope, 1991
19 Cheatham and Phelps 1995; Dixon-Reeves 2003; Robertson and Frier 1994; Sule 2009
20 Blanchett and Clarke-Yapi 1999
21 Johnson-Bailey, Valentine, Cervero, and Bolwes 2008
22 Kram's 1985
23 Jacobi 1991
24 Pascarella 1980
25 Austin 2002
26 Fassinger and Hensler-Mcginnis 2005; Mullen 2005
27 Kram 1985
28 Waldeck et al. 1997
29 Ragins and Cotton 1999
30 Glesne 1999; Merriam 1998
31 Gay and Airasian 2000
32 Pugach 2001
33 Patton 2002
34 Saldana 2013
35 Creswell 1998.
36 Johnson and Huwe 2003
37 Clark et al. 2000; Dixon-Reeves 2003; Tenenbaum, Crosby, and Gliner 2001
38 Hollingsworth and Fassinger 2002
39 Johnson and Huwe 2003; Schlosser et al. 2003
40 Grant-Vallone and Ensher 2000
41 King's 2003
42 Weidman 2006; Weidman and Stein 2003; Weidman et al. 2001
43 Cheatham and Phelps 1995; Dixon-Reeves 2003; Ellis 2001; Patton 2009; Robertson and Frier 1994; Sule 2009
44 Austin 2002; Jacobi 1991
45 Jacobi 1991; Roberts 2000
46 Jacobi 1991

Bibliography

Antony, James S. "Reexamining doctoral student socialization and professional development: Moving beyond the congruence and assimilation orientation." *Higher Education: Handbook of Theory and Research*, 17 (2002): 349–380.

Austin, Ann E. "Preparing the next generation of faculty: Graduate school as socialization to the academic career." *Journal of Higher Education*, 73 no. 1 (2002): 94–122.

Baird, Leonard L. "Helping graduate students: A graduate adviser's view." In Anne Pruitt, and Paul Isaac (Eds.), *Student Services for the changing graduate student population: New directions for student services*, 72 no. 4 (1995): 25–32.

Bargar, Robert R., and Jane Mayo-Chamberlain. "Advisor and advisee issues in doctoral education." *Journal of Higher Education*, 54 (1983): 407–432.
Blackwell, James E. Networking and mentoring: A study of cross-generational experiences of Blacks in graduate and professional school (Research Report). Atlanta, GA: Southern Educational Foundation, 1983.
Blanchett, Wanda J., and Marcia D. Clarke-Yapi. "Cross-cultural mentoring of ethnic minority students: Implications for increasing minority faculty." *Professional Educator*, 22, no. 1 (1999): 49–62.
Boote, David N., and Penny Beile. "Scholars before researchers: On the centrality of the dissertation literature review in research preparation." *Educational Researcher*, 34 no. 6 (2005): 3–15.
Bowen, William G., and Neil Rudenstein. *In Pursuit of the Ph.D.* Princeton, NJ: Princeton University Press, 1992.
Cheatham, Harold and Christine Phelps. "Promoting the development of graduate students of color." *New Directions for Student Services*, 72 no. 4 (1995): 91–99.
Council of Graduate Schools (2008). PhD Completion Report. Retrieved from www.cgsnet.org
Clark, Richard A., Sherry L. Harden, and W. Brad Johnson. "Mentor relationships in clinical psychology doctoral training: Results of a national survey." *Teaching of Psychology* 27, no. 4 (2000): 262–268.
Creswell, John W. *Qualitative inquiry and research design*. Thousand Oaks, CA: Sage, 1998.
Daniel, Carol Ann. "Outsiders-within: Critical race theory, graduate education and barriers to professionalization." *Journal of Sociology and Social Welfare*, 34 no. 1 (2007): 25–42.
Dixon-Reeves, Regina. "Mentoring as a precursor to incorporation: An assessment of the mentoring experience of newly minted Ph.D.s." *Journal of Black Studies*, 34 (2003): 12–27.
Ellis, Henry. "Graduate education in psychology: Past, present, and future." *American Psychologist*, 47 (1992): 570–576.
Ellis, Evelynn M. "The impact of race and gender on graduate school socialization, satisfaction with doctoral study, and commitment to degree completion." *The Western Journal of Black Studies*, 24 no. 35 (2001): 287–303.
Fassinger, Ruth E., and Nancy F. Hensler-Mcginnis. "Multicultural feminist mentoring as individual and small group pedagogy." In Carolyn Z. Enns, and Ada L. Sinacore (Eds.), *Teaching and social justice: Integrating multicultural and feminist theories in the classroom* (pp. 143–161). Washington, DC: American Psychological Association, 2005.
Faison, Jewel J. "The next generation: The mentoring of African American graduate students on predominantly White university campuses." Paper presented at the annual meeting of the American Educational Research Association, New York, 1996.
Fleming, Jacqueline. Blacks in college: A comparative study of student success in Black and White institutions. San Francisco: Jossey-Bass, 1984.
Flowers, Lamont A. "The impact of college racial composition on African American students' academic and social gains: Additional evidence." *Journal of College Student Development*, 43 no. 3 (2002): 403–410.
Gardner, Susan K. "The development of doctoral Students: Phases of challenge and support." *ASHE Higher Education Report*, 34 no. 6. San Francisco: Jossey-Bass, 2009.
Gardner, Susan K. "I heard it through the grapevine: Doctoral student socialization in chemistry and history." *Higher Education*, 54 no. 5 (2007): 723–740.

Gasman, Marybeth, Benjamin Baez, Noah D. Drezner, Katherine V. Sedgwick, Christopher Tudico, and Julie M. Schmid. "Historically black college and universities: Recent trends." *Academe*, 93 no. 1 (2007): 69–78.

Gasman, Marybeth, Laura. W. Perna, Susan Yoon, Noah D. Drezner, Valerie Lundy-Wagner, Enakshi Bose, and Shannon Gary. "The path to graduate school in science and engineering for underrepresented students of color." In Mary Howard-Hamilton, Carla L. Morelon-Quainoo, Susan D. Johnson, Rachelle Winkle-Wagner, and Lilia Sanitague (Eds.), *Standing on the outside looking in: Underrepresented students' experiences in advanced degree programs* (pp. 63–81). Sterling, VA: Stylus Press, 2009.

Gasman, Marybeth, Cynthia Gerstl-Pepin, Sibby Anderson-Thompkins, Lisa Rasheed, and Karry Hathaway. "Negotiating power, developing trust: Transgressing race and status in the academy." *Teachers College Record*, 106 no. 4 (2004): 689–715.Gay, Lorraine R., and Peter Airasian. *Educational research: Competencies for analysis and application*. Upper Saddle River, NJ: Prentice-Hall, 2000.

Glesne, Corrine. *Becoming qualitative researchers: An introduction*. New York, NY: Addison Wesley Longman, 1999.

Golde, Chris. "Should I stay or should I go? Student descriptions of the doctoral attrition process." *The Review of Higher Education*, 23 no. 2 (2001): 199–227.

Golde, Chris. "The role of the department and discipline in doctoral student attrition: Lessons from four departments." *The Journal of Higher Education*, 76 (2005): 669–700.

Golde, Chris and George Walker. Envisioning the future of doctoral education: Preparing stewards of the discipline. San Francisco: Jossey-Bass, 2006.

Grant-Vallone, Elisa J., and Ellen Ensher. "Effects of peer mentoring on types of mentor support, program satisfaction, and graduate student stress: A dyadic perspective." *Journal of College Student Development*, 41 (2000): 637–642.

Griffin, Kim A., David Perez, Annie Holmes, and Claude E. Mayo. "Investing in the future: The importance of faculty mentoring in the development of students of color in STEM." *New Directions for Institutional Research*, 14 (2010): 95–103.

Herzig, Abbe H. "How can women and students of color come to belong in graduate mathematics?" In Jill M. Bystydzienski (Ed.), *Removing barriers: Women in academic science, technology, engineering, and mathematics* (pp. 254–270). Bloomington, IN: Indiana University Press, 2006.

Hollingsworth, Merris A., and Ruth Fassinger. "The role of faculty mentors in the research training of counseling psychology doctoral students." *Journal of Counseling Psychology*, 49 no. 3 (2002): 324–330.

Howard-Hamilton, Mary, Carla Moerlon-Quainoo, Rachelle Winkle-Wagner, Susan Johnson, and Lilia Santiague. *Standing on the outside looking in: Underrepresented students' experiences in advanced degree programs*. Sterling, VA: Stylus Publishing.

Jacobi, Maryann. "Mentoring and undergraduate success: A literature review." *Review of Educational Research*, 61 (1991): 505–532.

Johnson-Bailey, Juanita. "Hitting the proverbial wall: Participation and retention issue for black graduate women." *Race, Ethnicity, and Education*, 7 no. 4 (2004): 331–349.

Johnson-Bailey, Juanita, Thomas S. Valentine, Ronald M. Cervero, and Tuere A. Bowles. "Lean on me: The support experiences of Black graduate students." *The Journal of Negro Education*, (2008): 365–381.

Johnson, W. Brad, and Jennifer M. Huwe. Getting mentored in graduate school. Washington, DC: American Psychological Association, 2003.

King, Margaret F. *On the right track: A manual for research mentors.* Washington, DC: Council of Graduate Schools, 2003.

Kram, Kathy E. Mentoring at work: Developmental relationships in organizational life. Glenview, IL: Scott, Foresman and Co, 1985.

Levinson, Daniel et al. *The seasons of a man's life.* New York: Knopf, 1978.

Lovitts, Barbara E. Leaving the ivory tower: The causes and consequences of departures from doctoral study. Lanham, MD: Rowman & Littlefield, 2001

Merriam, Sharan. B. Qualitative research and case study application in education. San Francisco, CA: Jossey-Bass, 1998.

Milner, H. Richard et al. "Voices of persistence and self-efficacy: African American graduate students and professors who affirm them." *Journal of Critical Inquiry into Curriculum and Instruction*, 4 no. 1 (2002): 33–39.

Mullen, Carol A. *The mentorship primer.* New York: Peter Lang, 2005.

National Center for Education Statistics. Doctor's degrees conferred by postsecondary institutions, by race/ethnicity and sex of student: Selected years, 1976-77 through 2014-15 (Table 324.20). Retrieved from https://nces.ed.gov/programs/digest/d16/tables/dt16_324.20.asp?current=yes

National Science Foundation. *2013 Survey of Earned Doctorates*, 2013. Retrieved from www.nsf.gov/statistics/sed/2013/data/tab9.pdf

Nelson Laird, Thomas, Brian Bridges, Carla Morelon-Quainoo, Julie Williams, and Michele S. Holmes. "African American and Hispanic student engagement at minority serving and predominately white institutions." *Journal of College Student Development*, 48 no. 1 (2007): 39–56.

Nettles, Michael T., and Catherine M. Millet. *Three magic words: Getting to Ph.D.* Baltimore, MD: The Johns Hopkins University Press, 2006.

Palmer, Robert, and Marybeth Gasman. " 'It takes a village to raise a child': The role of social capital in promoting academic success for African American men at a black college." *Journal of College Student Development*, 49, no. 1 (2008): 52–70.

Pascarella, Ernest. "Student faculty informal contact and college outcomes." *Review of Educational Research*, 50 (1980): 545–595.

Patton, Lori D. "My sister's keeper: A qualitative examination of mentoring experiences among African American women in graduate and professional schools." *Journal of Higher Education*, 80 no. 5 (2009): 510–537.

Patton, Lori, and Shaun Harper. "Mentoring relationships among African American women in graduate and professional schools." In Mary F. Howard-Hamilton (Ed.), *Meeting the needs of African American women: New Directions for students services* (No. 104, pp. 67–78). San Francisco: Jossey-Bass, 2003.

Patton, Michael Q. *Qualitative research and evaluation methods* (3rd ed.). Thousand Oaks, CA: Sage, 2002.

Pugach, Marlene. C. "The stories we chose to tell: Fulfilling the promise of qualitative research for special education." *Exceptional Children*, 67 no 4 (2001): 439–453.

Ragins, Belle R., and John L. Cotton. "Mentor functions and outcomes: A comparison of men and women informal and informal mentoring relationships." *Journal of Applied Psychology*, 84 (1999): 529–550.

Roberts, Andy. "Mentoring revisited: A phenomenological reading of the literature." *Mentoring and Tutoring*, 8 no. 2 (2000): 145–170.

Robertson, Piedad F., and Ted Frier. "Recruitment and retention of minority faculty." *New Directions for Community Colleges*, 22 no. 3 (1994): 65–71.

Saldana, Johnny. *The coding manual for qualitative researchers* (3rd ed.). Thousand Oaks, CA: Sage, 2013.

Schlosser, Lewis et al. "A qualitative study of the graduate advising relationship: The advisee perspective." *Journal of Counseling Psychology*, 50 (2003): 178–188.

Seifert, Tricia A., Jerri Drummond, and Ernest T. Pascarella. "African American students' experiences of good practices: A comparison of institutional type." *Journal of College Student Development*, 47 no. 2 (2006): 185–205.

Sule, Venice T. "Professional socialization, politicized race and gendered experience, and black female graduate students: A road map for structural transformation." In V. Barbara Bush, Crystal R. Chambers, and Mary Beth Walpole (Eds.), *From Diplomas to Doctorates: the success of Black women in higher education and its implications for equal educational opportunities for all* (pp. 111–130). Sterling, VA: Stylus Press, 2009.

Sweitzer, Vicki. "Towards a theory of doctoral student professional identity development: A developmental networks approach." *The Journal of Higher Education*, 80 no. 1 (2009): 1–33.

Tenenbaum, Harriet R., Faye J. Crosby, and Melissa D. Gliner. "Mentoring relationships in graduate school." *Journal of Vocational Behavior*, 59 (2001): 326–341.

Thomas, Gail E. "Participation and degree attainment of African-American and Latino students in graduate education relative to other racial and ethnic groups: An update from the Office of Civil Rights Data." *Harvard Educational Review*, 62 no. 1 (1992): 45–65.

Thompson, Garland L. "How HBCUs will help rebuild America: A roundtable discussion." *US Black Engineer and Information Technology*, 33 no. 2 (2009): 18–27.

Tinto, Vincent. *Leaving college: Rethinking the causes and cures of student attrition* (2nd ed.). Chicago, IL: University of Chicago Press, 1993.

US Census Bureau. The Black Population: 2010 (2011). Retrieved from https://www.census.gov/prod/cen2010/briefs/c2010br-06.pdf

Waldeck, Jennifer H., Victoria Orrego, Timothy Plax, and Patricia Kearney. "Graduate student/faculty mentoring relationships: Who gets mentored, how it happens, and to what end." *Communication Quarterly*, 45 (1997): 93–109. Weidman, John C. "Socialization of students in higher education: Organizational perspectives." *The Sage handbook for research in education: Engaging ideas and enriching inquiry* (2006): 253–262.

Weidman, John C., Darla J. Twale, and Elizabeth L. Stein. *Socialization of Graduate and Professional Students in Higher Education: A Perilous Passage?* San Francisco, CA: Jossey-Bass, 2001.

Weidman, John C., and Elizabeth L. Stein. "Socialization of doctoral students to academic norms." *Research in higher education*, 44 no. 6 (2003): 641–656.

Willie, Charles Vert, Michael K. Grady, and Richard O. Hope. *African-Americans and the doctoral experience: Implications for policy*. New York, NY: Teachers College Press, 1991.

Zhao, Chun M., Chris Golde, and Alexander McCormick. *More than a signature: How advisor choice and advisor behavior affect doctoral student satisfaction*. Paper presented at the annual meeting of the American Educational Research Association, Montreal, Quebec, 2005.

9 Beyond Respectable

Why Earn an Advanced Degree from an Historically Black College and University

Rikesha L. Fry Brown, Alonzo M. Flowers III, Adriel A. Hilton, and Michelle DeJohnette

Introduction

Since their inception, Historically Black Colleges and Universities (HBCUs) have served as an integral pathway for African Americans to pursue postsecondary educational opportunities.[1] Today, there are currently 103 HBCUs in the United States, including public and private, four-year institutions, medical schools, and community colleges.[2] HBCUs, unlike other colleges, are united in a mission to meet the educational and emotional needs of African American students.[3] Actualizing this mission has allowed HBCUs to successfully serve undergraduate, graduate, and professional students, particularly those of African descent. However, while much is known about the contributions, experiences, opportunities, and challenges facing undergraduate students at HBCUs, there remains a dearth of literature on graduate and professional students in this institutional context.[4]

Palmer et al. indicated that HBCUs account for a large percentage of African American graduate degree earners, despite the fact that only 10% of African American students attend HBCUs for graduate study.[5] For example, in 2009–2010, HBCUs accounted for 7,419 master's degree earners. Of these students, 75% (5,563) were of African descent. Most of these degree recipients were African American women, at 73%.[6] These 5,563 master's degree earners accounted for 7.3% of all African American master's degree earners, a large percentage considering that only 56 HBCUs awarded master's degrees during this timeframe. Even greater doctoral degree representation is seen among HBCUs. HBCUs awarded 2,079 doctoral degrees in 2009–2010. Most HBCU doctoral degree earners, 62% (1,635), were of African descent. Of these students, the balance between male-female recipients is more equitable, with 51% of doctoral recipients being women.[7] Given that only 10,417 doctorate degrees were awarded to African American students during this period, HBCUs accounted for 15.7% of all doctoral degrees awarded to African Americans. These data are even more impressive when considering that only 29 HBCUs awarded doctoral degrees during this timeframe.[8] Given these data, it is clear that HBCUs have a large impact on the overall percentage of African American graduate and professional degree earners, despite the limited number of institutions awarding these degrees.

Given the important role that HBCUs have in graduate and professional education and the limited knowledge regarding African American student experiences in these institutions, this study set out to fill this void. In particular, this chapter documents an exploratory study of graduate degree earners from HBCUs. Using data derived from master's, professional, and doctoral degree earners from HBCUs, we discuss factors that propelled students to attend HBCUs, their perceptions of the HBCU experience, and their overall assessment of the quality of the degrees they earned.

It is our hope that the information derived from this chapter will serve to provide more understanding of both the challenges and the opportunities facing African American students who attend HBCUs to earn advanced degrees. To provide a context for this discussion, the next section addresses relevant literature on African American students and HBCUs.

Relevant Literature

The HBCU

In general, HBCUs are defined as, "Black academic institutions established prior to 1964, whose principal mission was, and still is, the education of Black Americans."[9] Still, the National Association for Equal Opportunity in Higher Education has also designated some institutions that were established after 1964 as HBCUs.[10] The year 1964 represents a historical marker because it was the year that the *Civil Rights Act* was passed.

Whether out of the spirit of philanthropy, necessity, or fairness, the reason HBCUs were created in America and have survived for, in many cases, more than 140 years, is that they filled a void in this country.[11] Historically, African Americans were denied access to White institutions because of segregation laws that were prevalent at the time most HBCUs were created.[12] For instance, less than 3,000 African American students in the United States were enrolled in higher education by 1915, and most of them were men.[13]

HBCUs have marked their place in the history of this country. For many African Americans, HBCUs have been the door to higher education and to middle class America. HBCUs have a tradition of providing access to African Americans who otherwise might not have been given the opportunity for a college degree.[14] Despite the historical impact of HBCUs on the education of African Americans in this country, an imbalance remains between these institutions and their White counterparts.[15] The issue of disparate funding between HBCUs and predominantly White institutions (PWIs) has been the subject of litigation in America's courtrooms for years (e.g., *United States v. Fordice* 1992). Despite great differences in resourcing, these institutions have continued to provide educational opportunities to society's most marginalized and underserved students.

Prior Research on Student Success in HBCUs

Most studies on HBCUs have been conducted based on the linear comparisons of student success at both HBCUs and PWIs. Further, the experiences of graduate and professional students are often lumped into the narrative of the experiences of undergraduate students attending HBCUs. Within the context of this chapter, the academic success of graduate and professional students attending HBCUs will be framed based on factors of socialization, particularly peer and faculty interaction. Although research has demonstrated that student success is strongly related to satisfaction, the literature does not contain many studies examining the relationship between academic achievement and socialization at HBCUs. Roebuck and Murty noted that there is a general level of satisfaction and camaraderie among students who attend HBCUs that is not typically found among African American students who attend PWIs.[16] Harper, Carini, Bridges, and Hayek contended that student satisfaction and camaraderie remains a significant factor for academic success, particularly for students pursuing post-baccalaureate degrees at HBCUs.[17]

As seen in contemporary research of African American college success, the connection between institutional support and academic achievement has become an integral component of investigation. However, research focusing strictly on factors affecting advanced degree attainment for African Americans attending HBCUs remains limited. For African American college students, the level of institutional support either from peers or faculty members has a dramatic effect on academic development and matriculation.[18] While African American students pursuing advanced degrees, as a whole, continue to be underrepresented in postsecondary research, the HBCU experience continues to provide available context for inquiry. Kim noted that African American students at HBCUs are significantly more engaged in college experiences and develop considerably more cognitively and personally than those at PWIs.[19] In addition, the Department of Education stated that the purpose of HBCUs is to strengthen the African American community by providing educational programs to prepare future generations for anticipated global challenges.[20] On the whole, HBCUs remain educational environments in which African American students can come and actively participate in learning and obtain the engagement, support, and acceptance needed for intellectual growth and development. Presently, there has been a shift of the number of African Americans attending HBCUs to pursue advanced degrees as result of integration and increased competition from other institutions. Nevertheless, HBCUs still produce over 30% of bachelor degrees awarded out of 103 four-year colleges in this country.[21] Gray[22] noted that a large percentage of African American political leaders, scientists, engineers, lawyers, doctors, and doctorate recipients continue to graduate from HBCUs compared to other institutional types.

Factors Impacting Student Success

According to Patton and Bonner, "the HBCU has not only served as the exclusive avenue of access to higher education for African Americans with its promotion of a participatory ethos and an open door admissions policy, but it has also provided immeasurable benefits by way of student leadership potential and social development" (p. 18).[23] Johnson-Bailey, Valentine, Cervero, and Bowles pointed out that African Americans pursuing advanced degrees felt a sense of avoidance outside of the classroom from their White professors, as well as unintentional racism and social discomfort that caused them to miss out on research and teaching opportunities.[24] Kimbrough and Harper further detailed some of the negative experiences of African Americans while attending PWIs.[25] For instance, African American students expressed concerns about the lack of cultural awareness at their institutions. They reported that the faculty, staff, and student populations did not view them as full human beings with distinctive talents, virtues, interests, and problems. Similar to the undergraduate college experience, graduate and professional students also need to interact with peers and have faculty support for adequate academic development throughout the course of their matriculation. In general, the cultural climate at institutions of higher education greatly impacts retention and college graduation rates. According to the *Journal of Blacks in Higher Education*, institutions that have a nurturing environment have a great impact on student success.[26] Typically, African American graduate and professional students who attend HBCUs academically outperformed their African American counterparts who attend PWIs.[27] For the most part, their increased level of performance is a result of positive and supportive peer and faculty interaction.[28]

PEER INTERACTIONS

Swail, Redd, and Perna contended that satisfied and academically integrated African American students have well-established peer relations and few interfering social or academic problems.[29] Furthermore, these students tend to perceive the university as being nondiscriminatory, and they perform well in their courses. According to several academic researchers, college students spend a majority of their time with their peers;[30] therefore, peer influences significantly impact the lives and academic performance of college students. Moreover, peer cohesion among college students increases their chances of obtaining a college degree.[31] Astin further asserted that there is a strong link between positive peer interaction and college success.[32]

Peer influence among college students can be positive or negative. Singham indicated that peers can have a negative influence on educational aspirations.[33] Ogbu stated that academically gifted African American male students who disengage academically do so to gain group acceptance.[34] Thus, high-achieving African American males must learn to reshape their self-concept and balance peer relationships to accommodate their own academic development.[35] Specifically, the likelihood of college success increases with students who are able to navigate the campus climate despite incongruence in social values, norms, behaviors, and attitudes on campus.[36] Furthermore, research shows that participating in on-campus activities can foster peer cohesion.[37] For African American males, when compared to their White counterparts, campus involvement more often than not yielded positive effects on graduation rates.[38] In addition to on-campus activities, peer support plays an integral role in the process of students motivating students. African American students who engage in pre-college programs have demonstrated a positive relationship between peer interaction and academic achievement.[39] Still other sources of support have been noted to be important for African American college students.

FACULTY INTERACTIONS

African American students' interactions with faculty members are an essential element in their successful transition to the college environment. Students of color who are emotionally connected with faculty or staff members in the institutional environment have higher retention rates.[40] African American students often look to faculty to be mentors or to serve as role models throughout their college career. Palmer and Gasman found that models/mentors played a fundamental role in the academic development of African American male students.[41] Particularly, several of the participants in their study articulated that they admired their professors, and particularly those with whom they shared interests. Moreover, the participants expressed the view that having faculty members from their racial/ethnic background produced a greater sense of self-efficacy.[42] African American students who have faculty members who care for, support, and encourage them are more likely to report positive self-confidence in their academic performance.[43]

African American students who interact with faculty members who are African American tend to develop a stronger ability to cope academically with program rigor.[44] Frank contended that many African American students aspire to achieve the status of their African American mentors.[45] Thus, faculty who are mentors act as academic, social, and career guides for this student population. Grier-Reed, Madyum, and Buckley reported a correlation between social support and overall success and preservation in African American college students.[46] Demaris and Kritsonis consider faculty and student interactions to be one of the powerful predictors of student commitment and success.[47] Davis also emphasized the vitality of the student-faculty relationship for the academic development of African American students attending HBCUs.[48] Moreover, Davis noted that the type of interaction amongst student and faculty is what affects the student's academic performance. Faculty mentors can be inspirational to African American college students by motivating, encouraging, advising, and acting as role models.[49] According to Sutton, mentoring has the potential to decrease students' feelings of marginality, increase their sense of personal significance (that they "matter"), and provide important validation of belonging to the campus environment. Unfortunately, few research studies have examined the relationship between African American college students' achievement and the influence exerted by faculty members, if any, on their college success.[50] Future research studies should determine the role of faculty influence of motivation and encouragement as it pertains to African American college students. The next section will explain the methodology employed for this study.

Methodology

The researchers utilized ethnographic narrative case studies to extract themes from individual experiences. Ethnography is a qualitative methodology which entreats researchers to interpret phenomena from the perspective of individuals directly involved with or affected by phenomenal events, situations, or occurrences.[51] Ethnographic studies are built on the premise that conceptual, behavioral, and theoretical understanding is developed inductively, from the specific to the general.[52] Case studies using the ethnographic approach infer from three sources: 1) what people say; 2) the way they act; and 3) the artifacts they use.[53]

Participants for the study were contacted initially by email from among a population of ten individuals, known to the researchers, with earned graduate and professional degrees from HBCUs. Five individuals responded to the communication and agreed to participate in the interview protocol. The group consisted of three men and two women. Fletcher Thomas and Jaylon Reed earned juris doctorate degrees, while Conrad Johnson, Joyce Gayleston, and Lynn Davis earned doctor of philosophy degrees from HBCUs. It is important to note that pseudonyms have been used to protect the identity and privacy of the participants.

The interviews were conducted via email using a nine-question protocol. The open-ended questions focused on the decision to apply to and attend an HBCU, perceptions and misperceptions about HBCUs held by self and others, experiences at the HBCU and with respective staff, assessment of training provided, and benefits of degree pursuit at an HBCU. Participants were asked to respond to each question individually and as specifically as possible. Interview transcripts were examined for completion, quality, and connection to questions asked.

Analytic Technique

Responses were then analyzed for themes using an ideas grouping approach. Auerbach and Silverstein noted that the ideas grouping approach is an inductive research technique where narrative data are conceptually linked through the restriction of preconceived notions.[54] This tradition is informed by a modified grounded theory approach, where the purpose of the research is the generation of new/revised theory.[55] In particular, this analytic technique is most useful when little prior research exists on a given phenomenon. The ideas grouping approach, as articulated by Auerbach and Silverstein, employs several cyclical analytic steps.[56] First, statements or ideas are grouped together to create a master list of recurrent comments. Then, using a constant comparison method, these recurrent ideas are interrogated to determine the robustness of the identified theme. Recurrent ideas are then grouped together and linked conceptually to better understand relationships and processes. The result of this process is the expansion, elimination, and modification of recurrent ideas. This process results in the presentation of recurrent ideas, which, through this process, illustrates the most commonly articulated concepts portrayed through the participants' comments. The next section discusses the findings that resulted from this analytic process.

Findings

An advanced degree is a great accomplishment regardless of which type of institution attended. When asked how they had benefited academically, professionally, and personally, each of the participants noted that the aspects of relationship building and the levels of emotional connectedness provided for, fostered by, and maintained in their graduate and professional programs had been the most significant factors of all. The following themes emerged and may serve to explain the perceived respectability of HBCU graduate and professional programs and experiences in the lives of those who have successfully matriculated. We have organized the themes into the following areas: 1) students' decisions to apply to and attend an HBCU; 2) misperceptions and challenges associated with HBCU advanced degree programs; 3) assessment of HBCU quality; and 4) experiences with HBCU faculty.

Decisions to Apply to and Attend an HBCU

As with most students at any institution, for the participants of the present study, the decision to apply to and attend an HBCU rested heavily on the confluence of location, program of interest, cost, and the availability of funding. Most participants were accepted to a number of predominantly White institutions, many of which met these fundamental requirements. However, they were drawn by convenience and cost to pursue their studies at HBCUs.

Joyce Gayleston provided insight into the importance of convenience in selecting an institution. Like others, attending a college that had a close geographic proximity to their homes or work were integral selection considerations. For Joyce, the proximity to her work was a core selection factor.

> I was working at an HBCU so I enrolled in a graduate program [at that same institution] after completing a bachelor's degree on a part-time

basis. No. I did not apply to a non HBCU. . . . Convenience was one of the main deciding factors. Also I wanted to improve my chances at advancement in the job market.

For Conrad Johnson, attending an HBCU was a meld of several college-choice factors, primarily driven by the history of HBCUs and cost. However, Conrad was also drawn to the institutions for high-quality faculty members with extensive expertise in his field of study:

> I decided to attend an HBCU because of the historical significance of the institution. I attended all HBCUs from bachelor's to doctorate. In terms of graduate study, first for the master's and it was an opportunity to go for free. It was free because I received a Florida State University System fellowship. However, I was also motivated by the national reputation of Florida A&M as a whole as well as stellar faculty within the college of Arts and Sciences. They were nationally renowned, were published researchers. For my PhD, I attended Morgan State. I selected that institution due to costs and more importantly, because of the faculty . . . they had all served as college presidents and accreditation giants, and that was my goal, to study under giants.

With respect to the importance of cost, these findings were echoed by Fletcher Thomas, who cited "cost and potential scholarships" as his primary college-choice factors. These factors also served as a driving force in college selection for other students. For instance, Jaylon Reed cited cost considerations as one reason for attending an HBCU, but also noted he attended an HBCU to benefit from a supportive learning environment. He stated, "There were many factors. The most important factor was the environment. I needed one conducive to learning and inviting. Other factors included location, cost, and history."

Based on the responses of the participants, for some participants, the ultimate decision to attend an HBCU rested on more abstract and less tangible factors. Perceptions of the availability of encouragement and support, the opportunity for fair admission based on a holistic view of the student (i.e., scores, grades, research interests), and the history of the institution were also noted as important factors in the final decision, even despite fears and reservations. Lynn Davis stated:

> I received my undergraduate and first master's degree[s] from an HBCU and my second master's degree from a [PWI]. I really wanted to remain at the [PWI] to attain my doctoral degree . . . I felt that the department chair and faculty believed that I would not complete the doctoral program successfully . . . I decided to apply to an HBCU where I could interact with people of my own skin color and [be] given a fair chance. . . .

Lynn's comments complement those from Jaylon Reed and Conrad Johnson, who noted that they wanted to attend HBCUs for a supportive learning environment and for the historical significance of the institution. Thus, while college selection for HBCU students is based upon more common factors such as location, faculty quality, and convenience, the college-choice process was also heavily influenced by the desire to attend an HBCU for their advanced degree.

Misperceptions and Challenges Associated With HBCU Graduate Programs

Students based their decisions to attend graduate and professional programs on a number of factors, and many of their perceptions and the perceptions of others are influenced by society, both negatively and positively. Participants indicated being concerned, at least initially, that attending an HBCU for graduate and professional education deprived them of both cultural and experiential diversity, as well as opportunities for engagement both during the course of study and after graduating. Jaylon Reed indicated that for both potential students and their future colleagues, "the overall perception of African Americans . . . often clouds the true quality of an HBCU education." He noted that many negative perceptions about the HBCU experience were erroneous. One perception is that HBCUs are not diverse; he noted that "my law school was the most diverse law school in the nation for two years. In fact, the law school was 54% Caucasian. I think this swing in numbers and the interest of those individuals to protect the values and perception of their own education is aiding to bring this stigma to rapidly increasing halt."

All participants were aware of misperceptions and stereotypes about the quality of education at HBCUs. Fletcher Thomas noted concerns about the perceptions of HBCU quality. He stated, "At HBCUs, the opportunities for high-level work and advancement are limited because most business decision makers lack the foresight or courage to hire and/or retain HBCU graduates." Conrad Johnson also echoed the comments from his fellow HBCU graduates, noting that stereotypes existed about the quality of HBCU graduates. Further reinforcing this point, Joyce, like her counterparts, stated, "People assume that the programs at HBCUs are not good programs. Professors are not good teachers and ill prepared. People also assume that a 'standard' curriculum is not taught at an HBCU." In all, most participants noted that such perceptions were ill-informed stereotypes, not indicative of the quality of education received at an HBCU.

That being said, this is not to say that HBCU graduates do not face challenges in their educational experiences. One participant, Lynn Davis pointed out her discontent with the lack of resources available on the campus of the HBCU. Davis indicated that the necessity of utilizing the library consortium and contacts at other universities to secure research materials was wildly different from her research experience while attending a PWI. In essence, library holdings were limited, requiring students to rely upon interlibrary loans from other institutions. She noted that the time delay associated with such systems can inhibit creativity, momentum, and can lead to frustration.

Assessment of HBCU Quality

While recognizing the negative perceptions employers held about HBCU quality, Fletcher noted that such perceptions would erode: "those individuals who believe HBCUs do not produce high caliber students will become the minority as long as HBCUs maintain change at competent programming by way of funding and private and legislative financial support." Further, he noted that "many individuals who [think negatively about HBCUs] have never stepped on the campus of an HBCU or worked side-by-side with an HBCU graduate. HBCUs educate not only African American students, but students from all over the globe. In the 21st Century, many progressive business leaders understand the need for diversity."

Fletcher stated that employers who were willing to take on HBCU graduates benefited from well-educated individuals with a strong work ethic, experience in working with diverse communities, and fresh thinking. He contends that employers and colleagues that he has encountered in his career are "impressed with HBCU graduate programs mainly through [the] experience of working with an HBCU graduate and through conversations in which they gain more insight about the similarities between [PWI] and HBCU programs."

Conrad Johnson also noted that perceptions of HBCUs challenged graduates during the job search process, but that prospective employers were usually impressed with the quality of HBCU graduates once they had an opportunity to interact with them. Similar to Fletcher, he attributed the excellence of HBCU graduates to a strong work ethic, noting that they had to work harder, longer, and with higher quality than others in the workplace, but that it made them better hires.

When Joyce was asked about the quality of education she received, she commented, "Very well. I have been able to compete with others who are graduates of schools such as Penn State and University of Texas." Comparing the quality of education to highly selective PWIs was a common comparison made by the respondents; Conrad also compared his degree from an HBCU to other institutions such as Arizona State University and University of Maryland.

Lynn Davis contends that it was the training she received in her master's program that truly prepared her for her intended career path, but credits portions of her academic and professional success in her doctoral program and her decision to attend an HBCU. She stated, "I believe that HBCUs produce an excellent quality of students who are able to compete with students from [PWIs]." She explained that this quality is a result of an academic "environment that allows African American students to establish their identities, expose them to African American culture, and provide a foundation that will allow African American graduates to make informed decisions in a world that is still filled with racism and prejudice."

In all, interviewees agreed that attending an HBCU for their graduate and professional training was a rich and unique experience. For instance, Fletcher Thomas credited his training experience with preparing him for "thinking beyond societal norms." He contends that his training "helped me understand that breaking barriers . . . [is the] most important step in succeeding." Jaylon Reed credits his experience with providing him "many opportunities for exposure" that have served him very well in his career. Overall, respondents' perceptions of the HBCU graduate and professional student experience illustrated a high regard for HBCU academic quality.

Experiences With HBCU Faculty

Respondents all agreed that the faculty they encountered during their graduate and professional studies were competent, caring, compassionate, and invested in their students both professionally and personally. Jaylon Reed had postsecondary experiences at both White institutions and HBCUs. He provided a comparison of the interactions with faculty, noting that at the White institution, "the academic venture did not extend beyond the campus or the classroom." In this experience, he noted that the only exception was limited to one African American professor who worked at the PWI but had a commitment to serving the needs and wellbeing of African American students. Jaylon noted a marked difference between faculty-student interactions at HBCUs and PWIs. In terms of his HBCU experience, he stated:

> My experience was amazing. As expected they [faculty members] cared. They were available beyond office hours and often invited us into their homes for additional interactions. They seemed to know that my future mattered and they passionately accepted their role in the development of that process.

Joyce noted that professors took time out to establish relationships with students, stating, "I knew most of the professors." Similarly, Conrad Johnson also extolled the accessibility of faculty members at his HBCU. He noted that he had many high quality relationships with faculty. In this light, he stated the following:

> The interactions with faculty were excellent because they came with practical knowledge as having served as college presidents. They were very challenging, they challenged us to produce scholarship, be relevant thinkers, but really, they challenged us to be like, you might not be at University of Maryland or Arizona State, but you can produce quality

work. There were a lot of engagements outside of the classroom, we had time to sit down and engage with them outside of the classroom. To meet at Starbucks, to laugh, clown, go through papers, I don't think I would have had that in another program.

Such comments were common among participants. For instance, while Fletcher praised HBCU faculty as being "competent and compassionate," Gayle stated that her interactions with faculty were "Very positive. Very good relationships. Very good instruction and preparation in the degree program." In all, participants noted that they were pleased with the commitment of HBCU faculty. Their comments illustrate that these faculty members are dedicated to their respective fields of study, to high-quality interactions with students, to encouraging students to reach their highest potential, and to communicating to them that they "mattered."

Discussion

Overall, findings from this study contribute important knowledge to the African American graduate and professional student experience at HBCUs. This study showed that students attend HBCUs for a variety of reasons, including location, cost, and convenience. However, beyond these common rationales for college choice, respondents also indicated that they attended HBCUs as a result of their historical contribution to African American communities as well as the supportive environment fostered within these institutions. This finding is understandable, given that HBCUs have long served African American students when other institutions of higher education refused to do so. Further, these institutions are known for providing a college experience typified by a supportive environment, diversity, and dedication to serving the needs of the African American community.[57]

Findings also indicate that, while students often select HBCUs for graduate and professional school, because they are HBCUs they are aware of challenges associated with those decisions. Respondents noted that there are perceptions among employers that HBCU programs and faculty are not of quality. In particular, many employers also perceive that HBCUs do not teach the "standard" curriculum. These erroneous perceptions of HBCUs are obstacles to graduates in the workforce who, when vying for jobs, are often second-guessed and underestimated. It is possible that some of the negative perceptions of HBCUs are the byproduct of resourcing issues faced by these institutions. For example, one participant did note that obtaining access to library materials was more difficult, as students were reliant upon interlibrary systems to attain resources from other institutions.

That being said, respondents overwhelmingly lauded the quality of education they received at HBCUs. They noted that the programs were academically rigorous, that faculty members had exemplary qualifications, and that the environment was affirming. Specifically, students noted that HBCUs instilled within their graduates a strong work ethic that served them well in the workforce, enabling them to overcome misperceptions of HBCUs and to excel among their co-workers. Several respondents attributed this circumstance to faculty members who were encouraging and maintained high standards for excellence. In doing so, faculty members invested in relationships with students, taking extensive time inside and outside of class to talk with students, mentor them, discuss their future goals, and to illustrate that they "matter." Research from Sutton illustrated the multiplicity of benefits derived from faculty who communicate that students have personal significance (that they "matter").[58] Sutton noted that this increases their sense of belonging in the institution, leads to enhanced validation, and increases their overall satisfaction with their academic experience.[59] Indeed, prior research has shown that faculty members who invest in such relationships better prepare students by providing them with an enhanced confidence in their abilities[60] and greater levels of academic preparation.[61]

Conclusion

The Historically Black College and University has long been heralded for the production of African American baccalaureates. Despite the limited number of institutions offering post-graduate educational and professional opportunities, a significant number of African American advanced degree earners have matriculated through HBCUs. As such, research specifically focused on HBCU post-graduate students and degree earners is imperative to understanding the usefulness, utility, and necessity of HBCUs in today's ever-changing workforce climate. It is important to give voice to these institutions, these programs, and the students who study there. It is equally important to allow the students to speak for themselves. Hearing the voices of individuals who have matriculated and graduated from HBCUs informs the fields of education, workforce development, leadership, and psychology as well as policymakers, legislators, and governing entities about the impact of these institutions. Furthermore, such research highlights the programmatic needs and systematic inequalities faced by HBCUs and subsequently suffered by the students who study there. Finally, studies such as this highlight the existence of stereotypes and misperceptions applied to HBCUs and their students both during matriculation and after receiving their degrees.

Notes

1 Allen et al. 2007; Gasman et al. 2010; Palmer and Gasman 2008.
2 U.S. Department of Education 1993
3 Roebuck and Murty 1993; Palmer and Wood 2012
4 Palmer, Hilton, and Fountaine 2012
5 Palmer, Hilton, Fountaine 2012

6 Digest of Education Statistics 2010a
7 Digest of Education Statistics 2010b
8 Digest of Education Statistics 2010c
9 Roebuck and Murty 1993, p. 3
10 Roebuck and Murty 1993
11 Swygert 2004
12 *Sweatt v. Painter* 1950; *Hawkins v. Board of Control* 1950
13 Allen and Jewell 2002
14 Swygert 2004
15 Swygert 2004
16 Roebuck and Murty 1993
17 Harper et al. 2004
18 Harper 2010
19 Kim 2002
20 Department of Education 2008
21 Kim and Conrad 2006
22 Gray 1998
23 Patton and Bonner 2001
24 Johnson-Bailey et al. 2009
25 Kimbrough and Harper 2006
26 *Journal of Blacks in Higher Education* 2009
27 Hubbard 2006
28 Hubbard 2006
29 Swail, Redd, and Perna 2003
30 Gibson 2005; Horvat and Lewis 2003; Hubbard 2005; Newman and Newman 1999; Somers, Owens, and Piliawsky 2008
31 Astin 1993
32 Astin 1993
33 Singham 2003
34 Ogbu 2003
35 Barclay 2001; Brookins 2000
36 Astin 1993
37 Pascarella and Terenzini 1991
38 Pascarella 1985
39 Hubbard 2005; Palmer and Gasman 2008
40 Grier-Reed, Madyun, and Buckley 2008
41 Palmer and Gasman 2008
42 Palmer and Gasman 2008
43 Russell and Atwater 2005
44 Frank 2003
45 Frank 2003
46 Grier-Reed, Madyum, and Buckle 2008
47 Demaris and Kritsonis 2006
48 Davis 1994
49 Allen and Smith 2008
50 Sutton 2006; Moore, Ford, and Milner 2005
51 Dobbert 1982
52 Fetterman 1989
53 Spradley 1979
54 Auerbach and Silverstein 2003
55 Charmaz 2000; Glasper 1998
56 Auerbach and Silverstein 2003
57 Kim 2002

58 Sutton 2006
59 Sutton 2006
60 Palmer and Gasman 2008
61 Davis 1994

Bibliography

Allen, Walter R., and Joseph O. Jewel. "A backward glance forward: Past, present, future perspectives on historically black colleges and universities." *The Review of Higher Education*, 25 no. 3 (2002): 241–261.

Allen, Walter R., Joseph O. Jewell, Kim A. Griffin, and Da'Sha S. Wolf. "Historically black colleges and universities: Honoring the past, engaging the present, touching the future." *Journal of Negro Education*, 76 no. 3 (2007): 263–280.

Allen, Janine, and Cathleen Smith, C. "Importance of, responsibility for, and satisfaction with academic advising: A faculty perspective." *Journal of College Student Development*, 49 no. 5 (2008): 397–411.

Astin, Alexander W. *What matters in college*. San Francisco: Jossey-Bass, 1993.

Auerbach, Carl F., and Louise B. Silverstein. *An introduction to coding and analysis: Qualitative data*. New York: New York University Press, 2003.

Barclay, Janice A. High-achieving African-American high school students account for their access to and success in academically advanced program. Unpublished analytical paper, Harvard Graduate School of Education, Cambridge, MA, 2001.

Brookins, Sonja. Revisiting and increasing the talented tenth: Examining the experiences and performance of high-achieving and potentially high-achieving African American Students. Cambridge, MA: Harvard Graduate School of Education, 2000.

Charmaz, Kathy. "Grounded theory: Objectivist and constructivist methods." In Norman K. Denzin, and Yvonna S. Lincoln (Eds.), *Handbook of qualitative research* (2nd ed., pp. 509–536). Thousand Oaks, CA: Sage, 2000.

Davis, James E. "College in black and white: Campus environment and academic achievement of African American males." *Journal of Negro Education*, 63 (1994): 620–633.

Demaris, Michalyn C., and William A. Kritsonis. "A philosophical approach to minority student persistence on a historically black college and university campus." *Doctoral FORUM*, 3 no. 1 (2006): 1–6.

Digest of Education Statistics. Table 255. Selected statistics on degree-granting historically Black colleges and universities, by control and level of institution: Selected years, 1990 through 2010. Washington, DC: National Center for Education Statistics, 2010a.

Digest of Education Statistics. Table 304. Master's degrees conferred by degree-granting institutions, by sex, race/ethnicity, and field of study: 2009–10. Washington, DC: National Center for Education Statistics, 2010b.

Digest of Education Statistics. Table 306. Doctor's degrees conferred by degree-granting institutions, by race/ethnicity and sex of student: Selected years, 1976–77 through 2009–2010. Washington, DC: National Center for Education Statistics, 2010c.

Dobbert, Marion L. Ethnographic research: Theory and application for modern schools and societies. New York: Praeger Publishers, 1982.

Fetterman, David M. *Ethnography step by step*. Newberry Park, CA: Sage, 1989.

Frank, Anna Marie. "If they come, we should listen: African American education majors perceptions of a predominantly White university experience." *Teaching and Teacher Education*, 19 (2003): 697–717.

Gasman, Marybeth B., Valerie Lundy-Wagner, Tafaya Ransom, and Nelson Bowman III. *Unearthing promise and potential: Our nation's historically Black colleges and universities* (ASHE Higher Education Report). San Francisco: Jossey-Bass, 2010.

Gibson, Margaret A. "Promoting academic engagement among minority youth: Implications from Ogbu's Shaker Heights ethnography." *International Journal of Qualitative Studies in Education*, 18 (2005): 581–603.

Glaser, Barney. *Doing grounded theory: Issues and discussions*. Mill Valley, CA: Sociology Press, 1998.

Gray, William. "Leader lauds role of black colleges." *Boston Globe*, 1998.

Grier-Reed, Tabitha, Na'im H. Madyun, and Christopher G. Buckley. "Low black student retention on a predominantly White campus: Two faculty respond with the African American student network." *Journal of College Student Development*, 49 (2008): 476–485.

Harper, Shaun R. *The 2010 report on Black male students in public higher education*. Washington, DC: Congressional Black Caucus Foundation.

Harper, Shaun R., Robert M. Carini, Brian K. Bridges, and John C. Hayek. "Gender differences in student engagement among African American undergraduates at historically black colleges and universities." *Journal of College Student Development*, 45 no. 3 (2004): 271–284.

Hawkins v. Board of Control, 350 U.S. 413, 1950.

Horvat, Erin, and Kristine Lewis, K. "Reassessing the burden of 'acting white': The importance of peer groups in managing academic success." *Journal of Educational Sociology*, 76 (2003): 265–280.

Hubbard, Dolan. "The color of our classroom, the color of our future." *Academe*, 92 no. 6 (2006): 27–29.

Hubbard, Lea. "The role of gender in academic achievement." *Journal of Qualitative Studies in Education*, 18 (2005): 605–623.

Johnson-Bailey, Juanita, Thomas Valentine, Ronald Cervero, and Tuere Bowles. "Rooted in the soil: The social experiences of black graduate students at a Southern Research University." *The Journal of Higher Education*, 80 no. 2 (2009): 178–203.

Journal of Blacks in Higher Education. "Vital Statistics." 63 (2009). Retrieved from www.jbhe.com/book_rev/index.html

Kim, Mikyong M. "Historically black vs. white institutions: Academic development among black students." *The Review of Higher Education*, 25 no. 4 (2002): 385–407.

Kim, Mikyong, and Clifton Conrad. "The impact of historically black colleges and universities on the academic success of African American students." *Research in Higher Education*, 47 (2006): 399–427.

Kimbrough, Walter M., and Shaun R. Harper. "African American men at historically black colleges and universities: Different environments, similar challenges." In Michael J. Cuyjet (Ed.), *African American men in college* (pp. 189–209). San Francisco: Jossey-Bass, 2006.

Moore, James L III, Donna Y. Ford, and H. Richard Milner. "Recruiting is not enough: Retaining African-American students in gifted education." *Gifted Child Quarterly*, 49 (2005): 49–65.

Newman, Phillip, and Barbara Newman. "What does it take to have a positive impact on minority students' college retention?" *Adolescence*, 34 no. 135 (1999): 483–492.

Ogbu, John. Black students in an affluent suburb: A study of academic disengagement. Mahwah, NJ: Erlbaum, 2003.

Palmer, Robert T., and J. Luke Wood. "Setting the foundation for black men in colleges: Implications for historically black colleges and universities and beyond." In Robert T. Palmer, and J. Luke Wood (Eds.), *Black men in college: Implications for HBCUs and beyond* (pp. 1–17). New York: Routledge, 2012.

Palmer, Robert T., and Marybeth Gasman. "'It takes a village to raise a child': The role of social capital in promoting academic success for African American men at a black college." *Journal of College Student Development*, 49 no. 1 (2008): 52–70.

Palmer, Robert T., Adriel A. Hilton, and Tiffany P. Fountaine. Black graduate education at historically Black colleges and universities: Trends, experiences, and outcomes. Charlotte, NC: Information Age, 2012.

Pascarella, Ernest, and Patrick Terenzini. *How college affects students*. San Francisco: Jossey Bass, 1991.

Pascarella, Ernest. "Racial differences in factors associated with bachelor's degree completion: A nine-year follow-up." *Research in Higher Education*, 23 (1985): 351–373.

Patton, Lori, and Fred A. Bonner, II. "Advising the historically black Greek letter organization: A reason for angst of euphoria." *NASAP Journal*, 4 no. 1 (2001): 17–30.

Roebuck, Julian B., and Komanduri Murty. Historically Black colleges and universities: Their place in American higher education. Westport, CT: Praeger, 1993.

Russell, Melody, and Mary Atwater. "Traveling the road to success: A discourse on persistence throughout the science pipeline with African American students at a predominantly white university." *Journal of Research in Science Teaching*, 42 (2005): 691–623.

Sanchez-Leguelinel, Caridad. "Supporting slumping sophomores: Programmatic peer initiatives designed to enhance retention in the crucial second year of college." *College Student Journal*, 42 no. 2 (2008): 637–646.

Singham, Mano. "The achievement gap: Myths and reality." *Phi Delta Kappa*, 84 no. 8 (2003): 589.

Somers, Cheryl, Delila Owens, and Monte Piliawsky. "Individual and social factors related to urban African American adolescents' school performance." *The High School Journal*, 91 no. 3 (2008): 1–11.

Spradley, James P. *The ethnographic interview*. New York/Washington, DC: Bolt, Rinehart, and Winston. Summit, 1979.

Sutton, E. Michael. "Developmental mentoring of African American college men." In Michael Cuyjet, M. J. (Ed.), *African American men in college* (pp. 95–111). San Francisco: Jossey-Bass, 2006.

Swail, Watson S., Kenmeth Redd, and Laura Perna. "Retaining minority students in higher education: A framework for success." In *ASHE-ERIC Higher Education Report*. San Francisco: Jossey-Bass, 80 no. 2 (2003): 1–200.

Sweatt v. Painter, 339 U.S. 629. Cornell University Law School, Legal Information Institute Website, 1950. Retrieved from www.law.cornell.edu/supct/html/historics/USSC_CR_0339_0629_ZS.html

Swygert, H. Patrick. "The accomplishments and challenges of historically black colleges and universities." 2nd Annual African American Leadership, 2004.

U.S. Department of Education. *National excellence: A case for developing America's talent*. Washington, DC: Office of Educational Research and Improvement, 1993.

U.S. Department of Education. *Jacob K. Javits Gifted and Talented Students Education Program*, 2008. Retrieved from www.ed.gov/programs/javits/ index.html

United States v. Fordice, 505 U.S. 717, 1992.

10 In Excess of Legitimate Need
Title III and the Development of Graduate and Online Degree Programs at Morgan State University

Maurice C. Taylor

Introduction

Morgan State University (Morgan) celebrates its sesquicentennial in 2017, marking the institution's founding in 1867 by the Baltimore Conference of the Methodist Episcopal Church as the Centenary Biblical Institute. In 1890 the name was changed to Morgan College, and with a $50,000 grant from Andrew Carnegie, Morgan was able to retire its outstanding debts and purchase the Ivy Mill property and build its first academic facility, Carnegie Hall. The State of Maryland purchased Morgan College in 1939. Morgan achieved university status when, in 1975, the State Legislature first authorized Morgan to offer doctoral degrees. Subsequent legislation in 1988 further strengthened Morgan's authority to offer advanced programs and designated the campus as Maryland's Public Urban University.

Morgan is now classified by the Carnegie Foundation as a Doctoral University: Moderate Research Activity (R3) and enrolls more than 7,500 students actively pursuing the university's comprehensive array of undergraduate and graduate degree programs, including 16 doctoral programs and 14 online degree and post-baccalaureate certificate (PBC) programs. Much of Morgan's history with the State of Maryland, including the state's academic coordinating body, the Maryland Higher Education Commission (MHEC), can be summarized in the words of the White Laurelville residents opposed to Morgan's use of its newly acquired Ivy Mill property in 1917 as a "negro college" who complained in district court that "that a tract of seventy acres were in excess of the legitimate need of the respondent."[1]

Opposition to and neglect of Morgan and the other three "negro colleges" by the state are grounded in the enduring history of both de jure and de facto segregation throughout Maryland. The pernicious nature of segregation in Baltimore, particularly as it impacts the history and growth of Morgan, is well documented. Pietila[2] notes, for example, that former Morgan President, John Oakley Spencer, first sought to move the College in 1913 to Mount Washington but faced opposition from the Mount Washington Improvement Association and from the Mayor of Baltimore, James H. Preston. Mayor Preston proposed that in order to expand, Morgan should "take over the buildings of a reform school for delinquent black boys in southwest Baltimore." Morgan's effort to purchase its current site in 1917 was met first with an offer of a bribe to President Spencer and the filing of two lawsuits. When these efforts failed, more than 50 opponents, led by Edgar Allan Poe, the poet's grandnephew, chartered a special train to a hearing in Annapolis seeking to abrogate Morgan's charter through legislative action.[3]

A recent report by the Corporation for Enterprise Development (CFED)[4] notes that policymakers at all levels have influenced current economic and racial disparities in Baltimore. For example, in 1911, Mayor J. Barry Mahool and the City Council passed the country's first racially restrictive zoning law prohibiting members of one racial group from buying a house in a block dominated by another race.[5] The CFED reports[6] that Baltimore also formed a Committee on Segregation to enforce racially restrictive covenants, which prohibited the sale of homes to Black buyers. At the federal level, lawmakers developed a system of "Redlining" to prevent Black families from financing home purchases. By outlining Black neighborhoods in red on government maps, entire neighborhoods were considered poor credit risks and thus were not eligible for federally insured mortgages.

The outcome of these race based segregation policies has been described as Baltimore's "Negro Archipelago."[7] In 2015, former Baltimore Police Commissioner, Anthony W. Batts, told a White House panel that in Baltimore "I'm dealing with 1950s-level black-and-white racism. . . . Everything's either black or everything's white, and we're dealing with that as a community."[8] It is in this historical context and in the current racial climate that Morgan State University has had to make do.

Specifically, it is clear that the development of Morgan as a doctoral institution and the development of its inventory of online programs have occurred without sufficient support from the state, including MHEC officials, who consistently responded to the university's request for comparable funding as if any funds earmarked for Morgan were "in excess of legitimate need." The focus of this essay is how, in the absence of state support, Morgan was able to utilize federal funds, specifically the Department of Education's Title III Program, to develop its graduate degree programs and its online degree programs. To be clear, the development of Morgan's graduate programs, in particular its inventory of doctoral programs, as well as its online degree and post-baccalaureate certificate (PBC) programs, has occurred in the absence of financial support from the State of Maryland.

In Excess of Legitimate Need

Much like the complaints in *Diggs*, governors, the legislature, and officials at MHEC have regarded any amount of funding for Maryland's four public HBCUs as in excess of the institutions' legitimate needs. In fact, several commissions and reports authorized by the state documented a history of neglect by Maryland in funding for its HBCUs. A 1937 Soper Commission, for example, observed: "It is thus clear that the white population has had the advantage of generous state support for its higher education many years in advance of the Negro population. The contrast between the amounts of money received by the two racial groups would show, if possible of computation, an enormous differential in favor of the white race."

A decade later, the 1947 Marbury Commission conducted a comprehensive review of higher education in Maryland and found that none of the state's HBCUs were equal in quality to the corresponding institution maintained for the White population and that while Maryland maintained "extensive facilities for the graduate and professional education of white persons, there [was] no provision for the equivalent training of Negroes in the state." The 1950 Weglein Commission observed that "The continuous uphill struggle on the part of the Negro colleges to secure facilities on a par with white institutions is a factor which cannot be overlooked in a survey of this kind."

Subsequent to its notification in March of 1969 by what is now the Office for Civil Rights (OCR) at the Department of Education that Maryland was one of ten states operating a racially segregated system of education in violation of Title VI of the Civil Rights Act, the State drafted desegregation plans in 1974, 1985, and 2000, none of which were accepted by the Department of Education as having met the standards for dismantling Maryland's formally de jure dual system of higher education. In the latest (2000) Partnership Agreement between the State of Maryland and the US Department of Education Office of Civil Rights (OCR), among the state's nine commitments[9] were promises to avoid Unnecessary Program Duplication and Expansion of Mission and Program Uniqueness and Institutional Identity at the HBCUs and funding to enhancing Maryland's Historically Black Colleges and Universities.

Specifically, in this last Partnership Agreement, the state promised to provide enhanced operational funding to Bowie, Coppin, Morgan, and UMES consistent with the mix and degree level of academic programs, support for the development of research infrastructure, and support consistent with the academic profile of students; lower student-faculty ratios appropriate to support their missions; the expanse, functionality, and architectural quality of physical facilities; the appearance, attractiveness, and ambiance of the campus and surrounding public infrastructure, including roads, lighting, and public transportation; and funding to support students' quality of campus life.

In 2010, the Coalition for Equity and Excellence in Maryland Higher Education, Inc. (the Coalition), comprised of current students and alumni of the four public HBCUs in Maryland, as well as high school students who have expressed a desire to attend HBCUs in the future, sued MHEC seeking equitable relief to require the State of Maryland to honor its obligations to its Historically Black Colleges and Universities as required by federal statutes[10] and the United States constitution.[11] Specifically, the Coalition sought enforcement of the terms of the 2000 Partnership Agreement between Maryland and the United States Department of Education Office of Civil Rights (OCR).

Although acknowledging that there was "no basis to hold Maryland legally liable for any failure to provide such additional funding to the HBIs", in her 2013 ruling,[12] United States District Judge Catherine C. Blake found,

> "On the other hand, unnecessary duplication of academic programs at HBIs and non-HBIs 'was part and parcel of the prior dual system of higher education—the whole notion of 'separate but equal' required duplicative programs in two sets of schools—and . . . present unnecessary duplication is a continuation of that practice.'"[13]

Judge Blake observed that in Maryland's 2000 Partnership Agreement with the Office of Civil Rights, Maryland committed to developing unique, high-demand academic programs at the HBCUs and to avoid further unnecessary program duplication. Unfortunately, the state did not follow through on this commitment, and White enrollment at HBCUs only continued to decline following the Partnership Agreement, such that HBCU racial identifiability has continued to increase.[14]

The state refused to accept any culpability for allowing degree programs initially approved for Morgan, Bowie, Coppin, and UMES to be awarded subsequently to Maryland's traditionally White institutions (TWIs). A statement released by the office of (former) Governor Martin O'Malley following Judge Blake's ruling said: "[W]e are proud of the multitude of excellent academic programs that exist throughout the state, and we respectfully disagree with the court's conclusions regarding duplication."[15]

In summary, in its 2000 Partnership Agreement, the state again committed to enhancing operational funds for HBCUs. Frustrated with the failure of the state to keep that and the other eight promises made in the 2000 Partnership Agreement, a Coalition of HBCU alumni, and current and future students, sued MHEC in federal district court. Deciding that while the state's current funding formula(e) and practices could not be traced to the past de jure dual segregated system of higher education in Maryland, the current practice by MHEC of allowing traditionally White institutions to duplicate unique academic programs first offered by HBCUs is "part and parcel" of the continuation of "the whole notion of separate but equal."

Notwithstanding Judge Blake's failure to find a basis to hold Maryland legally liable for providing "additional funding" to its HBCUs, her finding of program duplication holds significant financial implications for the state. Academic degree programs, in particular doctoral programs, require financial support in the form of facilities, faculties, stipends, equipment, and supplies. In some instances, additional funding was provided to the state's TWIs to support degree programs that were duplications of academic programs awarded to the HBCUs. The remedy for duplication of HBCU degree programs by TWIs will require Maryland to provide the additional funding necessary to support an inventory of new and unique degree programs for the state's four public HBCUs that is comparable to those now offered at the TWIs.

Strengthening HBCUs—Title III Programs

Numerous reports commissioned by the State of Maryland document its long history of neglect in funding its HBCUs. To secure the additional funding needed to expand its academic program and degree offerings, particularly the number of graduate and online degrees, Morgan secured federal funds through the Strengthening Historically Black Colleges and Universities Program.[16] As defined by section 322(a) of the Higher Education Act of 1965, as amended (HEA), an HBCU is an institution established prior to 1964, whose principal mission was, and is, the education of Black Americans, and that is accredited by a nationally recognized accrediting agency or association.[17] One hundred and seven HBCUs are identified under this definition and are included in the White House Initiative on Historically Black Colleges and Universities.[18]

In establishing this program, Congress acknowledged that states and the Federal Government have discriminated in the allocation of land and financial resources to support Black public institutions under the Morrill Act of 1862 [7 U.S.C. 301 et seq.] and its progeny, and against public and private Black colleges and universities in the award of Federal grants and contracts.[19] Among the remedies provided by Congress for discrimination against Black colleges and universities by the states and the federal government in the allocation of land, financial resources, and grants and contracts are: Title III Part A, the Strengthening Historically Black Colleges and Universities Program, and Title III Part B, the Strengthening Historically Black Graduate Institutions (HBGIs) Program.

Part A of Title III provides financial assistance, i.e., Title III funds, to HBCUs to establish or strengthen their physical plants, financial management, academic resources, and endowment-building capacity. In general, Title III funds, a maximum of $1 million for up to five years, may be awarded to qualifying HBCUs to establish or strengthen the physical plants, financial management, academic resources, and endowments.[20]

Part B of Title III[21] allows for grants, a maximum of $1 million over 5 years, to be awarded to a limited number of HBCU postgraduate institutions determined by the US Secretary of Education to be making a substantial contribution to the legal, medical, dental, veterinary, or other graduate education opportunities in mathematics, engineering, or the physical or natural sciences for Black Americans. A "qualified graduate program" at an HBCU is one that provides a program of instruction in law or in the physical or natural sciences, engineering, mathematics, psychometrics, or

146 Maurice C. Taylor

other scientific discipline in which African Americans are underrepresented and has students enrolled in such program at the time of application for a grant.[22] Part B allows for HBCUs to use not more than 10% of the Title HBGI funds for the development of a new qualified graduate program. Morgan is just one of 16 HBGIs qualified to receive federal funds under Part B of Title III.[23]

Morgan offered its first master's degrees in education in 1964 and was granted university status in 1975 but received no funding to support the establishment of doctoral programs nor any funding to provide scholarships or stipends for graduate students. Morgan's first doctorate, Urban Educational Leadership, was approved by the state coordinating board in 1979. It would be another 15 years, i.e., 1994, before Morgan was approved to offer its next two doctorates in Engineering and History.[24] Following the funding initiatives outlined in Part B of Title III, Morgan developed doctoral programs in Bio- Environmental Sciences (PhD), Business Administration (PhD), Engineering (D.Eng.), Community College Leadership Program (Ed.D.), Industrial and Computation Mathematics (PhD), Mathematics Education (Ed.D.), Psychometrics (PhD), Public Health (Dr. P.H.),[25] Science Education (Ed.D.), and Social Work (PhD). In many instances, The Title III Part B HBGI grant allowed Morgan to provided stipends for graduate students in a number of these doctoral programs.

The additional doctoral programs resulted in (a) a significant increase in enrollment at Morgan; and (b) a change in Morgan's Carnegie classification from Master's Comprehensive University to Doctoral Research University (DRU). Figure 10.1 reflects graduate enrollment at Morgan over the past 15 years. Until about 2000, 520 students were enrolled across five doctoral programs, including Business Administration (PhD), English (PhD),

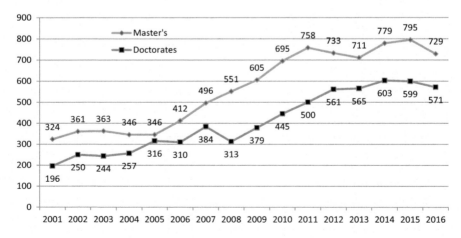

Figure 10.1 Enrollment for Graduate School from 2001 to 2016

Engineering (D.Eng.), History (PhD), and Urban Educational Leadership (Ed.D.). With funding from Part B of the Title III program, the addition of ten more doctoral programs led to an increase in enrollment from 520 in 2001 to 1,327 graduate students in 2016.[26]

In summary, in the absence of state support, Morgan was able to secure Title III Part B federal funds to support its increase in doctoral programs and the ensuing growth in graduate enrollment. Morgan qualified for the Title III Part B funds because it offered or developed a program of instruction in the physical or natural sciences, Engineering, Mathematics, or other scientific disciplines in which African Americans are underrepresented.[27]

Title III and Morgan Online

In 2009, the only online program approved for Morgan by MHEC was the post-baccalaureate certificate (PBC) in Psychometrics. Morgan was successful in securing a five-year Part A Strengthening Historically Black Colleges and Universities grant entitled Title III: Building, Supporting and Maintaining Morgan Online—Accessible, Flexible & Interconnected Strategies for Excellence in Education. The objectives for the initial five-year Title III grant (i.e., 2010–2015), were:

- increase the number of trained faculty offering online courses;
- increase the number of online courses being offered; and,
- increase the number of students enrolled in online courses.

Title III funds supported financial incentives for faculty to be trained in Quality Matters pedagogy for developing and teaching online courses. During the term of the Title III grant, 147 faculty members were trained to develop and teach online courses, and the number of courses offered to students increased from 87 to 194. Figure 10.2 represents student enrollment in online courses from 2008 to 2015.[28]

Figure 10.2 reveals that prior to receipt of the Title III grant in 2010, less than 300 students were enrolled in online courses and there were no hybrid courses. With the receipt of Title III funds in 2010, enrollment in online courses more than tripled to 920 students. By the end of the five-year grant period, almost 3,000 students (2,672) were enrolled in online courses at Morgan, and an additional 275 students were enrolled in hybrid (i.e., a combination of classroom based and online instruction) courses.

In 2014, a full-time Director was hired and assigned an institutional budget with continued Title III funding and an office within the University's Division of Academic Outreach and Engagement. Since the hiring of the Executive Director and the establishment of the Office of Morgan Online, the number of faculty at Morgan who have received Quality Matters (QM) training in both developing and teaching online courses has increased. As well, there has been an increase in the number of students enrolling in online

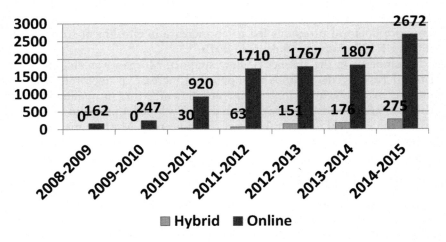

Figure 10.2 Online and Hybrid Course Enrollment by Academic Year: 2008–2015

courses during each academic term, including the winter session and in summer school. In 2016, for example, 102 Morgan faculty had been trained according to Quality Matters standards and offered 220 online courses. Student enrollment in online courses had increased to 3,680 and hybrid course enrollment was 574.

Morgan is now approved by MHEC to offer ten online degree programs in the Community College Leadership Doctoral Program (Ed.D.), (2+2) Bachelor of Science in Electrical Engineering (BSEE), Master's of Science in Electrical Engineering (MSEE), Master's of Science in Project Management (MSPM), Master's of Education in Community College Administration, Instruction and Student Development (M.Ed.), Master's in Business Administration (MBA), Master's in Social Work (MSW), Master's of Public Health (MPH), Master's of Public Health (RN-BS-MPH), and a Bachelor of Science in Applied Liberal Studies (BS). Additionally, Morgan now awards Post-Baccalaureate Certificates (PBCs.) in Psychometrics, Urban Sustainable Communities, Project Management, Advanced National Security, and Urban Journalism.

Implications for Other HBCUs in Maryland

Morgan is one of only two public colleges and universities in Maryland that is not governed by the University System of Maryland's Board of Regents.[29] Pursuant to Article 14 of the Education Article, Annotated Code of Maryland,[30] Morgan State University is a public corporation and an independent unit of state government and is not included in the University System of Maryland. Government of the University is vested in a 15-member Board of Regents appointed by the Governor, and Morgan's Regents are responsible for the management of the university and have all the powers, rights, and privileges that go with that responsibility which may not be superseded by any other state agency or office in managing the affairs of the university.

This measure of independence has allowed Morgan to speak directly to state officials at MHEC and in the state legislature regarding institutional needs and grievances. Likewise, independence has also allowed Morgan to aggressively pursue federal Title III funds and other federal contracts and grants to support the growth of its graduate and online degree programs.

Conversely, Maryland's three other HBCUs are governed by a 17-member Board of Regents who are appointed by the governor and who oversee the University System of Maryland's (USM) academic, administrative, and financial operations; formulate policy; and appoint the USM chancellor and the presidents of the system's 12 institutions. The Presidents of Bowie, Coppin, and UMES are constrained in their capacities to articulate the needs and grievances of their respective institutions. For example, the current ten-year USM strategic plan, Powering Maryland Forward,[31] was approved unanimously by the USM Board of Regents on December 3, 2010.

Powering Maryland Forward (the Plan) leaves behind the three HBCUs in the USM. The Plan fails to acknowledge even the significance of the impact of the African American population in meeting the Plan's five goals, opting instead to stress the demographic impact of two of Maryland's smallest minority groups. According to the Plan's summary of demographic trends impacting enrollment at USM institutions, the state's college and university enrollment will move from minority students making up just over 40% of the postsecondary enrollment in 2008 to almost 60% by 2020. The number of Hispanic and Asian students, in particular, will increase, doubling as a percentage of the enrollment over that period.

In contrast to the Plan's assessment, Maryland 2020: A State in Transition[32] reports that:

- over 1.6 million African Americans live in Maryland;
- African Americans are the largest minority group in the state; and,
- African Americans account for 28.9% of the state's population.[33]

The report observes that the Hispanic community in Maryland is relatively small, accounting for only 6.3% of the state's population,[34] and that the Asian community in Maryland accounts for 5.0% of the state's population.

The 32-page Plan refers to Historically Black Institutions (HBIs) only once as a suggested strategy for addressing the goals and challenges highlighted under the Plan's first goal or theme, "Access, Affordability, and Attainment—Helping the State of Maryland Achieve Its Goal of 55 Percent College Completion." In this way, the USM Plan may offer a nod to Bowie, Coppin, and UMES but does not acknowledge USM's role in the state's financial neglect of these HBCUs or the duplication of the HBCUs' degree programs by the USM's TWIs. Nor does the Plan offer any responsibility for USM over the next ten years in addressing such neglect, beyond asserting that

> In line with the recommendations of the Bohanan Commission, boost the success of the USM's Historically Black Institutions (HBIs) by identifying and providing the level of resources and support necessary to ensure student outcomes at a level equal to those at non-HBI institutions with the same general mission.[35]

In summary, because of independent authority granted by statute to Morgan's Board of Regents, Morgan's president(s) and its Regents have been able to pursue the growth of its graduate and online degree programs despite the lack of state support by relying on federal Title III funds. On the other hand, Bowie, Coppin, and UMES have, like Morgan, been disadvantaged by the history of de jure segregation throughout the state. Coppin, which is located in Baltimore City, has been impacted by the same race-based policies promulgated by a succession of mayors and city council officials that sought to block the growth of Morgan. The difference between Morgan and Bowie, Coppin, or UMES is that their institutional needs and grievances are filtered through the USM chancellor and USM Regents. Their ability to access Title III federal funds is limited by the degree programs approved for them by the USM.

Summary and Conclusion

In *Diggs v. Morgan College*, White residents who objected to a "negro college" in their community alleged in court that the land purchased by Morgan was "in excess of the legitimate need of the respondent." Maryland and its chief agent for higher education matters, the Maryland Higher Education Commission, have based their pattern and practice of funding Morgan on a similar belief that any funds spent on Morgan as well as on other HBCUs in the state are in excess of their legitimate need. A coalition of Morgan and other HBCU alumni, as well as current and prospective students, filed suit in 2010 to enforce the commitments made by the state in its 2000 Partnership Agreement between Maryland and the United States Department of Education Office of Civil Rights to avoid unnecessary program duplication and to provide funding to enhance Maryland's Historically Black Colleges and Universities.

Morgan's success in increasing enrollment and expanding academic degree and program offerings in the context of chronic under-funding by the state is a direct consequence of the university's ability to secure federal Title III funds established to Strengthen Historically Black Colleges and Universities. Specifically, in the absence of state support, Morgan was able to secure Title III Part B federal funds to support an increase in the number of science, technology, engineering, and mathematics (STEM) related doctoral programs and to benefit from the ensuing growth in graduate enrollment.

Morgan secured Title III Part A funds to support its Office of Morgan Online, and increase the number of faculty using Quality Matters pedagogy in the development of online courses and teaching online. Whereas prior to the initial five-year Title III grant, Morgan offered no online degree programs and enrollment in online courses was fewer than 300 students, current annual enrollment in online courses exceeds 3,000 students, and students may elect to earn degrees in ten online degree programs. By way of contrast, Maryland's other three public HBCUs, Bowie State University, Coppin State University, and the University of Maryland Eastern Shore, have not been able to use federal Title III funds to the extent that Morgan has, in large measure because development of degree programs must be approved by USM's chancellor and Board of Regents prior to approval by the Maryland Higher Education Commission.

Notes

1 From *Diggs v. Morgan College*, 105 A. 157, 133 Md. 264 (1918) where the complainants, White Laurelville residents, opposed Morgan's use of newly acquired Ivy Mill property in 1917 as a "negro college," alleging that "that a tract of seventy acres were in excess of the legitimate need of the respondent." Russell and Anna Diggs, Samuel and Jesse Lawder, George and Margaret Frankton, and William and Johanna Heck vs. Morgan College, a corporation duly incorporated under the Laws of the State of Maryland, Filed in the Circuit Court for Baltimore County, 1 August 1917.
2 Antero Pietila, Not in My Neighborhood: How Bigotry Shaped A Great American City. Ivan R. Dee (2010). Pg. 58.
3 Id at pg. 59
4 The Racial Wealth Divide in Baltimore. Corporation for Enterprise Development and J.P. Morgan Chase. January (2017).
5 Justin George and Mark Puente (reporters), The Baltimore Sun. March 14, 2015. www.baltimoresun.com/news/maryland/baltimore-city/bs-md-ci-baltimore-racism-20150314-story.html
6 Id at pg. 3.
7 Pietila, pg. 60.
8 George and Puente, The Baltimore Sun.
9 The nine commitments that Maryland made in the OCR Agreement are:
   1. Strengthening Academic and Teacher Preparation Programs
   2. Strengthening Partnerships with Elementary and Secondary School Stakeholders
   3. Strengthening Recruitment and Admissions
   4. Strengthening Retention and Graduation
   5. Improving Campus Climate and Environment
   6. Improving Diversity of Faculty/Staff and Governing/Advisory Boards
   7. Improving and Expanding 2+2 Partnerships
   8. Avoiding Unnecessary Program Duplication and Expansion of Mission and Program Uniqueness and Institutional Identity at the HBCUs
   9. Enhancing Maryland's Historically Black Colleges and Universities
10 Title VI of the Civil Rights Act of 1964
11 The Equal Protection Clause of the Fourteenth Amendment, and United States v. Fordice, 505 U.S. 717 (1992)

12 The Coalition for Equity and Excellence in Maryland Higher Education, et al. v. Maryland Higher Education Commission, et al. Civil No. CCB-06 Doc. 382 Filed 10/07/13 pgs. 43–44 of 60
13 Id. At pg. 44
14 Id at pg. 49
15 Scott Jaschik, A Win for Public Black Colleges. Inside Higher Ed. October 8, 2013.
16 20 U.S. Code § 1060 et. Seq; and 34 CFR 608 et. Seq
17 20 U.S. Code § 1061 (2); and 34 CFR 608.2
18 Saint Paul's College in Lawrenceville, Virginia, one of the 107 HBCUs on the list, closed on June 30, 2013.
19 20 U.S. Code § 1060(2)
20 20 U.S. Code § 1060 (4)
21 20 U.S. Code § 1063b(a)(1)
22 20 U.S. Code § 1063e(2)
23 Under 20 U.S.C. 1063b(e) and 34 C.F.R. §609.2, the 16 institutions with programs in law, medicine, or qualifying graduate degree programs eligible to receive a grant under Part B of Title III include; Morehouse School of Medicine, Meharry Medical School, Charles R. Drew Postgraduate Medical School, Clark Atlanta University, Tuskegee Institute School of Veterinary Medicine, Xavier University School of Pharmacy, Southern University School of Law, Texas Southern University School of Law and School of Pharmacy, Florida A&M University School of Pharmaceutical Sciences, North Carolina Central University School of Law, Morgan State University, Hampton University, Alabama A&M University, North Carolina A&T State University, University of Maryland Eastern Shore, and, Jackson State University.
24 Report to the Maryland Commission to Develop the Maryland Model for Funding Higher Education from The Panel on the Comparability and Competitiveness of Historically Black Institutions in Maryland Appendix 2, pg. 109.
25 The Public Health Program was begun with funding from a grant from the Kellogg Foundation.
26 The doctoral program supported with Title III, Part B funds that had the greatest impact on increased enrollment over this 15-year timeframe is the Community College Leadership Program.
27 20 U.S.C. 1063b(i)
28 Morgan had initiatives to develop online courses for several years prior to receiving a Title III grant in 2010 to support those initiatives.
29 The other is St. Mary's College of Maryland, a public honors college, located in St. Mary's County.
30 http://mgaleg.maryland.gov/2017RS/Statute_Web/ged/ged.pdf §14–101 et. Seq.
31 Powering Maryland Forward. www.usmd.edu/10yrplan/USM2020.pdf.
32 Maryland 2020: A State in Transition. Department of Legislative Services Office of Policy Analysis Annapolis, Maryland (September) 2008. http://dls.state.md.us/data/polanasubare/polanasubare_intmatnpubadm/Maryland_2020_A_State_in_Transition.pdf.
33 Id. at pg. 16.
34 Id. at pg. 10
35 Powering Maryland Forward. Proposed Strategy 1.c.3. pg. 13.

Bibliography

The Coalition for Equity and Excellence in Maryland Higher Education, et al. v. Maryland Higher Education Commission, et al. Fourth Amended Complaint filed. Retrieved September 2010, from https://lawyerscommittee.org/wp-content/uploads/2015/06/Docket-165-Fourth-Amended-Complaint.pdf

The Coalition for Equity and Excellence in Maryland Higher Education, et al. v. Maryland Higher Education Commission, et al. Court's Memorandum and Decision filed. Retrieved October 7, 2013, from https://lawyerscommittee.org/wp-content/uploads/2015/06/Coalition-v-MHEC-memorandum-decision.pdf

"Commission to Develop the Maryland Model for Funding Higher Education Final Report." December 2008. Retrieved from http://dls.state.md.us/data/polanasubare/polanasubare_edu/Commission-to-Study-the-Maryland-Model-for-Funding-Higher-Education.pdf

Diggs v. Morgan College, 133 Md. 264, 1918.

George, Justin and Mark Puente (reporters). *The Baltimore Sun*. Retrieved March 14, 2015, from www.baltimoresun.com/news/maryland/baltimore-city/bs-md-ci-baltimore-racism-20150314-story.html

Jaschik, Scott. "A win for public black colleges." *Inside Higher Ed*. Retrieved October 8, 2013, from www.insidehighered.com/news/2013/10/08/federal-judge-finds-maryland-discriminates-against-its-public-black-colleges

"Maryland 2020: A State in Transition. Department of Legislative Services Office of Policy Analysis Annapolis, Maryland." September 2008. Retrieved from http://dls.state.md.us/data/polanasubare/polanasubare_intmatnpubadm/Maryland_2020_A_State_in_Transition.pdf

Pietila, Antero. Not in my neighborhood: How bigotry shaped a great American city. Chicago, IL: Ivan R. Dee, 2010, 58–59.

Powering Maryland Forward. *University System of Maryland's 10-year strategic plan*. Retrieved from www.usmd.edu/10yrplan/USM2020.pdf

"The Racial Wealth Divide in Baltimore." *Corporation for Enterprise Development and J.P. Morgan Chase*. Retrieved January 2017, from http://cfed.org/assets/pdfs/Racial_Wealth_Divide_in_Baltimore_RWDI.pdf

Title III—Part A, the Strengthening Historically Black Colleges and Universities Program 20 U.S. Code § 1060 et. seq. and 34 CFR 608 et. seq.

Title III—Part B, the Strengthening Historically Black Graduate Institutions (HBGIs) Program 20 U.S. Code § 1063b et. seq. and 34 C.F.R. §609 et. seq.

Title VI of the Civil Rights Act of 1964, 42 U.S.Code § 2000d et seq.

United States v. Fordice, 505 U.S. 717.

11 Emerging Themes, Questions, and Implications for Professional Education at Historically Black Colleges and Universities

Adriel A. Hilton, Tiffany Fountaine Boykin, and Robert T. Palmer

Researchers have touted that Minority-Serving Institutions, especially HBCUs, empower, encourage, and push their students to fully participate in American society.[1] This rhetoric is especially evident regarding the HBCU's role in graduate education, particularly in professional programs of study. The primary objectives of this monograph are to: (1) provide a critical review of the historical nature of professional programs at HBCUs and the programs' impact on a global society; (2) provide context about the experiences of Black doctoral students in professional programs, outcomes for professional degree enrollment and attainment, student-faculty relationships, research opportunities, and the role of faculty in socialization processes for promoting positive Black doctoral student development and professional growth; and (3) address the future of professional education at HBCUs and what fundamental aspects are needed to ensure their survival, competitiveness, and growth. Given the historical sociopolitical policies and practices in the US higher education system, which at one time deemed Black men and women unworthy of postsecondary education and training and excluded them from full participation,[2] this volume is particularly noteworthy, as it examines the historical and contemporary significance of HBCUs, especially in producing Black doctorates. In its analysis of professional education, this work further confirms the continued relevance of and need for HBCUs in the 21st century and their global impact. The remainder of this final chapter recaps the monograph's salient points on areas of study including law, education, medicine, and social work, the experiences of Black doctoral students in professional programs at HBCUs, and HBCU advocacy. Implications for the future of professional education at HBCUs are offered.

The Elite Professions

HBCUs have long been at the forefront of shifting and creating societal change, and their law schools are no exception. HBCU law schools do not just produce lawyers but generate leaders who are primed and ready to advance the cause of civil rights with the same passion and commitment of previous generations of graduates, faculty, and administrators. Many societal advancements that have been made by African Americans can be credited, in large part, to HBCUs and their graduates. Just one example cited is Thurgood Marshall, a Howard University alumnus and the first African American appointed to the US Supreme Court.

Regarding HBCU education doctoral candidates, this volume argues that expanding the current model of recruitment, mentorship, development, and retention of the education doctoral candidates could potentially result in more teacher educators who serve as role models, leaders, and eventual policymakers. Today's 21st century K-12 classrooms are microcosmic representations of the increasingly diverse population that characterizes much of the nation. It is imperative that Black teacher educators train future teachers to create learning environments that enable student members to engage in a dialogue reflective of the unique sociocultural experiences that they bring to the setting.

In the field of medicine, this text maintains HBCUs have played a critical role in leading the charge of meeting the nation's goal to create a minority health professional pipeline to guide the future of America. HBCUs are uniquely equipped to foster the academic growth and success of culturally aware premedical, medical, and allied health professionals. While their academic rigor may mirror those of mainstream graduate medical education institutions, their missions often reflect meeting the needs of medically underserved communities of color. This monograph also raises the issue that historically Black health professional schools need to be cognizant of developing new models of sustainability and partnering opportunities in order to be strategic and proactive, rather than reactive. The traditional approach to leadership selection, which has too often been internal and relationship driven, needs to balance with retention of institutional memory by bringing in personnel with new experiences and concepts of innovation in a rapidly changing world. One such successful model cited of a merge creating a novel partnership of an HBCU with a research-intensive institution is the Emory University/Morehouse School of Medicine in Atlanta, Georgia.[3]

One of the more salient concepts this composition suggests is that social work education at HBCUs should be considered in the elite professional degree category (MSW/PhD), necessitated to meet the demands of the profession and the needs of individuals and communities from diverse backgrounds. HBCUs are in the forefront in establishing programs that not only make education and training available to Black students, but have developed a curriculum that makes them specifically knowledgeable and competent in Black issues. A particular point made is that HBCUs are able to position fieldwork opportunities for their graduate students directly within the urban and rural Black communities they hope to serve. For example, social work students at Howard University concentrate in Community, Administration, and Policy Practice and are required to take a required Resource

Development course that "provides students with knowledge and skills in strategic planning for resource development, program planning, grant proposal writing, financial management, entrepreneurship, and community and institutional capacity building and multi-level fundraising . . . [with] special attention given to the unique experiences and challenges faced by organizations in African American communities and other communities of color."[4]

Researching the HBCU Doctoral Student Experience

Presented in this work are research study findings, personal narratives, and theoretical analyses about the experiences of Black doctoral students in specific disciplines, outcomes for enrollment and degree attainment, relationships with faculty and advisors, research opportunities, and the role and socialization processes in promoting positive Black doctoral student development and professional growth. By paying particular attention to the HBCU setting in the more elite professions, it attempts to inform the reader of Black student trends in this area, including outcomes and experiences at HBCUs that could prove critical to matriculation and completion of professional advanced degrees for future students. This work also offers an understanding of some of the personal and professional challenges with which current and future Black students must contend, as well as strategies and best practices for faculty and administrators to best support these students.

Given the limited research on graduate students at HBCUs, this text showcases Black students' unique experiences attending professional degree programs at HBCUs. It highlights the essential support structures that might ultimately aid in retention and persistence, a better organizational fit, appropriate career decisions, and better expenditure of individual and institutional resources these students need to succeed. Hard to reach subgroups at HBCUs, including Black men, often succeed because faculty members take time during and after class to mentor scholars. Faculty do not simply work with students within the confines of the classroom but take time after class, including weekends, to support their efforts—acting as surrogate parents, confidantes, and academic advisors—playing a critical role in the lives of graduate and professional students.

Support during and after graduate and professional school is also important, particularly for Black students who depend on faculty members to help chart and catapult their career paths. These aspiring physicians, dentists, and pharmacists need access to individuals from similar ethnic and racial backgrounds in order to discuss how to navigate homogenous workspaces where they may encounter stereotypes and misconceptions. After graduation, relationships between HBCU faculty and former students continue to foster conversations on professional development and future goals and aspirations. Without positive feedback and support from faculty members, HBCUs could struggle to retain Black graduate students. For instance, Fountaine's study on Black graduate and professional students and faculty relationships determined that doctoral student-faculty engagement was positively linked to student persistence and a best predictor for positive experiences.[5]

Similar to faculty-to-student relationships, peer-to-peer relationships play an equally significant role for students at HBCUs. In school settings, students encourage each other to set high expectations and meet academic benchmarks. Researchers have confirmed that these peer relationships have helped graduate students overcome school-related challenges that impact attrition rates and can alleviate stressors associated with meeting academic benchmarks.[6] In addition, student cohorts provide opportunities for students to develop interpersonal skills, learn to work in small groups, and collaborate on research opportunities. Partnering on research projects may be particularly important for graduate and professional students that attend HBCUs because of limited departmental and university funding. Overall, HBCUs offer these students competitive and nurturing settings that encourage students to work together before and after graduation.

In regard to research training and research mentoring at HBCUs, this monograph stresses the importance of accentuating the relationship as well as the method utilized to increase research self-efficacy through appropriate research training. Such emphasis motivates HBCUs to find additional analytical methods designed to increase diverse researchers, as well as researchers with diverse cultural perspectives. This monograph distinguishes itself from other works; it neither makes efforts to reveal disparities between doctoral student achievements at HBCUs versus predominantly White institutions, nor does it compare the experiences of students at one HBCU over another. The editors and contributing authors collectively recognize that the influences that promote (or challenge) success among HBCU Black doctoral students in professional programs, independent of comparisons, are important and necessitate continued examination and visibility of HBCUs in the larger higher education conversation.

Advocating for HBCUs

Finally, this book addresses the future of professional education programs at America's HBCUs. An underlying objective of this work is to serve as a champion of advocacy for the continued necessity and relevance of the HBCU. The HBCU has and continues to serve as a bold catalyst in the development of Black advanced professional degree holders, thus adding to the success of higher education, the economy, and to the civic and social order of future generations in America.

While we can continue to see some progress, with HBCUs graduating more Black doctorates over the last 30 years, such progress has been relatively slow. Between 1977 and 2000, there was a 1% increase, from 3.8% to 4.8%, respectively.[7] And, even as late as 2010, Blacks' share of earned doctorates was 7.4%, considerably lagging behind that of White students,

74.3%.[8] Additionally, much of the research that actually has examined Black doctoral students has not necessarily investigated the implications of an HBCU setting.[9] And, even when it has, the aforementioned research often concentrated on Blacks in traditional PhD programs of study and less on professional programs, such as medicine, law, and social work.[10]

Moreover, today's HBCUs actually face lower Black student enrollments. Prior to the 1954 *Brown vs. Board of Education* decision, 90% of Black college-going students attended HBCUs.[11] However, after the passing of the *Brown* decision, Predominantly White Institutions (PWIs) began extending admission to more and more Black students. And, by the early 1960s, the number of Black college students attending HBCUs had decreased from 90% to 70%. This continued and by 1980, only 20% of Black college-going students were enrolled in HBCUs.[12] By 2000, that share had declined to 13%, and it stood at approximately 9% in 2015.[13]

Notwithstanding, recent data suggest that HBCUs continue to play an important and substantial role in the educational achievement of Black college students. For example, 50% of all Black public school teachers graduated from HBCUs, and more than a third of all Black college students who graduate with degrees in the natural sciences receive their degrees from HBCUs.[14] The statistics are even more noteworthy when considering production of Black doctorates, especially in professional disciplines. Thirty-three percent of all Blacks with a PhD in either science or engineering received their undergraduate degrees from HBCUs.[15] And, in 2016, HBCUs served as steadfast leaders in producing professional doctorates in general (i.e., medicine, law, veterinary medicine, etc.); Howard University, Florida Agricultural and Mechanical University, Meharry Medical College, Texas Southern University, Southern University Law Center, and North Carolina Central University ranked first, second, third, fifth, seventh, and eighth, respectively.[16]

Implications for the Future of Professional Education at HBCUs Future Research

Despite years of minimal funding, HBCUs continue to play a significant role in expanding Black academics and professionals. In addition to exploring student experiences, future research should focus on institutional and programmatic efforts at HBCUs. For instance, what policies, programs, and practices do graduate and professional schools at HBCUs offer that foster student engagement and a sense of community on campus? How do HBCUs build partnerships with community organizations so their students have the opportunity to apply their coursework in a real-world context while simultaneously contributing to their community? Also, as an emerging global society, what aspects of Black doctoral and professional students' experiences impact or foster global learning?

Another implication that has emerged from this volume is a deeper and more robust discussion about professional education at HBCUs. Indeed, while there has been research on doctoral education at HBCUs, albeit limited, and a stronger body of research on Black undergraduate student experiences at these noble institutions, there is scant literature that has documented the impact of professional education at HBCUs. In fact, to our knowledge, to date, this is the only volume that has focused exclusively on professional education at HBCUs (i.e., law, medical, and education) and the students enrolled in these critical professions.

Strategic Planning and Policy Considerations

The findings from this text also have implications for strategic planning and policy. For example, HBCU leaders and professional program administrators must consider how the mission of the HBCU has changed over time. Though the historic mission of these institutions was to educate Black men and women—who racism and segregation often excluded from participating in postsecondary educational opportunities in the same manner as Whites—one must consider how the HBCU is currently situated within today's higher education landscape and what that means with respect to Black people. A recent study revealed Black graduates of Historically Black Colleges and Universities felt more supported while in college and are thriving afterwards than are their Black peers who graduated from predominantly white institutions.[17] That tells us that the unique mission and commitment of these schools to the education of Black people must not be overlooked, but examined critically within today's society. HBCU presidents have agreed that contemporary missions for today's HBCUs should communicate HBCUs' responsibility to provide access and opportunity to Black students, as well as offer opportunities to prepare students for leadership.[18] This sentiment should then be emphasized in shared goals and learning outcomes associated with graduate professional programs of study at HBCUs.

Furthermore, HBCU leadership and graduate professional program administrators must consider how their missions align with a need to move forward in an ever-changing national, as well as global, context, including the global marketplace. They must examine their respective abilities to attract talent from a broad range of educational and ethnic backgrounds. By no means does this suggest that HBCUs stray from their core mission of providing educational opportunities for Black people. Rather, it's a call to action to continue building diverse student bodies that reflect changes in the current cultural landscape.

Another recommendation for strategic planning and policy is for HBCUs to explore institutional partnership opportunities for their graduate professional programs. This model has seen some success. For example in 1995, North Carolina A&T State University and the University of North Carolina at Greensboro (UNCG) entered into an agreement to begin a Joint Master's of Social Work Program supported by both universities. Similarly, in August of 2010, faculty and administrators at the two institutions launched a joint School of Nanoscience and Nanoengineering program. This text also highlights a partnership between Emory University and Morehouse School of Medicine in Atlanta, Georgia. Such multiple dual degree and exchange programs that HBCUs have established and continue to establish with PWIs function as critical components for HBCU efforts to strengthen their programs and ensure the long-term success of their schools.[19]

Intentionality on appropriate use of current research also has implications for strategic planning and policy. It is critical that HBCU policymakers and stakeholders maximize utility of research on HBCUs to ensure they are adequately funded. For example, researchers have noted that without improvements in fundraising, HBCUs will continue to struggle to provide supportive learning environments that encourage the pursuit of academic excellence.[20] Thus, leadership and graduate professional program administrators must think critically about how to involve donors and alumni in ways that encourage increases in both short-term and long-term philanthropic support. Such support is very much consistent with alumni of doctoral professional programs; essentially, as Blacks continue to make strides in education, they, likewise, gain the economic resources to make significant contributions to support the educational missions and upward mobility of their HBCUs and their programs of study.

Lastly, policymakers at the state level need to work with higher education commissioners and chancellors to prevent duplicate programs at PWIs, which have had adverse implications for HBCUs, and pursue legal action if necessary. The Coalition for Equity and Excellence in Maryland Higher Education, representing four Maryland HBCUs, sued the State's Higher Education Commission alleging that Maryland has failed to dismantle the vestiges of segregation from its prior de jure system of higher education. The Coalition has claimed that the state's continuing failures to Maryland HBCUs span the areas of funding, capital improvements, and unnecessary program duplication—including a graduate professional program in business—and have resulted in hampered efforts to recruit students.[21] The Court ruled that Maryland had in fact violated the constitutional rights of students at Maryland's four HBCUs by unnecessarily duplicating their programs at nearby predominantly White institutions. At the time of this printing, negotiations to provide remedy to the plaintiffs remained underway. Policymakers must be aware of the legal avenues they may have to take in order to equalize funding and prevent harmful policies and programs.

Conclusion

As the nation continues to transition under the Trump Administration, particularly given that there has been no explicit commitment to additional funding for HBCUs, the leadership and the administrators at HBCUs stand at a crossroads. It is remarkably evident that HBCUs continue to be a fundamental part of the nation's higher education landscape. Their importance to the success of the Black community, and to the nation, cannot be understated. While it is imperative that HBCUs remain true to their unique missions, it is also critical for them to consider, and even rethink, their role in American higher education. The HBCU is essential to Black professional degree attainment; that has broader implications for the nation's preservation and continuation of its role as a global leader. In order to advance the nation's agenda for global competitiveness, HBCUs must be proactive in addressing criticisms, often unfounded, of their continued existence. The HBCU legacy confirms that matriculation at and graduation from these institutions has increased the social capital of numerous Black students, especially those earning advanced degrees in the professions. But, these institutions cannot afford to rest on legacy alone; they must attend to the dynamic changes taking place in our society and showcase their importance and continued relevance.

Researchers have pointed out several factors that serve to restrict the capacity of professional education at HBCUs, including undeveloped missions implied by historical contexts for HBCUs, differential funding patterns for HBCUs and PWIs, and the continuing legacy of systemic racial discrimination by state governments in the treatment of HBCUs.[22] Each of those factors alone is sufficient to hinder the growth and opportunity of graduate professional programs at HBCUs. Notwithstanding, many HBCUs still manage to do more with less, standing poised to meet the needs of their students and ultimately producing significant numbers of Black doctorates in professional programs—Howard University, Florida Agricultural and Mechanical University, Meharry Medical College, Texas Southern University, Southern University Law Center, and North Carolina Central University, to name a few.[23] Ultimately, there will likely continue to be struggles grounded in the aforementioned factors as well as others. However, this realization should be acknowledged, but not be considered a deterrent. The contemporary economic, political, and social impact that HBCUs offer through production of Black doctorates tell us that we need more settings like HBCUs, not fewer. Thus, leaders and administrators of graduate professional programs at HBCUs enjoy a remarkable opportunity to counter narratives that lend to discounting the HBCU and continue transforming deficits tied to a legacy of compensating for a system of education that has far too often failed Black students.

Notes

1 Albritton 2012; Gasman et al. 2008
2 Albritton 2012
3 Ofili et al. 2013
4 Howard University, para. 16 2017
5 Fountaine, 2012
6 Ross et al. 2011
7 Nettles and Millet 2006

8 National Center for Education Statistics 2012
9 Palmer, Hilton, and Fountaine 2012; Nerad and Miller 1996; Nettles and Millet 2006.
10 Fountaine 2012; Palmer, Hilton, and Fountaine 2012.
11 Roebuck and Murty 1993, p. 43
12 Freeman and McDonald 2004
13 Anderson 2017
14 United Negro College Fund, n. d., "Our member colleges: About HBCUs"
15 Burrelli and Rapoport 2008
16 *Top 100 Degree Producers 2016*: Graduate and Professional
17 New, 2015
18 Ricard and Brown 2008
19 Albritton 2012
20 Albritton 2012
21 Palmer, Davis, and Gasman 2011
22 Taylor 2012
23 *Top 100 Degree Producers 2016*: Graduate and Professional

Bibliography

Albritton, Travis. "Educating our own: The historical legacy of HBCUs and their relevance for educating a new generation of leaders." *Urban Review*, 44 no. 2 (2012): 311–331.

Anderson, Monica. "A look at historically black colleges and universities as Howard turns 150." *Pew Research Center*, 2017. Retrieved from www.pewresearch.org/fact-tank/2017/02/28/a-look-at-historically-black-colleges-and-universities-as-howard-turns-150/

Burrelli, Joan, and Alan Rapoport. *Role of HBCUs as baccalaureate-origin institutions of Black S&E doctorate recipients* (NSF Publication No. 08–319). Arlington, VA: National Science Foundation, Division of Science Resources Statistics, 2008.

Fountaine, Tiffany P. "The impact of faculty-student interaction on black doctoral students attending historically black institutions." *The Journal of Negro Education*, 81 no. 2 (2012): 11.

Freeman, Kassie, and Nicole McDonald. "Attracting the best and brightest: College choice influences at black colleges." In M. Christopher Brown II, and Kassie Freeman (Eds.), *Black Colleges: New Perspectives on Policy and Practices* (pp. 53–64). Westport, CT: Praeger Publishers, 2004.

Gasman, Marybeth, Benjamin Baez, and Caroline Sotello, Viernes Turner. *Understanding Minority-Serving Institutions*. Albany, NY: State University of New York Press, 2008.

Howard University website, para 16, 2017. Retrieved from www.howard.edu/schoolsocialwork/programs/msw/courses.htm

National Center for Education Statistics. Doctor's degrees conferred by degree-granting institutions, by sex, racial/ethnic group, and major field of study: 20010–11. 2012. Retrieved from https://nces.ed.gov/programs/digest/d12/tables/dt12_336.asp

Nerad, Maresi, and Debra Sands Miller. "Increasing student retention in graduate and professional programs." *New Directions for Institutional Research*, 92 (1996): 61–76.

Nettles, Michael T., and Catherine M. Millet. *Three magic words: Getting to Ph.D*. Baltimore, MD: The Johns Hopkins University Press, 2006.

New, Jake. "Positive News for HBCUs." *Insider Higher Ed.*, 2015. Retrieved from https://www.insidehighered.com/news/2015/10/28/survey-finds-big-differences-between-black-hbcu-graduates-those-who-attended-other

Ofili, Elizabeth O. et al. "Models of interinstitutional partnerships between research intensive universities and Minority Serving Institutions (MSI) across the Clinical Translational Science Award (CTSA) Consortium." *Clinical and Translational Science*, (2013). doi:10.1111/cts.12118

Palmer, Robert T., Ryan J. Davis, and Marybeth Gasman. "A matter of diversity, equity, and necessity: The tension between Maryland's higher education system and its historically black colleges and universities over the Office of Civil Rights Agreement." *The Journal of Negro Education*, 80 no. 2 (2011): 121–133.

Palmer, Robert T., Adriel A. Hilton, and Tiffany P. Fountaine, T. P. *Black graduate education at historically black colleges and universities: Trends, experiences, and outcomes*. Charlotte, NC: Information Age Publishing, 2012.

Ricard, Ronyelle Bertrand, and M. Christopher Brown. Ebony towers in higher education: The evolution, mission, and presidency of historically black colleges and universities. Sterling: Stylus, 2008.

Roebuck, Julian and Komanduri Murty. *Historically black colleges and universities: Their place in American higher education*: ERIC, 1993. Retrieved from https://eric.ed.gov/?id=ED363683

Ross, Doreen, Alyson Adams, Elizabeth Bondy, Nancy Dana, Stephanie, Dodman, and Colleen Swain. "Preparing teacher leaders: Perceptions of the impact of a cohort-based, job embedded, blended teacher leadership program." *Teaching and Teacher Education*, 27 no. 8 (2011): 1213–1222.

Sleeter, Christine. Un-standardizing curriculum: Multicultural teaching in the standards-based classroom. New York: Teachers College Press, 2005.

Taylor, Maurice C. "On a wing and a prayer: The future of graduate education at HBCUs." In *Black graduate education at historically black colleges and universities*. New York: Information Ager Press, 2012: 223–252.

"Top 100 Degree Producers 2016: Graduate and Professional Diverse." Retrieved from http://diverseeducation.com/top100/GraduateDegreeProducers2016.php

United Negro College Fund, n.d., "Our member colleges: About HBCUs".

Index

Page numbers in *italics* denote figures.

achievement gap 51–2
advising, Black feminist approach to doctoral 4
advocating for HBCUs 158–9
affirmative action 47, 63–4
Affordable Care Act 65
African American students, projected increase in 63
Allen, Walter 79
American Council on Education (ACE) Leadership Academy 66
Antioch School of Law 31
apprenticeship model 106
Atlanta School of Social Work 93–4

Baltimore, Maryland 7, 141–2, 150
Batts, Anthony M. 142
bias, environment that shields Black students from explicit and implicit 15
Bioecological Systems Theory 14
Bishop Tuttle Memorial School of Social Work at St. Augustine College 93, 96–7
Black Lives Matter 38–40
Blake, Catherine C. 144
Bland, Sandra 39
Bohanan Commission 150
Bowie State University 17, 143–4, 149–51
Bronfenbrenner, Urie 14
Brown, Michael 39
Brown v. Board of Education 15, 37, 63, 159

camaraderie, of students at HBCUs 125
career-related functions, of mentoring 107, 109–14
Carnegie, Andrew 58–9, 141

Carnegie Classifications 3, 141, 146
Carter, Robert 37
case studies 128
Center for Child & Family Health (CCFH) 35
Charles R. Drew University of Medicine and Science 19, 57, 59, 67
Cheyney University 3
Civil Rights Act of 1964 47, 124, 143
Clark Atlanta University: ranking in awarding doctorate degrees to Blacks 4; social work education 93, 95
clinical programs, at HBCU law schools 34–6
coaching 107
Coalition for Equality and Excellence in Maryland Higher Education, Inc. 143–4, 161
community-centered approach 15, 17
community health centers 60
convenience, importance in selection of institutions 129–30
Coppin State University 7, 143–4, 149–51
Corporation for Enterprise Development 7, 142
cost, importance in selection of institutions 130
Council on Social Work Education (CSWE) Office of Social Work Accreditation 95
counseling, as mentor role 107, 113
Crump, Benjamin 40
cultural competency: advance with workforce diversity 59; concept 91; social work education 91–9
Cunningham, Kevin 39

dentists, Black produced by HBCUs 15
depression 16
desegregation 37, 143
DeVos, Betsy 48
Diggs v. Morgan College 150, 152
discrimination 15, 64, 92, 94, 145, 162
District of Columbia School of Law 31
doctoral students, and mentoring experiences at HBCUs 103–17
doctorate degrees: Blacks' share of recipients 7, 103, 157; increase in number awarded 4; number and percentage from HBCUs 4, 123, 158–9
doctorate programs, at Morgan State University 141, 146–7
Drew, Charles 67
Dubois, W. E. B. 93
duplication of programs 21, 143–5, 149–51, 161

Earl Carl Institute for Legal and Social Policy at Texas Southern 34
education doctoral students 47–54, 156; development 51–2; mentorship 50–1; recruitment 49–50; retention 52–3; review of literature 48–9
Ellis, Henry 109–10
Emory University 67, 156, 161
endowments 4, 16, 60, 65, 145
enrollment, decrease in 17, 159
Ethelyn R. Strong School of Social Work at Norfolk State University 96–7
ethnography 128
exosystem, university 14, 19–20

faculty: historically Black medical schools 60–2; mentoring by 50–1; percentage of Blacks in higher education 49; student experiences with at HBCUs 133–4, 135; student-to-faculty relationships 17–18, 103–17, 127–8, 157–8
familial protectionism 15
feminist approach to doctoral advising, Black 4
Fernandis, Sarah Collins 97
field training, in social work education 96–7, 156
Fisk University 93, 94
Flexner, Abraham 59
Florida Agricultural and Mechanical University 4, 20, 159, 162
Florida Agricultural and Mechanical University School of Law: clinical opportunities 35–6; founding 31; mission statement 33; as a top feeder school 37
Frazier, E. Franklin 92
Freedom Riders movement 39
friendship, as mentor role 107
Fulton, Sybrina 40
funding: differential patterns for HBCUs and PWIs 124, 142–5, 162; of Health Professional schools 65; Morgan State University and Title III programs 142, 145–51; philanthropic support 65, 161; research 61, 65, 76; for safe spaces 17

Gallot, Rick 38
Garner, Eric 39
gay men 4
globalization, fears regarding 20
global workforce 13, 15, 20–1
graduate degrees: as minimal educational credential 2; percentage from HBCUs 123
graduate students: enrollment at Morgan State University 146*f*; experiences at HBCUs 123–35; mentoring experiences of 103–17
Gray, Freddie 39
Great Depression 92

Hampton University, as a top feeder school for lawyers 37
Hawkins, Virgil Darnell 31
Hayes, George E. C. 37
Haynes, George Edmund 94–5
health: disparities among minority populations 13, 59, 62; inequities in 58, 59; primary care shortage areas 58; social determinants of 60
health professional schools, historically Black 57–67. *see also* medical schools, historically Black
Healthy People 2020 62
Higher Education Act of 1965 57
Hill, Oliver 37
Hispanic students, projected increase in 63
history of HBCUs in America 3, 124; importance in decisions to attend 130–1, 134; law schools 29–31; medical schools 57–9; social work education 91–5
Homelessness and Legal Advocacy Clinic (HALAC) 35–6

hostile environment, at predominately White institutions (PWIs) 13–14, 22
Houston, Charles Hamilton 37, 39
Howard University: alumni 15, 37–8; mentoring experiences of graduate students 108; professional doctorates awarded by 4, 103, 159, 162; ranking in awarding doctorate degrees to Blacks 4
Howard University School of Dentistry 16
Howard University School of Law: alumni 15, 37–8; founding 29–30; mission statement 33; students as social engineers 39–40; as a top feeder school 37
Howard University School of Medicine 19, 57, 59, 62–3; partnership with Georgetown University 67
Howard University School of Social Work 93, 95, 97, 156
Howard University Students for Justice 39
Hunter College 67

institutional financing 65
integration 63–4, 125
interviews, coding of 109

Jackson, H. Patrick Maynard 38
Jackson State University: mentoring experiences of graduate students 108; prominence in awarding doctorate degrees to Blacks 4, 103; social work education 95, 96
Jim Crow practices 30
Johnson, Harry E. 38
Johnson, Leroy R. 38
Jordan, Vernon E., Jr. 38
judges: lack of cultural competency 37–8; racial representation disparity 36

Kelley, Sharon Pratt 38
Kram, Kathy 106–7

Langston, John Mercer 29
Latino students, recruiting 16
law schools, HBCU 29–40; access and opportunity 31–2; clinical programs 34–6; history 29–31; impact on society 38; leaders generated by 155–6; mission statements 33–4; percentage of law students educated at 37; students as grassroots leaders 38–40; students as social engineer 29
law schools, lack of diversity in 32
lawyers, Black: percentage produced by HBCUs 15; racial representation disparity 36
leadership, historically Black medical schools and 62–3, 66–7, 156
LGBTQ students 16–17
Lincoln University 3
Lindsay, Inabel Burns 93

macroaggressions 14
Mahool, J. Barry 142
males, Black: drop in applications to medical school 19; mentoring and 105, 157; student-to-faculty relationships 18, 157
Mann, Horace 53
Marbury Commission (1947) 143
Marshall, Thurgood 15, 38, 156
Martin, Trayvon 39–40
Maryland, HBCUs in 7, 21, 141–51
Maryland Higher Education Commission (MHEC) 141–4, 147–9, 151
master's degrees: at Morgan State University 146; number and percentage from HBCUs 4, 123
MCAT 20
McNair Post-baccalaureate Achievement program 106
medical schools: acceptance rates 19; access for racial/ethnic minorities at traditional 64; drop in applications of Black males 19; emphasis on standardized test scores 20
medical schools, historically Black 57–67; creating clear identity 65; in educational marketplace 63–6; faculty development, challenges in 60–2; health equity 59–60; history 57–9; institutional financing 65; leadership 62–3; leadership selection 156; leadership strategies 66–7; mentoring 60–2; mission 58, 59, 65, 156; partnerships with other institutions 66–7; percentage of Black medical graduates from 58; research activities 60–2; threat of enhanced access for racial/ethnic minorities at traditional medical schools 64
Meharry Medical College 19, 57, 59; partnership with Vanderbilt

University 67; professional doctorates awarded by 4, 159, 162
mental health challenges 16
mentoring: of Black male students 105, 157; career-related functions 107, 109–14; definition 104; education doctoral students 50–1; experiences of graduate students 103–17; functions 106–7; medical schools, historically Black 60–2; overview of student-faculty 106; at predominately White institutions (PWIs) 104, 105; professional doctorates 75–86; psychosocial functions 107, 109, 114–16; research training 75–86; review of literature 104–5; role in student success 127–8; significance for women 105; student perceptions of 77–86
Mentoring at Work: Development Relationships in Organizational Life (Kram) 106–7
MHEC (Maryland Higher Education Commission) 141–4, 147–9, 151
microaggressions 14, 32
microsystem, university 14, 17–19
middle class, Black 18, 77
misperceptions of HBSUs 128–35, 157
mission statements/missions: of HBCU law schools 33–4; of HBCU medical schools 65; of HBCUs 20, 123–4, 160, 162; social work education 95
Morehouse College, as a top feeder school for lawyers 37
Morehouse School of Medicine 19, 57, 59, 67, 156, 161
Morgan State University 141–51; doctorate programs 141, 146–7; enrollment 141; founding 141; Graduate School enrollment 146f; history 141–5; independent governance of 148–50; master's degrees 146; mentoring experiences of graduate students 108; online programs 142, 147–8, 148f, 151; post-baccalaureate certificate (PBC) programs 142, 147–8; prominence in awarding doctorate degrees to Blacks 4, 103; social work education 95, 97; Title III programs 142, 145–51
Morrill Act 3, 145
Mubarak, Hosni 39
Murray, Dwayne M. 38

Nash, Diane 39
National Association for Equal Opportunity in Higher Education 124
National Conference on Social Welfare 92
National League on Urban Conditions Among Negroes (National Urban League) 93–4
Nation at Risk, A 48
networking 111–12
New York School of Social Work (New York University) 93–4
NIH research grants 61
non-traditional students 63–4
Norfolk State University, social work education at 95–7
North Carolina A&T State University 160–1
North Carolina Central University, as leader in professional doctorate degree production 4, 159, 162
North Carolina Central University School of Law: clinical program 35; founding 30; mission statement 33; as a top feeder school 37
nurturing environment 13, 16, 19–20, 76–7, 115, 158; HBCU law schools 32; impact on student success 126

Office for Civil Rights 143–4, 150
online programs, at Morgan State University 142, 147–8, 148f, 151
Overstreet, Morris 38

partnerships: institutional 67, 156, 160–1; research 158
peer-to-peer relationships 17–19, 158; education doctoral students 51; influence on student success 126–7; partnering on research projects 158
perceptions of HBSUs 128–35
physicians, Black: as percentage of profession 19; percentage produced by HBCUs 15
post-baccalaureate certificate (PBC) programs, at Morgan State University 142, 147–8
Powering Maryland Forward 149
predominately White institutions (PWIs): creation of institutes/programs targeting marginalized populations 16; duplication of programs 21, 143–5, 149–51, 161;

funding differences from HBCUs 124; HBCU faculty compared 133; HBCU quality compared 132–3; hostile environment 13–14, 22; institutional partnerships with HBCUs 67, 156, 160–1; institutional racism and tokenism 32; law schools 32; mentoring at 104, 105; number of Blacks enrolled in 47; social work education 91, 93, 95; student experiences and success compared to HBCUs 125–6
Preston, James H. 141–2
productivity, mentoring impact on 113
professional doctorates: leading institutions in degree recipients 4; mentoring 75–86; mentoring experiences of 103–17; percentage from HBCUs 159; research self-efficacy 75–86
professional schools, emphasis on standardized test scores 20
proposals, writing and submitting 113
protégés 106–7, 110–14, 116. *see also* mentoring
proximity, importance in selection of institutions 129–30
psychosocial functions, of mentoring 107, 109, 114–16
purposeful sampling 108
PWIs. *see* predominately White institutions

Quality Matters pedagogy 147–8, 151
quality of HBCU programs: misconceptions and stereotypes 131–2; student assessment of 132–3

racial discrimination 15, 64, 92, 94, 162
racism: in Baltimore 142; institutional in law schools 32; social work and 92; systemic 31, 39; unintentional 126
recruitment, of education doctoral students 49–50
Relman, Arnold S. 64
research: ethnography 128; historically Black medical schools 60–2, 65; mentoring efforts of HBCU graduate programs 75–86, 113; self-efficacy 75–86, 158; on student experiences in HBCUs 125–35; student partnering on projects 158

retention of students: education doctoral students 52–3; student-to-faculty relationships 17–18
Robinson, Spottswood William III 37
role model 32, 51–2, 57, 78, 84, 105, 107, 110–11, 127–8, 156
RTE theory 77, 83, 85–6

safe spaces 16–17
satisfaction, of students at HBCUs 32, 125–6, 135
scaffolding, role of faculty mentor in 110
Schmoke, Kurt 39
school choice 48
schools, diversity in enrollment 53
science, technology, engineering, and math (STEM) 1–2, 4, 14–15, 47–8, 150
Scrubbs, Courtney 39
segregation 7, 30, 58, 64, 124, 141–3, 150, 160–1
self-efficacy 75–86, 127, 158
separate but equal 30, 144
Shaw University 30
snowball sampling 80, 108
social capital 78, 162
social engineer 29, 37, 39–40
socialization process 50, 52–3, 76, 103–4, 106, 108, 116–17, 155, 157
social justice 29, 32–3
social work, projected growth in 91
social work education 91–9; black-focused curriculum 96; cultural competence 91–9; curriculum themes 95; as elite profession 156; field training 96–7, 156; formal curriculum in social work 95; HBCUs and degrees conferred 95; history through 20th century 91–5; interdisciplinary knowledge 97–8; lessons learned from HBCUs 98–9; mission statements 95
Soper Commission (1937) 143
Southern University, social work education at 95
Southern University Law Center: founding 30–1; as leader in professional doctorate degree production 4, 159, 162
Spelman College, as a top feeder school for lawyers 37
Spenser, John Oakley 141–2
sponsorship 107

St. Augustine College, Bishop Tuttle Memorial School of Social Work at 93, 96–7
standardized test scores, emphasis on 20
STEM 1–2, 4, 14–15, 47–8, 150
stereotypes about quality of HBCU graduates 131, 157
Sterling, Alton 39
Stone, Jesse N., Jr. 38
Strategic planning and policy 160–1
Strengthening Historically Black Colleges and Universities Program 145
Strengthening Historically Black Graduate Institutions Program 145
student demographics, shift in 63
student departure 1–2
student experiences at HBCUs 123–35, 157–8; decisions to apply and attend 129–31; factors impacting student success 126–8; with faculty 133–4, 135, 157–8; faculty interactions 127–8; misconceptions and challenges 131–2; peer interactions 126–7; prior research 125–8; quality of HBCU programs 132–3
Student Nonviolent Coordinating Committee 39
student persistence 158
student-to-faculty relationships 17–18, 157–8; Black males 18, 157; in graduate schools 103–17; role in student success 127–8. *see also* mentoring
Sweatt, Herman 30
systemic barriers, preparing students to counter 15

teachers: average incoming salary 49; downward trend in enrollment in preparation programs 47; higher achievement gains with minority teachers 48; limited presence of African Americans 48; median salary 49; percentage of graduates from HBCUs 47
Texas Southern University 4, 20, 159, 162
Texas Southern University Thurgood Marshall School of Law: clinical programs 34–5; founding 30

Texas State University for Negroes. *see* Texas Southern University
Title III programs 142, 145–51
Title VI of the Civil Rights Act 143
tokenism 32
Traditionally White Institutions (TWIs): duplication of programs 21, 143–5, 149–51, 161; social work education 91, 93, 95. *see also* predominately White institutions (PWIs)
tuition, increasing cost of 65

Undergraduate Research Opportunity Programs 106
underrepresented minorities, as health professionals and researchers 60–2
United States v. Fordice (1992) 124
University of Maryland Eastern Shore 143–4, 149–51
University of North Carolina at Greensboro 160–1
University of the District of Columbia 20
University of the District of Columbia David A. Clark School of Law: clinical program 35; establishment 31; mission statement 33
University System of Maryland 148–51
US population, percentage of Blacks in 19, 103

Washington, Booker T. 93
Washington, Forrester Blanchard 93–4
wealth, building 18
Weglein Commission (1950) 143
Westry-Robinson, Briana 38
White enrollment in HBCUs 144
White House Initiative on Historically Black Colleges and Universities 145
Whitney Young Jr. School of Social Work at Clark Atlanta University 93
Wilberforce University 3
Wilder, L. Douglas 38
Willrich, Penny 38
women: percentage of degrees from HBCUs 123; racist behavior encountered by women of color 14; significance of mentoring for 105
Women's Suffrage League 93
workforce readiness 14
workplace hostilities 20

Zimmerman, George 39